LONDON WAS OURS

Diaries and Memoirs
of the London Blitz

AMY HELEN BELL

I.B. TAURIS

LONDON · NEW YORK

New paperback edition published in 2011 by I.B.Tauris & Co Ltd
6 Salem Road, London W2 4BU
175 Fifth Avenue, New York NY 10010
www.ibtauris.com

Distributed in the United States and Canada Exclusively by Palgrave Macmillan
175 Fifth Avenue, New York NY 10010

First published in hardback in 2008 by I.B.Tauris & Co Ltd

ISBN: 978 1 84885 849 7

A full CIP record for this book is available from the British Library
A full CIP record is available from the Library of Congress

Library of Congress Catalog Card Number: available

Printed and bound in Sweden by ScandBook AB
from camera-ready copy edited and supplied by the author

This book is dedicated to the memory of my mother, Ann Martha Bell, who died in 1980 at the age of 36. Her absence taught me that all silences hold the possibility of music.

CONTENTS

ACKNOWLEDGMENTS

My love of British History came as a by-product of my fascination with Professor Stephen Brooke's unraveling sweater sleeve. I took course after history course, until the sleeve was rolled up and the sweater eventually disappeared. By that time I was hooked. Sandra den Otter kept the flame alive, nurturing this project and me with many delicious lunches. Thanks to you both for your guidance and friendship.

Queen's University, where this book began, was a wonderful place to be a graduate student, with amazing faculty, supportive fellow students and staff, and a tasty annual bake sale. Thanks to Professors Geoff Smith, Harold Mah, Maggie Berg, Bob Malcolmson, Karen Dubinsky and Tim Smith for your help and kindness, and to the lovely Professor Sonya Rose at Michigan who offered valuable feedback. Muchas gracias also to my incredibly amazing academic girlfriends for reading portions of this book: Erin Lemon, Jennifer Marotta, Helen Harrison, Lisa Smith, Joy Frith, Jenne MacLean and Krista Kesselring.

The excellent staff at the research facilities I visited in England made my work much easier. Thanks to Tony Richards and the staff of the Imperial War Museum's Department of Documents and Dorothy Sheridan and Joy Eldridge at the Mass-Observation Archives. Thanks to the staff members at the Hackney Archives, Bexley Local History Library, Waltham Forest Archive, Kensington

Local Studies Library, Lewisham Local History Library, Ealing Local
History Library, Islington Council Central Reference Library,
Richmond Local Studies Archive, Brunel University Library,
Wandsworth Local History Library and the Enfield Local History
Library.

Thanks to the trustees of the Imperial War Museum for access to
the collection, and to those who archived their diaries and memoirs
with the IWM, and their copyright holders: B. Garman, Bruce
Gordon-Smith, Joyce Smith, Ms Penelope E. Nichol, Canon J. H.
Rumens, Mrs Ann Regan-Atherton, Dorothea Ridgway, M. M. King,
David M. Reynolds, Keith Nicholson, Mrs Ouida V. Ashcroft, David
J. Champion, Phyllis M. Damonte and Mrs H. Faber. Every effort
has been made to contact copyright holders and the author and the
Imperial War Museum would be grateful for any information which
might trace those whose identities or addresses are not currently
known. Thanks also to the trustees of the Mass Observation Archive,
University of Sussex for permission to publish extracts from wartime
diaries, which are copyright © The Trustees of the Mass Observation
Archive.

Many thanks to Lester Crook, Liz Friend-Smith and the staff at
I.B.Tauris, for their help, encouragement and excellent advice.

Thanks to my husband Rupert, whose skills as a literary agent and
as a baby-tamer helped to complete this project, and to my dad Big
Ed who gave me free rein to be anything, and is proud that I ended
up loving history as he does.

INTRODUCTION

At this time I was not the only one who hugged London to my beating heart. London was ours from the hour the blacked-out night hid its beauty until the morning siren signaled the coming day, most triumphantly ours when the full moon rose and shone on its age-old face and we knew the Germans would not be coming.[1]

In this passage from her autobiography, Joan Bright Astley describes a community of unified and exhilarated Londoners. My book, an analysis of the first-person accounts of Londoners writing about the bombing raids on London from September 1940 to May 1941, suggests how participants themselves wrote and rewrote the history of the London Blitz. In the following pages, I elaborate an original theory of the British memory of the Second World War, in which individual memories and cultural representations form the new *lieux de memoire*.[2] I examine three main private narrative forms: diaries, letters and autobiographies. Letters and diaries provide a near-immediate recitation of daily experiences, as well as individual hopes and fears often forgotten or air-brushed with nostalgia after the war, while participants' memoirs present a retrospective which elaborates on the narrative and historical context of the Blitz. Both sets of sources place the writer and the Blitz firmly at the centre of their war history. My analysis thus recognizes the significance of London as a

space and *place* during the raids, how writers like Astley saw themselves as participants in a moment of change, and how retrospective
accounts have conflated the entire Second World War into the Blitz
experience.

Three new strands of enquiry have revitalized the topic of civilian
experiences during the Second World War. The first is Jonathan
Rose's innovative methodology of reading first-person sources. In
The Intellectual Life of the British Working Classes (2001), Rose develops a
'history of audiences', using working class autobiographies to access
reading experience and responses of the 'common reader'.[3] The
second strand is heralded by the publication of Sonya Rose's book,
Which People's War? (2003), which explores the transformation of
wartime political culture and conceptions of citizenship. Sonya
Rose uses a wide variety of sources, including newspapers, films,
diaries and letters, Home Office Reports, radio scripts and novels,
to get as close as possible to what people would have seen, heard
and read at the time, in order to understand how public culture
filtered wartime experiences.[4] Her analysis reveals that a heroic,
populist and utopian construction of national identity and citizenship
dominated public and political culture at the time. The third strand
is the emerging interest in crime during wartime, which challenges
the populist notions of citizenship and universality and paints a
darker picture of London during the war.[5] Together these strands
provide fascinating glimpses of London during the Blitz, based on
participants' writings. These works underline the role of the
individual in creating national identity, and they allow the possibility
of dissent from utopian conceptions of citizenship and civilian
morale in wartime.

Participant narratives of the Blitz comprise an important and an
overlooked aspect of Second World War history. The rapidly
expanding field of the historiography of memory has tended to over-
generalize, turning the concept into what Henri Rousso has called a
'value' instead of an objective phenomenon.[6] Hence 'collective' or
'national' memory is understood literally, and all memory becomes
social.[7] As Susan Sontag notes, memory is individual, irreproducible

and dies with each person. Left behind – in cultural objects such as photographs or memoirs – is collective instruction.[8] In this sense collective memory is better understood as a social framework that can organize individual histories and memories.[9] We are now at a crucial moment of remembrance of World War Two. We live at the moment when individual memory – corporeal and transitory – gives way to cultural representations that lack the immediacy of first-hand recollection, and whose canon of memorialized images, anecdotes and assumptions about the war increases annually. The danger is that the national memorial culture will be reduced to memorializing earlier forms of remembrance, 'erasing history in the very act of its recuperation'.[10]

In this book, I restore the voices of individuals to the collective memory of the Blitz and the war, revealing variations, heterogeneity and the existence of dissenting points of view to those expressed in wartime official or propagandic narratives, and providing a corrective to simplistic Whiggish notions of civilian 'morale' and inevitable victory. Letters, diaries and memoirs provide an intimate glimpse into the private world of Londoners, disclosing personal and family strategies for coping with the privations, stresses, and dangers of war. Such sources also link these private and public worlds, revealing personal conceptions of national identity, most specifically in the debates over what form the social and geographical reconstruction of London should take.

Linking the everyday lives of Londoners during the Blitz to the wider spheres of national politics connects the importance of the individual to wider national history and its identity and symbols. People in London were not members of a national community because the propagandists who coined the phrase 'The People's War' said they were. They were members of this community because they believed themselves to be, and they wrote themselves into a national narrative in their diaries and memoirs. Although politicians and policy makers may have controlled the organs of the state, a complete understanding of Britain at war must look to the people who constituted the nation.

London Was Ours

The beginning of the Blitz – the German bombing raids on London from September 1940 to May 1941 – accompanied the end of the Battle of Britain, in which German and British planes fought for air supremacy in southeast England. Coming after the fall of France, the Blitz was the first test of Britain standing alone against the Germans, heralding the threat of invasion in September 1940. The Blitz provided the first tests of civilian morale, subjecting people to prolonged raids, disruption of services, and destruction of property and life. From September 7, 1940 to May 11, 1941, 15,775 Londoners were killed and 1,400,000, or one in six, were rendered homeless. The Blitz encompassed the historical themes that have come to characterize the Second World War in Britain: civilian fortitude under the bombing, and the emergence of a new national unity.

'London was ours', Astley writes, and this sense of possessiveness runs through the letters and diaries of Londoners living through the Blitz. Isabelle Granger described this solidarity in a letter to her friend Harrison Brown in Canada:

> December 1, 1940. You wouldn't mind London at all now – it seems shorn of most of its worst aspects, glares stubbornly and gaily at us all encouragingly. And the ordinary people who belong in London are still here, are just as good as any of these more easily distinguished allies. The people who are here now are here for a purpose, they are purposeful, determined, very good-tempered people.[11]

Granger presents London as a newly unified community, shorn of negative pre-war connotations, and anthropomorphized into a symbol of courage. She emphasizes the importance of 'ordinary people' who belong in London, and whose purpose it is to win the war.

London during the Blitz also symbolizes a unifying moment in memoirs. In *Best Wine Last* (1978), Alec Waugh wrote poetically about the winter of 1940:

London had glamour during that first winter of the Blitz. It was an empty city, but it was still an English city. Austerity had not been felt. Clothes rationing did not start until the summer of 1941. People still looked smart. The streets were not shabby though they were littered with broken glass. You could eat well. Wine cellars were still well stocked. There was a sense of pride in having provided the first check to the German menace. One felt oneself to be at the centre of big events. When I went into the country for the night on a tour of duty, to Winchester or Swanage, I did not get the long sleep I had expected. I felt restless, wondering how things were in London.[12]

Waugh defines London in the Blitz as an 'English city' because of its continuing bourgeois elegance and communal patriotic pride at having repulsed the first attempted Nazi invasion. Waugh also places himself at the centre of the action, as a member of a unified community of Londoners. His memories of London are central to the importance he gives his own role in the war, and comprise a key part of the historical narrative that deemed British victory inevitable because of Britons' innate civility and moral rectitude. Both contemporary and retrospective narratives place the writer and London at the centre of the war experience.

Assumptions of inevitable victory and national unity also inform the first generation of Blitz histories. In the quarter century after VE Day, storytelling narratives of the war assumed the inevitability of Britain's victory, and reflected more a wistful Whiggish historical view than an assessment of Britain's war resources.[13] Early social histories, including Richard Titmuss's *Problems of Social Policy* (1950), emphasized the transformative postwar effects of social cohesion in the face of war and government policies ostensibly implemented to protect and reward the people.[14] The theme of the moral justice of British victory in a Manichean morality play continues even more starkly in John Lukacs's more recent *Five Days in London: May 1940* (1999). Historians who challenge the positivist reading of Second World War historiography tend merely to reverse the binary by citing a massive historiographical cover-up of the negative aspects of the war. Angus Calder argues in *The People's War* (1969) that the war strengthened old powers of wealth, privilege and bureaucracy, masking tyrannical aims by appealing to the 'scorned and underprivileged sections of society' with the promise of a better life after the war through wartime slogans like 'The People's War'.[15] Other historians focus on postwar mythologizing of the war through the imposition of cultural norms on individual recollections. Tom Harrisson's *Living Through the Blitz* (1976) draws on the vast collection of contemporary diaries, surveys and letters in the Mass Observation Archive to demonstrate how postwar myths of solidarity perverted the actual experiences of those who lived through the Blitz:

> The record from a third of a century ago can seem improbable today because it reads so differently from the contemporary, established concept of 'what really happened' in that war. There has, in particular, been a massive, largely unconscious cover-up of the more disagreeable facts of 1940–1. ... It amounts to a form of intellectual pollution: but pollution by perfume.[16]

The belief that the actual events of the war have been obscured by a dominant myth – in accordance with the way in which people unconsciously adjust their memories – is also the theme of Clive Ponting's *1940: Myth and Reality* (1990), and Angus Calder's *The Myth of the Blitz* (1991).[17] But although they aim to reveal the truth of ordinary people's lives during the war, variations on 'myth' only reinforce elitist models of popular memory. While I agree that people in London during the war often made sense of a frightening and chaotic reality in terms of heroic mythology, I do not believe that a myth, or collective memory of the war, exists separately from the people who created it.[18] Missing in the historiography of the Second World War in Britain, a lacuna this book will fill, is a thorough analysis of participants' memories and a consideration of how they write about their roles and experiences. This book provides a more nuanced account that reintegrates the memories of participants into history – without accusations of false consciousness – and links British and continental European history and historiography of the Second World War.

An Archive without Borders

Like historians, participants have recognized the political importance of the memories of the Second World War, but they have not recognized the power of the pen they wield in their own hands. My research reveals an extensive and original bibliography of private narratives written during, or remembering, September 1940 to May 1941 in London. This material comes from the Imperial War Museum, the diary collection of the Mass Observation Archive, the Working Class Autobiographies Collection at Brunel University, the local history collections of the borough libraries in and around London, and published accounts. The bibliography of written narratives of the Blitz is a living archive without borders, as participants continue to write, donate their writings and publish.

The way I use diaries and autobiographies in this work is markedly different from their use by other historians. I consider the experiences described therein, but, just as importantly, I emphasize *how* writers narrate those experiences. As James Olney argues, metaphor provides the link through which autobiographers and life writers recapture their lost selves, and order the world around them.[19] Hence the metaphors writers use are as important as their referent subjects. My analysis of private writings reveals how writers thought about their own roles as witnesses, about their national identity, and about the historical importance of the Blitz in particular and the war in general, as much by how they wrote and what they left out as by the stories they tell. This method restores the individual contingencies and contradictions to histories of the war, and it creates a popular history of a war that depended so much on ideas of 'the people'. My method also permits an escape from continuing historiographical notions – imbedded in so many retrospective visions of the war – that the war's events and British victory were inevitable.

Chapter Synopses

In the book's chapters I explore how Londoners envisioned and re-envisioned London during the Blitz. To position themselves as authoritative historical witnesses, Londoners asserted the cultural importance of the metropolis and its essential modernity during the Blitz. In doing so, they validated their writings as participants. The first and most obvious topic for their pens was the damage to the physical geography of London. The meanings they ascribed to the changed space were profoundly indebted to cultural attitudes towards the geography of London and its 'slum' neighborhoods. People writing during the Blitz described a unique wartime social geography of London, through their perceptions of the war's effects on class relationships and ties of kinship, love and sex. In their memoirs, Londoners again asserted the importance of their cultural role by reframing the London Blitz as a pivotal historical point in modern British history.

The first chapter, *Looking at London*, establishes the importance of analyzing the form as well as the content of first-person sources, and explores the importance of metaphor to participants' experiences and memories of the Blitz. Instead of the pastoral metaphors of 'Deep England' identified in other histories, Londoners' descriptions of the metropolis during the Blitz reveal a new vision of modernity, the legacy of mass culture in the metropolis, the influence of the sociological observation movement of the 1930s and the persistence of World War One metaphors of the paradoxical nearness of death in the midst of life. The concept of witnessing was so strong that descriptions of London were most often expressed in metaphors of seeing, watching and hearing the Blitz, which also echoed the shared cultural language of modernity. The London Blitz was thus the first experience of a modern war in Britain, not only because of the targeting of civilians thorough sustained mass bombing, but more importantly because civilians participated in redrawing the modern urban space by inscribing on it their own importance.

The middle chapters in the book centre upon another form of witnessing: the use of the diary and the memoir to record frustrations, privations and other emotions that had no outlet in wartime. These three chapters reveal how writers, sometimes unwittingly, expressed their anger, resentment and boredom with the staples of the wartime collective experience: air raids, rationing, volunteer and paid work, familial unity and endless waiting. In Chapter Two, *Raids and Rationing*, I explore how Londoners responded to bombing raids and the rationing of food. While the language of national unity and British fortitude implied the universality of both experiences, social divisions lurked within images of crumbling barriers. Social tensions between classes and genders revolved around questions of access to food and shelter, and accentuated the contrast between public shelters and availability of food in shops, and the greater luxuries of both food and shelter in hotels, clubs and restaurants.

Another aspect of national unity surfaces in Chapter Three, *Workers and Civil Defence*. The slogan, 'the People's War', created in response to the production crises of 1940, emphasizes the importance of the worker and implies a cross-class productive unity. But the temporary nature of conscription and voluntarism – the methods of expanding the sphere of labor and civil defense in London – did not yield fundamental changes in class-consciousness or even class relations. The motives for war work expressed by diarists and memoirists make this clear. Instead, the geographical difficulties of raids and their effects, such as disrupted transportation and destruction of property, made work conditions more difficult.

Chapter Four, *Children and the Family*, explores another aspect of continuity in class divisions. While public appeals to morale emphasized the communal and familial nature of London during the war, class divisions continued to inform attitudes towards the working class family, newly visible in public shelters and through the evacuation schemes. Diaries and memoirs also reveal exacerbated family tensions and the hardships endured by the most vulnerable family members, children and the elderly.

In Chapter Five, *Love in the Blitz*, I build on the material, social and cultural geography, as laid out in the earlier chapters, to examine the sexual geography of London during the Blitz. Both those who feared a newly liberal sexuality in the Blitz and those who wanted to lay claim to it emphasized how the geography of blacked-out streets, dark sandbagged entrances, public shelters and the dissipation of parental authority created new tensions between sexual pleasures and dangers. Yet diaries and memoirs reveal a continuing emphasis on long-term monogamous relationships, and on the marital and procreative aspects of sexuality. The liberatory sexual geography of London in wartime was, therefore, a cultural construction for which we can find no solid evidence in first-person sources.

The final chapter, *Remembering the Blitz*, examines how participants rewrote and recalled their Blitz experiences with the hindsight of victory. Their memories as participants and the national significance they ascribed to the war offer a window into changing popular conceptions of the Second World War, which evolve with each generation. The series of fiftieth anniversaries in 1989, 1994 and 1995 highlighted the heroic, celebratory and unified aspects of the civilian experience in wartime, in which the Blitz, and the war in general, has come to stand for a moment of unsurpassed British greatness: 'Our Finest Hour'. In contrast to other European nations, whose war memories are constrained by a history of invasion and defeat and years of collective suppression, individual and public memories of the Blitz are part of a phenomenal British investment in the national symbols of the war.

1

LOOKING AT LONDON

September 6, 1940. The night before last, I watched the battle over East London, from Paddington Street – most beautiful, with the searchlights, and parachute flares, and the fiery balls from our guns which are said to be tracer bullets, and the sky lit up by gun-flashes, like sheet-lightning, and a wonderful background of stars. The guns were faint, I think about Stratford. I'm so sorry you had such a noisy night, Nancy said it was awful. Do you use wax ear-balls? I think this is important.[1]

Rose Macaulay's letter uses powerful aesthetic descriptions and metaphors to convey images of the Blitz to her sister. Like other writers during the Blitz, Macaulay positioned herself as an authoritative historical witness by asserting the visual nature of her own Blitz experiences. Analyzing the literary and descriptive forms through which writers described the Blitz reveals the strategies they used to emphasize the importance of their own positions as witnesses, and of London as the political and cultural centre of a nation at war. Their descriptions of seeing, watching and hearing the Blitz are indebted to aesthetic and political writings of the 1920s and 1930s that underline the central themes of visuality and observation to the experiences and descriptions of the modern metropolis. Descriptions of the Blitz also reveal the ambiguity of the aesthetic pleasures of the Blitz and of the modernity of the metropolis under threat of destruction. Blitz writings reveal the Blitz as one of the first battles of a modern war, as civilians witnessed the destruction of raids and helped to rewrite the centrality of London as a modern urban space by inscribing on it their own importance.

Imagining London in 1940

At the outbreak of war, London became a symbol for the entire British nation-state. After the Zeppelin raids of the First World War and interwar aeronautic advances, Britons recognized that London was a potential target. The popular fictional predictions of H. G. Wells and the newsreels of bombing in Spain's civil war increased public concern over Britain's vulnerability from the air.[2] London became a nation-wide symbol of resistance to the German bombing raids in part because it was bombed first. The mass bombing raids on London that began on September 5, 1940 were the fiercest ever seen in Britain, and would continue almost unabated until November, with daily fears and rumors of invasion. By the time Coventry was bombed and gutted on November 14, 1940, and although its destruction was much greater, London had already become the national symbol of civilian courage. As the *Daily Express* reporter Hilde Marchant wrote on November 13, 1940, 'Bombs make the Provinces love London more.'

London also became a convenient metonym for the rest of England. Both wartime travel and communication were fraught with difficulty, and those wanting to write or talk about the state of England in wartime were restricted in their movements. In *England's Hour* (1941), written for wartime publication and a North American audience, Vera Brittain wrote that at first she had intended to travel around England in a wartime version of Priestley's *English Journey* (1934):

But when the Battle for Britain intensified, and the Battle of London assumed characteristics which few of us had pictured before they appeared, the difficulties of travel combined with the time limit necessarily imposed upon a topical book made the projected long journeys impossible. Moreover, it became clear to me that the world's eyes were concentrated on London; and such travels as I was able to undertake seemed to show that a tour of the more remote areas of the country would ... differ little from similar impressions in peacetime.[3]

Brittain compared London during the Blitz to the front lines in the Great War to argue that London in 1940 was fundamentally different from the London of the past and the rest of England. Thus she privileged her viewpoint (having written 'more than one book' about the Great War) and drew upon the cultural and historical debates about representing the Great War. The knowledge gap between those at home and those who experienced the Front was a central theme of post-Great War writing, including Brittain's own memoirs.[4] As Vera Brittain pointed out, London was the new battlefield of the modern war. The bombing attacks on London while the armed forces were inactive reversed the traditional role of protector and protected, as in as in the popular joke: 'Thank Gawd', said one old lady, as she inspected the ruins of her local shopping street. 'Thank Gawd Jack's safe in the army!'[5] Personal correspondence reveals the role reversal as well, as in a Hackney soldier's letter to his wife on March 21, 1941: 'Dear Lily, I hope you are alright after the heavy raid on London. Do answer at once, I feel worried and can't get out to phone. Believe me that is the worst part of it, when one hears of a heavy raid and has to wait to hear that things are alright.'[6]

The possibility of random civilian deaths in London made comparison to a battlefield more than metaphorical. Geographically vulnerable, and with increased diplomatic and military importance after the fall of France, London had a new international visibility in 1940. Churchill's broadcast to the nation on September 11, 1940, as the Blitz began and fears of invasion were at their highest, presented London as a symbol of the fortitude of the British nation. Churchill contrasted the Germans' attempt to destroy civilian morale to fearlessness of Londoners in the past:

He [Hitler] hopes, by killing large numbers of civilians, and women and children, that he will terrorize and cow the people of a mighty imperial city, and make them a burden and anxiety to the Government and thus distract our attention unduly from the ferocious onslaught he is preparing. Little does he know the spirit of the British nation, or the tough fibre of Londoners, whose forbears played a leading part in the establishment of Parliamentary institutions and who have been bred to value freedom above their lives. ... All the world that is still free marvels at the composure and fortitude with which the citizens of London are facing and surmounting the great ordeal to which they are subjected, the end of which or the severity of which cannot yet be foreseen.[7]

Churchill presented London's ordeal as not only heroic, but as visibly heroic on an international stage, underlining the importance of the capital at war.[8]

After the fall of France in June 1940, London became the capital of Allied freedom, housing exiled governments and broadcasting to Europe through the British Broadcasting Company (BBC). London was also the site of journalistic drama for North Americans and the rest of Europe, as journalists like Edward Murrow reported back to America on conditions in London.[9] International journalists, especially the large contingent of American reporters who formed their own community at the Savoy Hotel, helped to create an image of London as a People's Front that was waiting for, and then enduring, aerial attacks by the Germans. American journalistic accounts most often described the London Blitz as a drama in which plucky Londoners defeated the raiders through their fortitude. In *Bomber's Moon* (1941), Negley Farson recorded the changing skyline and London characters in written and charcoal sketches. He emphasized the poetic urban landscape:

London, when you can see its sky-line at all, seems particularly beautiful under the black-out. And you may read a bitter, sad defiance in its silver stone. But for most nights of the month it is just a black nothingness in which you move your feet gingerly for fear you will meet something. You hear the sound of passing feet. And you begin to read them. I think I know some of them now – particularly that rush of hurrying footsteps in the early morning, after the 'All Clear' has gone. They are hurrying home.[10]

Farson was careful to impose meaning on the 'black nothingness' of London during the Blitz. 'Reading' the steps asserts the continuity of the everyday in the face of potentially terrifying absences and presents an image of brave Londoners enduring the raids and anxious to continue with their everyday lives and work.

The more propagandistic American accounts were often treated with suspicion by Londoners themselves. One female diarist, a thirty-five-year old journalist, recorded her reaction to reading published accounts by American journalists: 'September 12, 1940. Am rather amused to read the articles of American correspondents to New York – they have their facts, they don't really exaggerate and yet somehow the impression they give is wrong. I don't know about other countries but here the whole damn thing is so matter of fact, writing up by professional men just doesn't get the picture.'[11] By rejecting the high drama of the American account, the diarist reinforces her own position as an inside witness and a courageous Londoner. Another diarist wrote a scathing reaction to the book *London Front* (1941), a collection of letters written to America from 1940 London: 'Gosh, what a terrible book! It made me swear not only with irritation, but with shame that such stuff should have been, as it apparently was, accepted, and in fact lapped up, by Americans as an expression of a British point of view. It's full of moaning and martyrdom and fake heroism … no war work, rationing, blitz, or restrictions.'[12] Such criticisms demonstrate the confidence writers had in their own experiences, and their unwillingness to accept the metaphors presented in media accounts, particularly those from America.

Stephen Spender recalled in his memoir a fireman in his National Fire Service brigade during the Blitz who was never asked to keep the log because he was illiterate. But Spender saw his illiteracy as a historical boon: he was the only man in the station who told the truth about his firefighting experiences. The others had almost completely substituted descriptions that they read in the newspapers for their own experiences.[13] Spender's distrust of journalism echoed that of Robert Graves who, on leave during the First World War, was unable to talk to those in England because 'they spoke a foreign language. It was newspaper language.'[14] Like the soldiers of the Great War, Londoners had the confidence and the authority of witnesses who could reject public images that did not correspond to their own experiences. Although journalistic accounts no doubt influenced readers and listeners abroad and at home, they also functioned as a foil against which diarists could project the validity of their own experiences and interpretations of the London Blitz.

The Historical Witness

Diarists' conceptions of their own historical importance emerge in the authorial motives they present in their narratives. Most war diarists believed strongly in the importance of their task for themselves, for their families and for posterity. For example, Nell Bosanquet asked her mother to forgive her for the 'diary trend' in her letters, but 'every bit of the day something seems to happen that is worth telling.'[15] Like prisoner-of-war diarists, writers during the Blitz sought to recreate absent communities and their own identities through their writing.[16] They did this by recording the historical events around them through the lens of their own subjectivity. Self-disclosure was vital to the task of the Blitz diarist, because it added legitimacy to his or her narrative. Harold Nicolson, a writer, wartime Member of Parliament (MP) for the National Labour Party and Parliamentary Secretary to the Minister of Information from 1940 to 1941, articulated his frustration with his failure to provide enough personal detail in his diary: 'The day-to-day impressions of a greengrocer in Streatham would be more interesting. I must try henceforth to be more intimate and more illuminating. ... I find some relief in putting down on paper the momentary spurts and gushes of this cataract of history.'[17] The diarist's task was to provide relief for him or herself, and interest for posterity.

Blitz diarists' sense of their own historical importance was bound up in the daily details of their lives. For instance, Vere Hodgson kept a detailed diary during the war years, intending to circulate it among her family all over the world to show how she, and England, were bearing up. In her 1976 foreword to the published diary, *Few Eggs and No Oranges: A Diary showing how Unimportant People in London and Birmingham Lived through the War Years 1940–1945*, she wrote: 'Later I was able to type it, and it records fairly accurately the hopes and fears and daily drudgery of an ordinary person during many weary springs, summers, autumns and winters.'[18] Though he would never have described himself as an ordinary person, Henry 'Chips' Channon felt his diaries were so vital that he buried them in the garden in a tin box in case of invasion.[19]

Diarists who were published during the war were also conscious of their role as historical witnesses. Published diaries were usually kept by journalists, or those working in publishing – people who had access to publication channels and who could present an 'official' view of the war. Bound by censorship restrictions, as well as the need to appeal to a wartime audience, they reinforced the public narratives of victory of Churchill and others by emphasizing the courage of the British populace in the face of raids and the historical durability of London. Yet many unpublished diaries reflect their dissatisfaction with official narratives, whether of American or British journalists. Keeping a diary was one way in which diarists felt they could add to or correct the official views.

Such confidence in their own pens owed much to the advent of sociological writing in the interwar era. In the 1930s, George Orwell had pioneered a new type of sociological observation in his political writings.[20] The new science of sociology also influenced the Mass Observation research group. Formed in 1937, Mass Observation gathered the data of volunteer and paid 'observers', which they then published in four books between 1937 and 1940: *May 12th*, (1937), *Our First Year's Work* (1938), *Britain by Mass-Observation* (1939) and *War begins at Home* (1940). Mass Observation was a curious blend of sociological and anthropological observation of humans, whose observers emulated scientific and journalistic styles in their desire to provide neutral and factual information about the working classes.[21] The impulse to record the opinions and feelings of Britons propelled Tom Harrisson of Mass Observation to solicit monthly diary submissions in a newspaper advertisement in 1937, which offered volunteers the opportunity to be 'self-observers'. The diarists who contributed to Mass Observation during the war differed from other wartime diarists in that they knew their diaries had an audience – they sent off a missive to the panel each month.[22] Some Mass Observation diarists felt encouraged by the regular correspondence and audience. A twenty-four-year-old female civil servant wrote on October 4, 1940: 'Tonight a fresh missive from Mass-Observation which inspires me to fresh efforts with this diary. In fact, today's record seems to have come out like a minutes book. But it stops me from wondering whether I can stick this life much longer, if nothing else.'[23]

Diarists and letter writers during the war wrote in an atmosphere of censorship, paper rationing and reduced wartime publishing.[24] Censorship was touted as a way to prevent the leakage of military information to the enemy, though government agencies extended censorship beyond military matters in an attempt to assess and direct public opinion. Peter Quennell, working as an editor in the Ministry of Information, described the process for editing press copy. Every day an assistant seated on a central chair read aloud the set of rules to which editors had to adhere, entitled 'Stops and Releases': 'No reference to a certain type of bomb! No mention of the latest raid! Numbers of lives lost in the last twenty-four hours required particularly close attention. The numbers themselves were suppressed; instead, according to the latest rules, we removed "35" and substituted "some casualties," reserving "considerable casualties" for a genuine disaster.'[25] A network of censorship offices around the country monitored private postal and telegraphic correspondence and removed passages with details of military or government actions that they deemed bad for morale. The censorship officers also read letters to gather military and intelligence information and to gauge public morale, especially during the difficult years of 1940 and 1941.[26] Letter writers and those who sent diaries through the mail had to contend with these difficulties. Diana Cooper's father's letters were so mangled by the censor that she described them in her diary as 'something you cut out for Christmas decoration'.[27] Censorship was a particular problem for Mass Observation diaries, which were submitted to the organization in monthly installments through the mail. Naomi Mitchison recorded on February 19, 1941: 'I talked mostly to Mary and a little to Judy. She says that the censor's pen got parts of my letters and diary, which were copied (with dashes in places – but I don't think I ever said worse than bloody!) and came to her … Judy says she has a certain amount of struggle about getting war diaries through. I think Mass-Obs. ought to get on this and make their position clear with the censor's office: *please note*.'[28] Censorship of personal writing not only demonstrates the importance the government put on individual civilian morale, but also reinforced diarists' belief that their perceptions and opinions were not being publicly represented. Moreover, the lack of reliable information in the press about bombing incidents and casualties made many diarists feel a greater responsibility to record Blitz incidents in their neighborhoods.

The concept of an official wartime narrative was belied by the actual content of the books published during the war, which were without exception vague in detail and patriotic, if not jingoistic, in tone. Basil Woon's book *Hell Came to London* (1941) was subtitled 'A Reportage of the Blitz During 14 Days'. The author claimed to be an ex-newspaper man, and his avowed aim in publishing his book was to refute American accounts that London had faltered in any way during the Blitz. He also acknowledged his debt to newspapers of London, 'which, night after night, under the most appalling

conditions, often with bombs actually falling on their roofs, lived up
to the highest tradition of journalism and gave the people the facts'.[29]
This judgment is considered at best a bit of wishful thinking on
Woon's part: the newspapers were considerably hampered by
censorship and communications delays. Nevertheless Woon
emphasized 'the people's' right to information. He offered them his
own personal account, highly colored by patriotic sentiment: 'If you
saw the Western Front during or just after the last war you know
something of how portions of the East End look today. Whole
streets of Poplar, Hackney, Wapping, East and West Ham, Bow,
Shoreditch, Stepney and other districts are little more than rubble
heaps. But while the little homes of the poor lie pitifully smashed in
their hundreds, ships are still loading at the docks.'[30] The East
Enders became the gallant and brave little soldiers, playing, Woon
suggested, a similar role to the privates and officers on the Western
Front in the First World War. Woon was not blessed with a sense of
historical irony, or he had forgotten the slaughter of the Somme.
Once again, participants in a war wanted to add their own voices and
experiences to these unsatisfactory published accounts.

Metaphors of Modernity

To position themselves as authoritative historical witnesses,
Londoners established the historical and cultural importance of their
writings. They did so not only in the act of writing itself, but also in
the ways in which they wrote. Analyzing the forms which structure
writings of the Blitz reveals as much about London in 1940 as their
content does. As James Olney argued in his early work on autobiographical writings, metaphor provides the connection between the
self and the world.[31] A metaphor refers to a thing, idea or action by a
word or expression normally denoting another thing, idea or action,
suggesting a common quality between the two. Metaphors establish
relationships of similarity between the self and the world, between
the past and present self, and between the writer and the reader.
Since, as Regina Kunzel has noted, the mediation of experience by

language and its encoding in particular rhetorical conventions shapes our access to the past, the images and metaphors used by Blitz writers can themselves reveal how writers saw themselves and their environment.[32]

Diaries and memoirs of the Blitz consistently use metaphors and images that assert the cultural importance of the modern metropolis during the Blitz. As Michel de Certeau argued, the city is both the machinery and hero of modernity. As pedestrians walk the city, they read it as a text, but also write it in a series of 'migrational metaphors'.[33] So it was with writers during the Blitz. Their writings also follow a tradition set out in interwar tourist guidebooks, which emphasized the modernity of London, read in the signs of 'the spectacle of its movement, congestion and even dirtiness'.[34] The spectacular nature of modern London revealed itself not only in movement, but also in a visual world of images, performances and glances that were central to the urban experience. Historians have traced the visual culture of London, particularly in the nineteenth century, through mirrored music halls and the new department stores and shopping arcades.[35] These commercial institutions changed the physical landscape of the city, and pointed to a profound change in the modern aesthetic. Like Walter Benjamin's Paris arcades in the late nineteenth century, music halls and department stores transformed use and exchange value into visual commodity value, as people were taught to derive pleasure from the spectacle alone.[36]

By the 1940s, music halls were no longer at the forefront of popular culture, but department stores were even more central to urban popular culture. London department stores, such as Debenhams, Peter Robinson, John Lewis, D. H. Evans and Selfridges in Oxford Street, Liberty's on Regent Street and Harrods in Knightsbridge, were landmarks and symbols of the visual variety and commodity display of the modern city. During the Blitz, department stores also became emblems of the triumph of London's fortitude. When John Lewis's Oxford Street premises were bombed in late September 1940, the firm replied with a 'Churchillian blast of defiance' in their in-house magazine: 'We shall defend our partnership with the utmost energy. What matter if we are bombed out of John Lewis? We shall fight on at Peter Jones!'[37]

The continued commercial life of the city symbolized patriotism and high morale.[38] Department stores offered the perfect symbol of London commercial institutions, and of the visual display of the modern metropolis. On October 14, 1940, a female architect living in London linked morale and continuing consumption in London's Regent Street shopping district: 'Each time I go to London I am astonished at its indestructibility. The broken houses might be in process of demolition, the craters in the roads repairs to drains or cables. One can walk down Regent Street in full October sunshine, buy a hat at Dickens and Jones, lunch at Lyons corner house while sirens wail.'[39] Yet Londoners perceived damage to department stores in raids as particularly threatening. Joyce Weiner wrote in her diary:

> Nov 24, 1940. The face of London changed. [Blasted] houses like stage sets faced a gaping world. Unimaginable dust and chaos marked the spot where houses once had been. … The middle class adequacy of John Lewis a dangerous tottering frame of a building – great gobs of Peter Robinson like pieces of served-up pastry rest uneasily in the road. London is deserted, cold, with the winds whistling through its empty screens of damaged stone.[40]

The raid damage deflated the 'middle-class adequacy' of the department store. The incongruous domestic image of masonry as pastry emphasized the fragility of the store, and by extension of the commercial and cultural life of the city. The final image of an empty deserted city, in which nothing and no one is to be seen, points to the fears of the end of British civilization in the war.

Diarists also used stores to map the restricted boundaries of London during the Blitz. In *Outside Information* (1941), Naomi Royde-Smith described how the Blitz changed her shopping schedule:

> As Elizabeth Bowen pointed out this evening, London is no longer a city but a congeries of villages … I was a Londoner

for thirty years. Sloane Square, Sloane Street, Knightsbridge,
Buckingham Palace Road, Bond Street, Regent Street, Heal's,
Selfridges, Fortnum and Mason's, Harrods and Truslove and
Hanson's, were mine to shop in or at: I had my hair sham-
pooed in Conduit Street and, on the same afternoon, bought
French silk at Barker's. In September I got as far north as
Liberty's, as far south as Hampton's. This morning I have done
all my shopping in the Strand.[41]

Shopping in the metropolis is the barometer of the continuing life of
the city. Instead of the Blitz bringing London together, Royde-Smith
described a London whose commodities were restricted and whose
neighborhoods were contracted. The metropolis in this image is
reduced to groups of self-contained villages.

Storeowners responded in placards and advertising to the damage
to their stores. Both contemporary and historical accounts of the
Blitz delight in quoting from the humorous signs placed on bombed-
out stores: 'More open than usual' is often cited. One window display
used modernist metaphors in its response to the destruction of
London. A twenty-year-old male civil servant drew a picture in his
diary of a shop window in Coventry Street on October 18, 1940, in
which a mannequin's naked and upside-down legs protruded from a
placard that read 'BLAST'.[42] Not described in the diary, but next to
this segment of the display was a damaged female mannequin
wearing a gas-mask and torn clothes. The placard echoed both *Blast!*,
the short-lived Vorticist journal published during the Great War, and
the danger of bomb blast in London during the Blitz.

The reference to *Blast!* demonstrates how indebted writings and
cultural references of the Blitz were to early twentieth-century
cultural influences. One of the most significant was the legacy of the
First World War. Writers like Vera Brittain drew on their experiences
of the Great War to make explicit comparisons between the two
conflicts. But the cultural influence of the Great War also surfaced in
the tone, forms and metaphors of Blitz writing. Writers used a flat
and ironic tone, contrasted pastoral metaphors with the horror of

war, and remarked on the seeming absurdity of the possibility of
mechanized death in the midst of life. A diary entry by Harold
Nicolson illustrates all of these themes:

> August 26, 1940. At noon I hear aeroplanes and shortly after-
> wards the wail of the siren. People are becoming quite used to
> these interruptions. I find one practises a sort of suspension of
> the imagination. I do not think that the drone in the sky means
> death to many people at any moment. It seems so incredible as
> I sit here at my window, looking out on the fuchsias and the
> zinneas with yellow butterflies playing round each other, that
> in a few seconds above the trees I may see other butterflies
> circling in the air intent on murdering each other. One lives in
> the present. The past is too sad a recollection and the future
> too sad a despair.[43]

The short sentences and flat tone emphasize the irony of mechanized
warfare, in contrast to the beauty of the garden with its flowers and
butterflies. These images echo Great War poetry, such as that of
Wilfred Owen, Charlotte Mew and others, and Great War memoirs
and novels published in the 1920s and 1930s. The image of the
butterfly echoes the final scene of Erich Maria Remarque's novel *All
Quiet on the Western Front* (1929) in which Paul Baumer follows a
butterfly to his own death.

Nicolson's flat ironic tone is also indebted to the work of
modernist authors. Modernism, dated from approximately 1910 in
Britain, was a loose artistic and cultural movement that attacked the
principles of modern progress. Using a variety of experimental
artistic forms, modernists sought to achieve the unity and harmony
that the modern project had promised, but not quite delivered.[44]
Modernism could be rebellious, individualistic and avant-garde – as
in Wyndham Lewis's *Blast!*, for instance – or traditionalist and
nostalgic. Poets such as T. S. Eliot and W. H. Auden straddle both
aspects, in their trajectories from early modernist experimentation to
more traditional poetic forms and subject matter in the 1930s. In the

rest of the chapter, I will trace in Blitz writings three themes that characterize modernism: the importance of the metropolis, visuality and a profound ambiguity. Through their references to these themes, Blitz writers asserted their importance as witnesses, and the centrality of London as a modern urban space.

The Modern City

Just as the city is central to modernity, so is it central to modernism. As Raymond Williams argued, the shift from the city to the metropolis was crucial to the creation of modernism. The metropolis is characterized by 'crowds of strangers', by the individual lonely in the crowd who performs repetitive and mechanical activities, and by an impenetrable and mysterious geography.[45] British modernist writing, in particular, fed off these themes of urban alienation, and pointed to the degradation of mass culture and decay symbolized by the metropolis. The Georgian poets' return to pastoral metaphors, T. S. Eliot's poem *The Wasteland* and the leftist 'Auden' poets of the 1930s emphasized the worthlessness of modern mass media, and its association with alienating mechanical reproduction. Both mass culture and urban life threatened the elite symbols of national culture, the rural and genteel image of English identity, and its literary inheritance.

Londoners writing during the Blitz transformed this tradition of modernist urban mistrust by asserting the centrality of both mass culture and the urban experience to their participation in the war effort and their vision of the Blitz. Writers used visual metaphors to legitimize their own roles as witnesses and the centrality of the urban space of London to the experience and conception of a modern war.[46]

The transformation of London from an embarrassment to a focus for pride can be traced in the diary of Harold Nicolson, who wrote on February 14, 1940:

Dear London! So vast and unexpected, so ugly and so strong! You have been bruised and battered and all your clothes are

tattered and in disarray. Yet we, who never knew we loved you
(who regarded you in fact like some old family servant,
ministering to our comforts and amenities, yet slightly incongruous and absurd), have suddenly felt the twinge of some
fibre of identity, respect and love. We know what is coming to
you. And our eyes slip along your old untidy limbs, knowing
that the leg may be gone tomorrow, and that tomorrow the
arm may be severed. Yet through all this regret and dread
pierces a slim clean note of pride. 'London can take it.'[47]

Nicolson's account implicitly reveals how London, specifically the
poorer East End, moves from the perceived seat of degeneration and
decay to the focus of civilian morale during the Blitz. Londoners,
indebted to modernist metaphors, transform London in the act of
writing to the apex of a new cultural and national pride.

Visual Metaphors

As one of the key features of the modernist metropolis was the
movement of crowds of strangers, the most important modernist
figure was the privileged spectator. As the seminal modernist writer
Charles Baudelaire defined him, the modernist spectator, or *flâneur*,
was an aimless urban wanderer/observer who easily traversed the
divided spaces of the metropolis.[48] The *flâneur* was protected by his
anonymity and free to gaze on the urban spectacle before him, yet
also had to fear the contagion that proximity to the degenerative
urban crowd and forms of popular culture generated.[49] Londoners
writing during the Blitz were influenced by the modernist idea of the
privileged spectator, but instead of fearing the alienating aspects of
mass culture, they embraced its forms in their metaphors linking the
Blitz with newspapers, films and photographs.

   One of the most frequent metaphors in Blitz diaries and memoirs
is the act of reading. The bright lights of bombing raids were
especially compelling to observers in a city blacked-out since
September 1939. The raids were so intense, diarists claimed, that they

could have read by the light of London fires. Metaphors of newspaper readings emphasized the long tradition of London newspapers and illustrated magazines as well as the ferocity of the raids.[50] Mrs M. Morris wrote on December 30, 1940: 'We could hear planes overhead but it was not until we walked across Westminster Bridge that we realized the full horror of the situation. The whole City was ablaze. It was like bright daylight and had we felt so inclined it would have been possible to read a newspaper. We could see the dome of St Paul's standing out against an awesome background of flame.'[51] Vere Hodgson saw the fires the same night: 'After I wrote my diary last night there were Terrible Fires in London. We went up on the roof to look. At Shepherd's Bush flames were leaping, and towards the City they were gigantic. As I walked up the road I could see the smoke. A great red glow filled the sky – I had no need of a torch – I could see every step that I took and could have read a book if I had wished.'[52] Metaphors of reading did more than underline the intensity or brightness of the fires. They also emphasized the spectator who could observe London with the assurance of historical and aesthetic specificity. The image of reading a newspaper during a raid also emphasized British fearlessness and pragmatism in the face of danger.[53]

Modernists tended to mistrust visual forms of popular culture, such as films and photographs, as empty forms of mechanically reproduced objects.[54] Diarists and commentators reversed the trend, comparing London during the raids to films, theatre or photographs. These forms of media were increasingly important in the modern metropolis, and vital to portraying and preserving images of London at war.[55]

During the war, London itself became the subject of propaganda films such as *London Can Take It* and *Fires Were Started* in 1940 and 1941. But propagandistic filming of the city was constrained by the ambiguous messages of images of the devastated city. Censors were worried that the shots of bombed buildings might hurt civilian confidence and morale. At the height of the Blitz, the chief censor required that each panning shot of London 'start from an undamaged building ... conclude on an undamaged building and ... not linger over damaged buildings.'[56] The scenes of devastation that Londoners saw as they traveled through the city seemed so unreal compared to the censored films of London that diarists and memoirists compared London not to British films, but to American ones. Mollie Panter-Downes compared the scene after a bomb exploded outside the Café Royal on September 14, 1940 to a movie set:

> The scene the next morning was quite extraordinarily eerie. The great sweep of Regent Street, deserted by everyone except police and salvage workers, stared gauntly like a thoroughfare in a dead city. It would have been no surprise to see grass growing up out of the pavements, which were covered instead with a fine, frosty glitter of powdered glass. ... Scenes like this are new enough to seem both shocking and unreal; to come across a wrecked filling station with a couple of riddled cars standing dejectedly by its smashed pumps makes one feel that one must have strayed on to a Hollywood set, and it's good to get back to normality among the still snug houses in the next street.[57]

The image of the dead city evokes ghost town movie sets and old Westerns.[58] Panter-Downes conjures up images of a deserted, still and dead city to express fears for London's survival.

In his memoir, *Ain't it Grand (Or This Was Stepney)* (1981), Jim Wolveridge described how damage from the raids eventually forced him to leave the East End and his impoverished youth. His description of leaving Stepney in a rain of ash and emerging into the sunshine of Ealing was both a visual comparison of the ferocity of the raids in the East End and the rest of London, and a dramatic metaphor for moving into a hopeful future. He compared the raids over Stepney to a film:

> Aldgate bus station had been bombed in the night, and all the buses in the depot were burning. There was the biggest fire I

had ever seen, and smoke was climbing a mile high. Bits of burning rags and paper were raining down on High Street, and we had to walk through it, dodging the flaming stuff as best we could. It was a bit like the film version of the 'Last Days of Pompeii', and we got a rousing send-off. All that first week of the Blitz there had been so much smoke and dust that we couldn't see the sky, and when we got to Ealing we saw clear blue skies, and it was a shock to realize it was still summertime. I'd escaped from the East End at last, but it had taken a war to uproot me. And now I'm back in Stepney again, it seems I can't escape, maybe this is where I belong.[59]

Wolveridge underlined the spectacular nature of the raids, and the intensive devastation of the East End.[60] Images and metaphors comparing the dead city to forms of mass culture expressed writers' attempts both to assert the modernity of London as a metropolis and to express fears of the city's possible destruction in the devastation of bombing raids.

The photograph was and is the most popular means of representing the Blitz. As Walter Benjamin argued in *A Short History of Photography* (1931), the photograph is also the privileged mode of representation of modernism, in the alienation of its posed studio subject, the mechanical nature of the reproduction of negatives and the urban proletariat as a new artistic subject.[61] Easily reproduced and distributed in illustrated newspapers, magazines and books, photographic representations of the Blitz depicted the architectural damage from air raids while emphasizing signs of continuing life in the city. Photographs of London during the Blitz were heavily censored to protect civilian morale and to conceal from the Germans information about the success of their raids.

Obtaining permission to take photographs in 1940 was a complex process. To get a photography permit from the Ministry of Information, a photographer or cinematographer had to have accreditation, usually from a newspaper or public agency.[62] Authorized photographers then submitted their photographs to the Official Censor before they were published or distributed. Photographers tended to self-censor their pictures in hopes of a speedy return of their photographs, and sometimes the public reaction to the presence of a photographer meant that shots were censored before they could be taken. Cecil Beaton, a society and fashion photographer, recorded in his diary how he was prevented from photographing the remains of a wax head among the wreckage of a hairdressing establishment: 'The usual officious passer-by appeared', demanding to see his papers and insisting that photographing the heads 'wasn't right – the Ministry of Information would not want to show anything like that. I explained that, in any case, my photographs had to be submitted to the censor. But the discontent had started and was now gathering momentum.'[63] A police constable was called and Beaton was escorted to the police station.

Beaton, whose photography had been influenced by Surrealism in the 1930s, and other wartime photographers sought to capture the visual incongruity of bomb sites. Objects in the debris, such as the wax head, offered a poignant reminder of the vulnerability of people and businesses to raids. Beaton described seeing such an incongruous bombed-out street scene in his diary:

> October 12, 1940. One feels a sinking of the heart at the sight of even more bomb damage: windows blown in and tumbled wreckage of rubble in the road. A small dwelling – its front cut away – gives a doll's house effect, with the parlour, where the evening meal was being eaten at the cloth covered table, a teapot and a bowl of tomatoes exposed to passers-by. Pictures have been knocked crooked by the blast. Skyed high in the air remain the useless bath and lavatory with the pathetic little roll of toilet paper still affixed to the door, and the staircase leads to an upper floor that no longer exists. James is writing a book called *London Under Fire* for which I am doing the photographs. Besides the vandalistic damage, we must show the tenacity and courage of the people, and we do not have to look far. Signs are posted: 'We have no glass, but business continues.' As soon

as the worst rubbish is cleared away, the notice appears, 'Open as usual'.[64]

The written scene, rich in visual imagery, has the quality of a photograph already, in the visual contrast of the toilet paper and the unscathed bowl of tomatoes with the general destruction. Both the debris and the posted signs' reaction to it emphasize continuing life in the city, damaged but not devastated. Beaton makes explicit the visual nature of witnessing and depicting the Blitz.[65] The aesthetic pleasure derived from scenes of destruction such as this points to the final theme of modernism: ambiguity.

The Ambiguity of Modernity

Modernism as an artistic reaction to the experience of modernity was characterized by a fundamental ambiguity: the desire for order in the face of disorder. The desire to observe and to discover hidden meaning in the metropolis also became, in early twentieth-century modernist writing, an assertion of the desire to impose order on the city through art. By pointing to the degeneration of the urban space the modern writer could position himself as a savior and assert the validity of his writing. The modernist metropolis was therefore both a risk and a resource in modernism's struggle for cultural authority.[66] The ambiguities of modernism also point to the partiality and uneven modernization of cities such as London, in which civic innovations and building entailed the destruction of older historic buildings.[67]

The Blitz, like Victorian urban planning, was a form of creative destruction, a final push of the city into modernity. Such destructiveness, and the aesthetic pleasure that writers recorded feeling in their witnessing of it, gave their writings a profound sense of ambiguity which surfaced in sublime metaphors of 'terrible beauty' and in a loose surrealism which lingered in vague threats and uncanny associations. These metaphors underline Blitz writers' implicitly ambiguous relationship to the visual metaphors of newspapers, photographs and films that emphasize the city's modernity, but whose recorded spectacle is the city's apparent destruction.

Modernists were not the first to consider the possible destruction of the city of London. In 1757, Edmund Burke, in *Enquiry into the ... Sublime and Beautiful* defined the sublime as the perception of beauty in terror:

> I believe no man is so strangely wicked as to desire to see [London] destroyed by a conflagration or an earthquake. But suppose such a fatal accident to have happened, what numbers from all parts would crowd to behold the ruins, and amongst them many who would have been content never to have seen London in its glory?[68]

The sublime was the sense of aesthetic pleasure derived from large-scale suffering and destruction, and has been identified as the paradigmatic modern/postmodern aesthetic value permeating popular culture to the point of becoming commonplace.[69] While Burke's sublime destruction was theoretical, the invention of modern artillery made nineteenth- and twentieth-century battlefields the epitome of beauty in terror. George Frederick Dallas, a soldier in the Crimean War, described being under enemy fire while hidden on a mountain face above Sebastopol in 1854 as 'the most beautiful and horrific sight I ever witnessed. The romantic situation we were in lighted up by the constant bursting of shells, the awful noise and reverberation through the hills, & the knowledge of the very important position we were in charge of, all combined to make it a most exciting position to be placed in.'[70] The visual beauty of the lights of the cannonade and the view of the city was enhanced by the excitement not only of battle, but also of being a participant and a witness. Descriptions of terrible beauty also demand a certain distance: the ability to see the battlefield from afar.

The First World War made witnessing these battlefield images possible for civilians. The air attacks made on London by German Zeppelins in 1915–1916 and airplanes in 1916–1917 had a negligible death toll of between 600 and 800 people, but signaled London's vulnerability to the technological advances of warfare. Two daylight raids, one on June 13, 1917 targeting the Royal Albert Docks, Liverpool Street Station and Poplar, and one on July 7, 1917 hitting Shoreditch, St Pancras and the City, produced together 832 casualties at the rate of 121 casualties per ton of bombs dropped, which strongly influenced the interwar predictions about the likely effects of future raids on London.[71] At the height of the German attacks, 250,000 people took shelter in the Tube stations and tunnels under the Thames, and many Londoners evacuated the city. Michael MacDonagh, journalist for *The Times*, recorded in his diary his impression of a Zeppelin bombing raid on January 17, 1917:

> I saw last night the most wonderful spectacle of beauty and terror combined that I have ever seen, or that, perhaps, it is possible for anyone ever to see outside the arena of war. ... It was pitch dark. Then suddenly a golden glow lit up the eastern sky, making everything as clear as day; and looking down the Thames I saw a high column of yellow flames rising, as I thought, from the river. This quickly died down, and the sky immediately became overspread with the loveliest colours – violet, indigo, blue, green, yellow, orange and red – which eddied and swirled. ... Dazzled and awestruck, I saw that London, so dark a few moments before, was made glorious as if by a marvellous sunset the like of which had never been seen before. ... Its disappearance was accompanied by a terrific explosion, rising and shattering and dying away with an angry growl. ... It had something of the terror of the unknown and uncanny. I thought if God ever came out of the sky He would appear like that in awful majesty. But, of course, it must be an air raid.[72]

Writers used many of the same descriptions to describe raids during the Blitz: the colors, the glowing sky and the sunset. Though MacDonagh was careful to point that out the raid was the greatest spectacle outside the battlefield, this distinction could not be made during the Blitz, when London itself was the arena of war.

London's sublime destruction was one of the main metaphors in writing about the Blitz. Terrible beauty was a striking metaphor for the danger, contingency and unreal visual beauty of the raids: the lights of the planes, guns, and fires against a blacked-out sky. Again and again diarists and memoirists describe raids as 'magnificent and terrible', 'the most beautiful and the most horrific spectacle I ever saw', and 'very Beautiful'.[73]

Vivienne Hall's diary describes the beauty of the sky during a raid on September 23, 1940: 'A Lovely starlit night, the sky, seemingly laced with searchlights and stars of bursting shells and the usual noises to make it more obvious that beauty has no part in this world of our making at the moment.'[74] Florence Speed also pointed out the irony of such destructive beauty on November 1, 1940: 'Incredibly lovely sight. Have been watching from the roof formations of planes[,] several in action at once, criss crossing and streaking across the sky, patterning the blue with snow white smoke trails. Odd that anything so beautiful, brings death and destruction.'[75] Bruce Lockhart compared the airplanes above London to tropical fish in the Pacific Ocean, an image whose beauty he found impossible to reconcile with the destruction they represented.[76]

The aesthetic pleasure of witnessing the Blitz could conflict with the writers' role as historical witnesses. Their motives for writing necessitated that they put themselves in the frame, even if it deflated sublime imagery. Edith Grimshaw wrote:

April 16, 1941. To have a picture of this raid imagine yourself standing in a darkened street and whichever way you looked the sky is aglow with the light of many furnace-like fires and every building around you is floodlit with the white glare of parachute flares. Also, the many coloured tracer shells which look like giant strings of beads, winging their way through flight paths in the sky, searching out the intruder planes, plus flashes from the hundreds of incendiary bombs. All the while the drone of the planes in the sky and the roar of the guns seeking them out is like the sound of a mighty orchestra. The whole scene has a kind of terrible beauty. Winnie and I viewed this from the fire escape stairs.[77]

Towards the end of the bombing raids, people in London were so obsessed with the visual display of raids that they stood outside to watch the lights and fires. After the raids on May 11, 1941, the *Daily Express* condemned the 'gawkers' and 'blitz-trippers' who crowded the streets the next day:

> But the day being Sunday and a day of rest, thousands of people had nothing to do. So they came in droves to look at the seared ruins, to block the streets, to trample on hoses, to hold up fire engines, to gawk at the weary, blistered firemen, to fill the roads with their cars, to hamper the police, to stare at the grimy, half-clad homeless. It was a day out.[78]

Burke's prediction of the aesthetic pleasure people would take in the destruction of London had come true.

Another aspect of the ambiguity of modernism is the sense of dislocation and discontinuity that permeates much of the private writings of the Blitz. To express their sense of loss and alienation in the face of the destruction of the city, Londoners turned to strange juxtapositions and metaphors of the uncanny. Writers were indebted to surrealism, though not formal surrealism. Blitz writers seemed to use automatic writing: a literary technique of surrealist writing which produces an uninterrupted chain of associations. The images produced by this technique can be read, according to Michel Riffaterre, as an extended metaphor within the limits of the text.[79] In the case of Blitz writings, surrealist metaphors can be read as expressions of the more traumatic elements of the bombing raids. Writers used surrealist metaphors to convey the darker side of modern warfare: the juxtaposition of terror and beauty and the eerie and uncanny aspects of London in the Blitz.

Surrealism began as a European movement, pioneered by artists such as André Breton and Salvador Dali, who strove to abolish the frontiers between dream world and reality and mine the unconscious for a revolutionary approach to reality and art.[80] Breton himself had been profoundly influenced by his experiences as a medical student in neuropsychiatry facilities for wounded soldiers during the First World War, where free association and dream interpretation were used as treatments for the soldiers' psychological disturbances, generally termed neurasthenia. Breton drew on these experiences in his art, which celebrated the relationship between dreams and reality. Breton saw surrealism in art as a liberatory process of desublimation, an antidote to the traumatic psychic sublimation Sigmund Freud observed in similar wounded soldier case studies.

The Surrealist movement, particularly active in the interwar era, sought irrational clues and unexplained connections in art, and juxtaposed different realities through a variety of mediums, including painting, sculpture and performance art. The Surrealist agenda was to conflate the seeing subject and the object – the interchange between the surrealist seeing and being seen – as part of their construction of human subjectivity as a fluctuating relationship between vision, body and space.[81] The English Surrealist group was centered in London, where the International Surrealist exhibition opened in 1936.[82] British culture revealed the popularization of Surrealism through the fashion photography and photographic portraits of Cecil Beaton and Lee Miller, who worked for British *Vogue* after 1940, as well as the auto-ethnography of Mass Observation and the films of one of its founders, Humphrey Jennings.[83]

The war decimated the English surrealists as an artistic group but popularized Surrealism as a mode of expression.[84] As Breton found in World War One, the setting and psychic strains of war encouraged the expression of the irrational. London during the war seemed to be a ready-made surrealist setting, with blacked-out streets, sandbagged doorways and shelters, random encounters in streets and shelters and the spectacular 'terrible beauty' of raids. Writing diary entries or letters during the raids to relieve tension and fear was similar to

Surrealist automatic writing, in which artists tried to write without thinking in order to bring forward associated words and images from the unconscious mind.

London during the Blitz became the perfect symbol of the Surrealist juxtaposition of realities, just as Berlin during the war became the Expressionist city of a Nazi World made real.[85] Yet London became surreal not as an artistic creation, but in the surreal aspects of the experiences of its inhabitants. Their writings reflect the surreal aspects of a city being bombed nightly, peppered with bursts of patriotism. As the writer and editor John Lehmann described: 'London had suddenly become two cities. The one, the daytime city where we went about our business much as before, worked in our offices and discussed what plans we could make for the future. ... The other London was the new, symbolic city of the blackout, where one floundered about in the unaccustomed darkness of the streets, bumping into patrolling wardens or huddled strangers...'[86] The chance encounter in the dark streets added to London's menacing mien:

> Strangest of all at night were the London terminus stations: King's Cross appeared like some weird imagining of John Martin, the long trains waiting like prehistoric beasts, smoking and hissing under the huge, gloomy cavern of the glass roofing only discernible by the rows of faint blue lights far above. Shadowy figures of porters and policemen moved around the bales and packages heaped in dark corners. ... The whole city was in a great conspiracy of secrecy, confusing yet curiously stimulating; when one went into a club or restaurant or drinking place one felt one had reached some beleaguered subterranean den or cave in the mountains...[87]

The conspiracy of secrecy signified both the shared nervous tension in London and the dream-like intensity of the city during the Blitz. London in this description becomes an uncanny city, in which a mysterious landscape, strangely familiar, evokes terror.

The surreal visual aspects of London during the Blitz were an uncanny geography and the strange juxtapositions of objects and people in the blacked-out streets. He or she who traveled though London during a raid was a new kind of *flâneur* discovering the irrationality of the city. In his diary on October 30, 1940, S. G. Champion described being out during a raid on an errand for the wardens. He and his companion were sheltering in a pub, when they heard two bombs dropping. Everyone ducked for cover, but got up amidst jokes when there was no explosion. He looked out the door and saw the building across the street was on fire from an oil bomb. He and his companion continued down the street, but got nervous in the increasing intensity of the raid: 'Seeing a white concrete building next to the public house, we made for it in the hope that it was a shelter. We were out in double quick time on discovering that it was a petrol station.' Finally they reached the hospital to deliver a swab: 'We had taken only a few steps when the guns restarted and faint cries for help came from the darkness. Thinking someone had been hit by shrapnel we drew the attention of a passer-by. He said it was a drunkard, so we left it at that. Several moments later, a man stopped at the Warden's Post, having apparently fallen into the River Rum.'[88] The fires, bombs and guns of the air raids gave random encounters in urban space an added unreality.

Even the most pragmatic of witnesses felt the dream-aspect of raids. Max Cohen's memoir, *What Nobody told the Foreman* (1953), detailed the conditions of work during the war. His description of the fantastic beauty of the raids was parenthetical to the life of work that his book details, and he wrote explicitly of their dream-like nature:

Many recollections of that hectic time return: of nights when all hell seemed to have broken loose, when a mad cacophony of guns and bombs assailed the black empty streets with crashing and shattering explosions, when the house was shaking with a violent bout of *delirium tremens*, when into the turmoil of conflicting noises came the dry scratching rattle of shrapnel on the roof. Nights when through the uncurtained bedroom window came a bewildering display of pyrotechnics, flashes and flickering and explosions of red, yellow, green, white, chasing and tumbling over one another and mingling with one another in a fantastic series of cosmic fireworks. And yet once again we would wake in the morning unscathed. The hectic air-raid would seem a mere nightmare of the imagination.[89]

The raids and their dangerous beauty were, as in Lehmann's account, juxtaposed with the rationality of daytime life, signifying the ambiguities of a city at war.[90]

Aesthetic metaphors expressed the fearfulness and strangeness of the raid. Alan Goodlet referred to raids as 'the Devil's picnic' and Max Cohen described them as 'a witches cauldron' of cosmic fireworks, metaphors suggesting both evil and otherworldly pyro-technics.[91] Harold Nicolson also used metaphors of otherness to describe what was once familiar:

> April 16, 1940. After typing this I go to bed. I get off to sleep all right, but the blitz gets worse and worse, and the night shrieks and jabbers like an African jungle. I have never heard such a variety of sounds – the whistle of descending bombs, the crash of anti-aircraft, the dull thud of walls collapsing, the sharp taps of incendiaries falling all around. The British Museum opposite my window turns rose-red in the light of the fire of the University. Every now and then it turns sharp white when a magnesium flare descends. Then rose-red again. It goes all night and I sleep fitfully.[92]

Nicolson's African jungle metaphor draws on the tradition of imperialism and metaphors of the jungle as savage and mysterious. It also reflects the long tradition of portraying East London as an exotic, mysterious and impoverished 'Other'. The impressionistic journalism of Henry Mayhew in particular, published in 1861 as *London Labour and the London Poor*, used metaphors of imperial exploration to describe journeys into Whitechapel, Bethnal Green, Wapping and Limehouse areas of east London. Such language and imagery set the tone for subsequent writings, and influenced such disparate figures as the early social scientist Charles Booth, who described 'Darkest London'; preacher, reformer and Salvation Army founder William Booth who published *In Darkest London and the Way Out* in 1890; and American journalist Jack London, who published *People of the Abyss* in 1903. These accounts emphasized the exoticism of urban poverty and the cultural mores of the 'tribal' poor in the East End. In this passage Nicolson reveals his uneasiness at the strange geography of London during the raids and displaces an older metaphor of tribal savagery of the London poor onto the Germans and onto the city as a whole under siege.

London's geography was uncanny not only during the raids, but also in the strangeness of the streets in the days after. The writer Mrs Robert Henrey described her street after a bomb had hit:

> The bomb that had fallen on our garage had made a sorry sight of our village street. It had shattered every window, and filled the glass strewn road with wares of all descriptions. One was obliged to tread carefully over boxes of sardines from the general store and bottles of perfume from the ladies' hair-dressing establishment run by our local chief warden. But the queerest assortment of goods was pitch-forked into the centre of the road from the old curiosity shop run by a gentleman of eighty-nine who had a patriarchal white beard. There were officer's leggings and stage swords that had once flashed on the boards of Drury Lane in epic melodramas, women's white boots that buttoned up the side, billiard balls and telescopes and South American riding saddles. A policeman had picked up from the gutter a collection of African spears, with which he was gesticulating in the light of dawn.[93]

As Nicolson did, Mrs Henrey used the metaphor of Africa to denote strangeness and described the spectacle of the goods in the street as an imperial exhibition. The spear-waving policemen is an example of the most respected figures of authority made strange by the effects of the bomb; instead of collecting or inspecting the spears he gesticulates with them, becoming tribal in the strange new jungle of London.

Sometimes the uncanny and dream-like nature of raids in London could be menacing. The Surrealists' own emphasis on liberation ignored the darker aspects of their exploration of the unconscious, in which the return of repressed unconscious material, in the form of the 'uncanny', disrupted unitary identity, aesthetic norms and social order.[94] Michael MacDonagh used the term 'uncanny' in his description of the World War One air raid, twinned with a religious metaphor comparing the raids to a manifestation of God in the world. In World War Two accounts, the beauty and the terror of raids were not linked to greater spiritual economies, but existed without a system of meaning, making them seem random and surreal.

The dislocation of London during the Blitz could be beautiful, but was also ominous. Mrs M. Morris described the threatening aspects of uncanny juxtaposition in her diary entry of May 9, 1941: 'We went for a walk round the West End after lunch, and it was a renewed shock to me to see London as it is now. After twenty months of war there is a smell of death and destruction everywhere – blasted windows – clocks without hands – great mounds of yellow rubble. There is a poisonous tang of damp plaster and coal gas, a reminder that eighteen thousand Londoners have died here.'[95] Her association of the ruined landscape with death and bereavement was rare among diaries and memoirs, and stands in sharp contrast to the journalistic images of heroic and plucky London. The dream-like images and the description of clocks without hands also echoed Salvador Dali's disturbing painting of melting clocks, *The Persistence of Memory* (1931). Art historian Jose Milicua recently uncovered evidence of surrealist torture cells built in Barcelona in 1938 in which curved walls, angled furniture and confusing geometric patterns point to the darker uses to which avant-garde art could be put.[96]

Sickness and anxiety over the sight of London's dislocation were explicit in Vera Brittain's diary entry of September 17, 1940: 'To get to Paddington, we ordered a taxi; it was a nightmare journey like one of Wells' terrible fantasies. Went along Mile End Road, then through City. Dislocation appalling everywhere; yawning gaps where buildings had been; immense detours, huge traffic blocks, piles of rubble, craters in street. Made me feel too sick for words.' During this time she was writing *England's Journey*; nothing of this fearful tone and nightmarish landscape appeared there.

The most literary of wartime diarists was undoubtedly Virginia Woolf. Written shortly before her final descent into madness, Woolf's description of a journey through blitzed London reveals a surreal landscape and embattled consciousness. Her description was fragmentary and impressionistic, a series of hallucinatory images filled with a sense of menace and danger:

Sept 10, 1940. Back from half a day in London – perhaps our strangest visit. ... The house about 30 yards from ours was struck at one this morning by a bomb. Completely ruined. Another bomb in the square still unexploded. We walked around the back. Stood by Jane Harrison's house. The house was still smouldering. That is a great pile of bricks. Underneath people who had gone down to their shelter. Scraps of cloth hanging to bare walls at the side still standing. A looking glass I think swinging. Like a tooth knocked out – a clean cut. Our house undamaged. ... I suppose the casual young men & women I used to see, from my window; the flat dwellers who used to have flower pots & sit on the balcony. All now blown to bits.[97]

The surreal images are even more striking and disturbing because they are stripped of their context. While Mrs Morris wrote in a linear narrative and Brittain alluded to Wells, Woolf described only disconnected scenes, such as the image of the mirror swinging like a tooth. She also alluded to the death of people in the shelter, the human trauma behind the images of physical destruction. Her journey continued:

> Then into Lincoln's Inn. To the N.S. office, windows broken but house untouched. We went over it. Deserted. Wet passages. Glass on stairs. Doors locked. So back to the car. ... And then miles & miles of orderly ordinary streets – all Bayswater, & Sussex Sqre as usual. Streets empty. Faces set & eyes bleared. In Chancery Lane I saw a man with a barrow of music books. My typist's office destroyed. Then at Wimbledon a Siren – people began running. We drove, through almost empty streets, as fast as possible. Horses taken out of their shafts. Cars pulled up. Then the all clear. The people I think of now are the very grimy lodging house keepers, say in Heathcote Street; with another night to face; wretched old women standing at their doors; dirty, miserable.

A sense of danger permeates the passage, as people run at the sound of the siren and those in the car drive out of a sense of urgency. The potential humor of the sight of the man with his barrow of books is deflated by images of dead and miserable Londoners.

Visual descriptions of London during the Blitz emphasized both aesthetic legacies of modernism, the liberatory wonder and visual pleasure of the 'terrible beauty' of the raids and fires, and the anxiety produced by the uncanny and surreal landscape of London. Modernism was also ambiguous in its relationship to the artistic past. The tension between the two facets of modernism – the artistic and critical insistence on an elite and individual culture versus the symbols and representation of democratized mass culture – fed into debates about the effects of modern war on the city and its culture.

Peter Quennell's description of his favorite London landmark illustrates the tension between elite and popular culture in the city. His experience of the Blitz was punctuated by a frustrating job at the Ministry of Information, makeshift flat arrangements and unhappy love affairs.[98] Quennell contrasted the marble statue visible from his office window to the wartime degradation of London:

> Visible from the Ministry [of Information]'s windows was a lonely marble nymph. Stationed at the bottom of Berkeley Square, opposite the disfigured remains of Landsdowne House. ... There she stood, and happily, still stands – a pensive naiad dropping above a fountain that had long since ceased to flow, her smooth shoulders and gracefully moulded breast worn by years of London rain, her bowed neck, the twist of her body and the line of the arms that hold the urn, forming a harmonious fluid curve ... she symbolized all the charms of peace, all the graces and virtues that a modern war destroys. Since parks and squares had lost their railings ... they had become refuse-littered dust-bowls. The ruins one passed every day had at least a tragic and heroic look; and burned out City churches, their steeples scorched and discoloured by fire, possessed a kind of dreadful beauty. Far worse were degrading minor details – telephone boxes that stank of urine, scrawled over with obscene inscriptions; the heavy sickening stench of Underground platforms where one picked one's way through lines of corpse-like figures asleep among their household goods. My nymph, although eternally silent and aloof, spoke a language that I could understand. Even the rough graffiti that disfigured her marble flanks could not spoil her air of deep repose.[99]

The nymph stood for the vanishing British culture of civilization that Quennell saw the Blitz destroying. For Quennell, the war was degrading, exposing the ugliness and poverty of the city, and defacing the traditional elite values that had created the nymph with the graffiti of social decline. Like Orwell in *1984* and Evelyn Waugh in *Brideshead Revisited*, Quennell expressed nostalgia for elite forms of culture and anxiety about the effects of war on postwar values and society. Among the diarists and memoirists of the Blitz, he is in the minority.

Diarists' and memoirists' descriptions of London during the Blitz were heavily indebted to modernist metaphors. Civilian writers used metaphors of reading, watching films and photography to link raids to the familiar, and to emphasize their own importance as viewers. Like the Crimean soldier and the Great War journalist in London, Londoners during the Blitz were awed, saddened and excited by what they saw during the Blitz, and by their own privileged position as witnesses. The use of modernist and surrealist imagery points to the new artistic and historical interrelationship between the spectator and the London they watched. The images of London they helped to create were so strong that they disguised the continuing social inequalities and general privations of the Blitz, creating an imagined wartime London whose existence is still presumed to be real in many histories of the Blitz. In the following chapters, I contrast this imagined aesthetic map of London to the social experiences of raids, rationing, work, family life and sexuality during the Blitz.

2

RAIDS AND RATIONING

At 8:30 we heard a most terrific explosion and the sound of everything falling. Dirt and rubble trapped us in the shelter. ... With the help of our neighbors we managed to make a hole big enough for us to crawl through. I shall always remember what I saw then: Just a pile of rubble where our bungalow had stood. Beside us was a large gaping hole. Everything we had possessed had gone into that hole. I had planted rows of spinach in the garden. Not a bit remained. An apple and a pear tree had completely disappeared. ... Human nature is a funny thing for, believe it or not, although we had lost everything we possessed, the thing I mourned for most was my precious spinach.[1]

In Grace Foakes's memoir, she described how she and her children survived a bomb that destroyed her home in Hornchurch and killed her neighbors. Fixating on the loss of the spinach was not just an effect of psychological shock, but also a reaction to the restricted diet of rationing to which home-grown vegetables were a welcome addition. After the hit, Grace Foakes had nowhere to go. As the bomb that destroyed her house was the first bomb to fall in Hornchurch, there were no reception centers set up, and she and her children had to walk the streets by day and sleep in shelters at night.

Grace Foakes's experiences during the Blitz illustrate the social inequalities that lurked beneath the metaphors of imagined community in London. Despite the symbolic images of a united London, the city's organizational, geographical and class differences contributed to an uneven social experience of the Blitz. In this chapter, I examine the social experiences of bombing raids and food rationing in the context of civilian morale and national fortitude. While observers presented an ideal of unbroken civilian morale and British steadfastness, diaries and memoirs reveal a London community engaged in debates over entitlement and divided along lines of ethnicity, gender and class.

On September 11, 1940, the *Daily Express* asserted that 'bombs show no class distinction' and that the raids had transformed London from 'an uneven city' to a 'common state'. But the demographics of London in the fall of 1940 had changed since the beginning of the war. Many with the means and opportunity to leave London had done so. Parents were encouraged to evacuate their school-age children in a state-sponsored program, and many children were privately evacuated. Voluntary evacuation was not just for children, as Margaret Kennedy described her encounters with some evacuated bourgeois women in Wales in July 1940: 'The expensive hotels are filling up with expensive evacuées. We call them the Gluebottoms because they seem able to do nothing but sit. In the lounges and on the beaches you find them in hammock chairs, complaining of the personal inconvenience to which this war has put them.'[2] An evacuation of a less comfortable kind was forced on all 'enemy aliens' in Britain. They had to appear before tribunals at the outbreak of war, and classified: 'A' class aliens were interned, 'B' class were restricted and the majority of aliens, grouped into 'C' class, had free movement. On May 16 and 17, 1940, with the fall of France looming, all 'B' class aliens, over 27,000 people, were hastily rounded up and interned, while 'C' class had to endure new restrictions, reflecting and adding to the fears and anxieties of the public.[3] Even men who had served in the First World War were refused entry into the volunteer defence services or Home Guard if they had a foreign-born father, though by May 1941 London Civil Defence Regional

Commissioners recommended that aliens could be full-time paid volunteers.[4] Conditions for internees, which were in many cases appalling, and the injustice and inconsistency of the Home Guard policies were frequently attacked by the trade unions, the Communist Party and the editorials of *The Jewish Chronicle*.[5] The government eventually seemed to realize that interning and deporting aliens was a waste of labor. In the fall of 1940 over a thousand detainees were released to work in agriculture or industry, though many would remain imprisoned until 1944. The public was less concerned about the internment of the political detainees such as Oswald Mosley, his wife Diana and many of Mosley's supporters, who were imprisoned in May 1940.[6]

Although political speeches and press articles described Londoners as a collective grouping and a united community, not all people in London were considered equal citizens. Frances Faviell of Chelsea described in her memoir how many of her friends had left London, and friends who were not British were treated with suspicion, 'a queer hostile questioning attitude to any of their friends who had any vestige of foreign blood in them'.[7] The new recruits of the wartime Ministries were especially suspicious, and the 'foreigners' were soon excluded from her social circle. Despite these provisos, Faviell, seemingly unaware of what her own comments revealed about the chauvinism of wartime London, described the Blitz as a period of crumbling barriers, when those who were left talked to each other in the streets, shops and shelters.[8]

Though the British Union of Fascists was banned in 1940, anti-Semitism continued to surface in London. The Trades Advisory Council found that even with increased demands for wartime labor, employers still discriminated against Jewish applicants and employees. Anti-Semitism was most overt in the East End, where the 1936 Battle of Cable Street between Jews and fascists was still fresh in memory, but it also existed throughout London and Britain. Jews served as what Ritchie Calder called 'the objects of transferable vengeance' and were often blamed for getting Britain into the war, dominating the black market, and being cowards.[9] Anti-Semitic remarks pepper diaries of the Blitz, including that of Florence Speed of Brixton, who described acts of cowardice by Jews. A retired seventy-one-year-old man drew a line in his Mass Observation diary between Jew and 'Englishman' on December 14, 1940: 'I had my hair cut yesterday by a Jew. I remarked upon his accent and told him he was no Englishman but I might have guessed had I troubled to look at his nose in the glass in front of me as he snipped away at my hair.'[10] George Orwell heard rumors of greater numbers of Jews in shelters, and resolved to examine the shelter crowds:

> The other night I examined the crowds sheltering in Chancery Lane, Oxford Circus and Baker Street Stations. *Not* all Jews, but, I think, a higher proportion of Jews than one would normally see in a crowd of this size. What is bad about Jews is that they are not only conspicuous, but go out of the way to make themselves so. A fearful Jewish woman, a regular comic-paper cartoon of a Jewess, fought her way off the train at Oxford Circus, landing blows on anyone who stood in her way.[11]

Even the newspaper *The Catholic Herald* described the East End shelter of Tilbury as a 'brothel', where the 'ubiquitous Jew and his family spread disease and the young Jewish Communist' added 'fuel to the red fire'.[12] A fifty-three-year-old woman noted in her Mass Observation diary the disquieting increase in anti-Semitism: 'October 29, 1940. I have heard an alarming amount of anti-Jewish sentiment expressed lately and if things go badly for us in the war I foresee the time when we shall start pogroms – German fashion.'[13] Many tried to refute this image of Jews, including the newspaper *The Jewish Chronicle*, which celebrated in headlines 'Jewish People's Exemplary Courage' and 'London Jewry's Splendid Fortitude'. The paper was also careful to note in news stories the incidences of cooperation between Jews and Gentiles, and later in the Blitz they note that the anti-Semitism in shelters had decreased as conditions in shelters improved.[14] Hilde Marchant, a journalist for the *Daily Express*, noted in her account of the Battle of Britain that Jews had behaved like 'good citizens', and the Mayor of Stepney credited the Blitz with bringing the Jews and Gentiles of that community together.[15]

Ethnicity and politics were not the only dividing factors in London in 1940. Even those who stayed in London during the Blitz did not always see themselves as Londoners. In a letter on September 23, 1940, Diana Cooper, living in the Savoy Hotel with her husband Duff, wrote: 'I am not, as you know, made of the stuff Londoners are made of. My instinct is to flee.'[16] Though Cooper accepted a particular image of steadfast Londoners, she defined herself against it. Many other governmental and bureaucratic officials who were in London during the Blitz identified more with their country homes. Even those in the West End, particularly in the first month of bombing, saw the Blitz as an East End spectacle, and journalists and government officials 'toured' the blitzed areas for copy. John Colville, Assistant Private Secretary to the Prime Minister, went with Mrs Winston Churchill to Chingford to join the Mayor on October 4, 1940 to 'tour the place' with the Mayor and see the damage: 'The saddest sight was the homeless refugees in a school. ... One woman said: "It is all very well for them", (looking at us!) "who have all they want; but we have lost everything."'[17] In these cases, looking at or 'touring' the bomb damage highlighted a power imbalance – the observers returned to unbombed homes and amenities, while those bombed-out no longer had the privacy of homes to which to retreat.

Morale

In the interwar period, official government estimates assumed a death rate of 50 people per ton of bombs dropped on urban areas. The numerous treatises published in the 1930s on the dangers of bombing in a future war emphasized both the vulnerability of British cities to aerial attack, estimating the damage from air raids at 500 times the damage of Zeppelin raids, and the likelihood of civilian panic and rioting. Then would follow a similar process of psychological breakdown into apathy and callousness as had affected soldiers in the First World War. Concerns about civilian morale haunted planning committees and created a public demand for increased police and army troops in London and provincial centers. The belief that civilian bombing would cause mass psychological trauma led a number of eminent psychiatrists to present a report to the Ministry of Health calling for the creation of immediate treatment centers in bombed-out areas, twenty-four hour outpatient clinics outside cities, special hospitals in safer areas and mobile teams of psychiatrists and child guidance teams.[18] Though the dreaded immediate mass hysteria did not occur during the heavy raids of September 1940, the government still feared the effects of long nighttime raids on morale.

Morale was 'the woolliest and most muddled concept of the war', frequently invoked by the government and in the media but rarely defined with any clarity.[19] The difficulty of definition arose partly from the lack of criteria against which public opinion could be measured, and partly from the inconsistencies of approach used by the authors of different intelligence reports to the Home Office.[20] Dr Stephen Taylor, Director of the Ministry of Information's Home Security Division in 1941, catalogued in October the material factors affecting morale: food, warmth, work, leisure, rest and sleep, a secure base and security of dependants. The corresponding mental factors were: the belief that victory was possible, that sacrifices were being shared equally, and that the leadership was effective. Taylor conceded, however, that these factors were difficult to assess in large groups, and that morale must ultimately be measured 'not by what a person thinks or says, but by what he does and how he does it.'[21] This distinction reveals the paradox of governmental concerns about 'morale'. Home Intelligence Reports on popular attitudes did give some indication of morale but did not illuminate the link between what people thought and felt and how they acted. The only possible evidence for a break in morale would be segments of the population succumbing to mass hysteria or failing as a group to perform their allotted tasks.[22] Furthermore, other than the vague indications of absentee reports and crime statistics, there were no ways to express dissenting views to political leaders short of mass demonstrations in the streets.[23]

Britishness

When the expected civilian panics during raids failed to materialize, both public war narratives and private writers tied the steadfastness of the public to the idea of Britishness. The resistance of Londoners to the bombing raids was seen as quintessentially British, as in M. Mogridge's 1942 memoir:

> A people who can remain steadfast under bombardment from dusk to dawn for weeks on end deserve to win, and Fate, in the end, gives the prize to the deserving. The victory of London was not won with weapons it was won in the human heart, and hearts of such calibre can do many things.[24]

The belief that civilian morale was a deposit on ultimate victory was not unusual. The direct experience of bombing raids inspired compassion and diminished the desire for reprisal raids, but many still distinguished between the German bombing tactics and those of the British.[25] Anthony Weymouth wrote in his diary:

> September 25, 1940. Although we are bombing military objectives in Berlin, we are, it goes without saying, damaging in the process property and inflicting casualties on civilians. It cannot be otherwise. This is obviously a very different principle to that adopted by the Nazis. They say that they are attacking targets of military importance – these, of course, legitimately include railways and utility works generally – and they maintain (if I understand their viewpoint correctly) that, if in the course of these operations civilians get hurt, well that's just too bad. But the random dropping of bombs on suburbs, on villages, anywhere, in fact, sooner than take them back to Germany – is

ample proof that their pilots have been told not to be squeam-
ish in their choice of targets.[26]

Weymouth represented the British as more civilized in their
military strategy and in their reaction to fear. The irony of these
passages is poignant in the light of 1943–45 Allied bombing raids on
Germany, in which the Allies dropped 2.7 times more bomb tonnage
than fell on London during the Blitz, and the infamous eight
hundred bomber fire-raid over Dresden on February 13–14, 1945,
which killed 30,000 Germans in one night.[27] The resistance of civilian
populations to bombing could not be causally linked to democracy,
as the pre-war experience of the Spanish Civil War, and the wartime
experiences of Germany, made clear. But victory allowed the British
to weave the experience of the raids into a narrative of Britain's
superior fortitude and endurance in a way not accessible to losing
European countries who had suffered more physical damage.[28]

The civilian endurance of bombing raids during the Blitz fed into
pre-existing ideals of British identity as essentially domestic, home-
loving, anti-heroic but fiercely protective.[29] Steadfastness emerges in
civilian narratives as the defining British characteristic. Writer and
journalist James Lansdale Hodson wrote in 1941: 'The British
character is akin to the mills of God. It grinds exceedingly slow but,
in the long run, infinitely small.'[30] Stephen Spender wrote in *Civilians
at War* (1945) that morale is an innate British national characteristic:

British morale springs from within, and not from without. That
which is a phenomenon in British History is the extent to
which a people, insular, uninterested in domination and expansion, have yet spread the pattern of their whole thought and
rule over the world. The magic of their success is their faith in
their own way of life, their incredulity when confronted with
the customs of other people. Their will to resist has nothing to
do with theories, and little connection with causes; it is the
resistance of their whole nature, their whole history, the whole
pattern of their culture, against any attempt to impose on

them the behaviour of another nation. ... War for them is simply an ultimate way of asserting the reality of their own experience.[31]

The 'magic' of the imperial successes of a seemingly opaque people 'uninterested' in expansion is the same magic that Spender believed would lead the British to ultimate victory.

Spender's characterization of Britishness also contains an element that was less amenable to wartime patriotic strains. He identified the British as fervent chauvinists, who clung to their way of life in the face of all obstacles. This aspect of national identity contradicted the exigencies of wartime bureaucracy. Writer Peter Conway also described Britishness as a chafing against too many rules: 'the Englishman resents direction and control. He hates petty official-dom, red tape and irritating regulations.'[32] The British national character would naturally scorn the bureaucracy of rationing, blackout regulations and shelter rules. Thus, being sufficiently British during the war could mean fortitude in the face of raids and privations, as well as a contradictory resistance to the official rules and regulations designed to enforce safety standards and 'fair shares' in the distribution of goods. The link between Britishness and good civilian morale was tenuous, if not paradoxical.

The Bombing Raids

By the second week of German bombing of civilian targets in London in September 1940, the raids no longer constituted the first part of the German strategy of *blitzkrieg*, because the struggle for air supremacy over Britain necessary for German invasion had been won by the Royal Air Force (RAF). The planned German invasion, Operation Sealion, was abandoned on September 17 and not rescheduled. The military aim of the air raids – after September 18 almost exclusively night raids – was therefore to disrupt the manu-facturing, transport and administrative systems in London, and to demoralize the civilian population and encourage them to sue for

peace. The first phase of the Blitz lasted from the beginning of
September to mid-November 1940, after which German bombers
widened their targets to include provincial cities such as Coventry.
From September 6 onwards, with one night's respite on November
2, London endured 76 consecutive nights of bombing. The majority
of the bombs dropped were high explosives, estimated at 27,500
tons, along with incendiaries, oil explosive bombs parachute mines
and delayed-action bombs.[33]

The East End, particularly Stepney, received the highest concentration of hits in September, though the *Luftwaffe* expanded their
targets to include other boroughs in October.[34] The bombing of
Buckingham Place on October 13 was widely publicized in order to
promote the idea of air raids as a universal experience. Constantine
Fitzgibbon claimed that 'it undoubtedly heartened the people of the
East End to know that their perils were being shared by the highest
in the land. In a curious way, this knowledge was almost as good for
morale as the anti-aircraft barrage.'[35] While the optimism of this is
perhaps overstated, the widening of the bombing from the East End
did help reduce the class tensions that the Germans hoped would
bring down the British Government.

Although the air raids on Britain continued almost nightly in
November and December 1940, only six out of a hundred or more
raids were directed against London. Bombing raids on smaller British
cities, such as Coventry, Manchester and Hull were more structurally
devastating, but attention still focused on London.[36] The next major
raid on London was on the City and came on December 29, 1940.
The combination of the desertion of the City on a holiday Sunday
night, the tidal ebb of the Thames and the use of incendiary bombs
caused massive property destruction.[37] The Guildhall and the area
surrounding St Paul's were destroyed, though St Paul's emerged
relatively unscathed, and became a symbol for London's fortitude.
Another heavy raid occurred on January 11, 1941, in which a bomb
hit the Bank underground station, killing shelterers and blasting a
hole in the roadway in front of the Royal Exchange so wide that the
Royal Engineers had to build a bridge across it.[38] A lull followed until

March, when the Germans sent over bombers approximately once a week throughout March and April. Two major raids on April 16 and April 19, known as 'The Wednesday' and 'The Saturday', were reprisal raids that Hitler ordered in response to the bombing of Berlin. Each raid dropped over a thousand tons of high-explosive and incendiary bombs.[39] The last raid of the Blitz occurred on May 10, 1941. It lasted seven hours, killed over 1,400 and injured 1,800.[40] Londoners feared even more extensive attacks but, as the Germans turned their offensive towards Russia, the London Blitz was effectively at an end.

A chronological narrative of the Blitz imposes an order on the events that might otherwise seem random and incomprehensible to those who experienced them. The Mayor of Stepney, Frank Lewey, wrote towards the end of the war that trying to recall the order of events during the Blitz was difficult: 'The whole affair was so overwhelming and confusing that few who took part in it have been able to arrange their memories in ordered sequence. One man whom I asked for his impressions thought a moment, scratched his head, and said: "Well, guv'nor, it was the biggest bloody rush wot I've ever known."'[41] The duration and ferocity of the raids seemed unfathomable at the time. And as reports on raids in other areas in London were censored, people often relied on word of mouth reports or vague newspaper accounts for information. The emotional and psychological strain of not knowing the extent or duration of raids is a factor often forgotten in retrospective histories of the Blitz.

Shelters

Once the bombing raids began in August 1940, it became clear that the prospective death toll had been overestimated, as had the fears of mass civilian hysteria. The largest structural problem created by air raids was the provision of shelters for long raids and the problem of repairing homes and re-housing the homeless. Time spent in shelters, more than any other wartime experience in London, is cited in wartime and postwar assertions of the growth of solidarity among

Londoners. Yet the evolution of shelter provisions and the debates surrounding them in the months of the Blitz reveal the social tensions and continuing inequality in the metropolis.

In November 1938, after becoming responsible for Britain's Air Raid Precautions, Sir John Anderson commissioned the design of a cheap and simple domestic outside shelter, the 'Anderson'. Made from an arch of corrugated metal, the Anderson had to be buried in a hole in the earth seven feet six inches long by six feet wide, to a depth of up to four feet. By September 1940, 2,300,000 Anderson shelters had been produced, sufficient to provide for 12,500,000 people, nearly a quarter of the population. The Anderson was supplied free to those earning under £250 a year in danger areas, and others could buy them for £7 plus the cost of erection.[42] In addition, the government strengthened railway arches, excavated trenches in parks, built oblong brick surface shelters and reinforced basements to provide public shelters. Their policy was to provide small but numerous shelters, in order to avoid the deleterious effects on morale of a direct hit on a large shelter.

However, the duration of raids and the switch to nighttime bombing betrayed the surface shelters' unsuitability for longer stays. Despite the public rejection of surface shelters, and preference for shelters below ground level, it took months for the government to overcome its fears of a 'timorous troglodyte' mentality and allow the official occupation of Tube stations as shelters.[43] On September 20, 1940, the *Daily Express* reported Anderson's admonition that the Tubes be used only in emergencies: 'The present mass of Tube-squatters who come from remote districts each night are to be rehoused nearer their homes in basement offices, shops and factories, now closed for the night.'[44] The image of 'masses' of 'squatters' revealed the fears and stereotypes of the Tube-shelterer as weak, and prone to irrational fears and a herd mentality. Anderson tried to assert the similarity of protection offered by all types of shelters, despite 'the fact that the public have shown a preference for some shelters and have left others empty'. Herbert Morrison, as Home Secretary, rejected the use of Tube stations as shelters again on October 11, despite the fact that they continued in general use.[45] Even when the Tube station tunnels were expanded for use as shelters, Morrison warned Londoners against fantasies of safety: 'Be on your guard against all who seek to make this deep shelter cry a means of defeatist agitation.'[46] Shelter provisions were a hotly contested political as well as social issue. Communists used the inequality and inadequacy of shelter provision as a political platform. They were suspected by the government and credited themselves with organizing all popular demonstrations for expanded shelters.[47] Whether popular demonstrations, such as the one at the Liverpool Street Station on September 8, 1940 which forced down the locked gates, were influenced by Communist agitation or were spontaneous expressions of popular feeling is impossible to determine.

Despite the ideal of a breakdown in social barriers in shelters, there was rarely a mix of classes in public shelters. Only 4 per cent of the London populace used Tube shelters, 9 per cent used the other public shelters and 27 per cent opted for domestic shelters during the Blitz.[48] Others presumably sought the safest corners in their homes. These totals fluctuated throughout the Blitz, with an estimated 175,000 people using Tube shelters in late September, 160,000 in October, 125,000 in November, down to a 75,000 low in December. After the raids on the City, the total jumped back to 100,000, and at the end of January, 65,000 people were using Tube shelters though there had been no raids for weeks.[49] Though at first even the latrines in Tube stations were closed at night, creating a stench of unventilated bodies and overflowing latrine buckets, Transport and local authorities soon installed bucket lavatories and bunks in the stations, and the London County Council and welfare organizations began in mid-September to provide drinking water, canteens and even lending libraries. Yet the early days cemented many peoples' impressions of the shelters, and kept them away for the whole of the Blitz. Marie Lawrence expressed her distaste in a diary entry of August 27, 1940: 'Well we put our rugs together and found that it was nearly full and instead of there being 50 people there were 60. It was a most funny sensation as we sat there. Looking along the tunnel to see all kinds of people with their children all sitting on cramped forms. It made you feel you were a refugee.'[50]

Most middle class families had Anderson shelters in their back-yards, or stayed in the basements of their homes. In areas of homes without gardens, such as Pimlico where only 235 gardens were big enough for Anderson shelters, local authorities strengthened 8,000 coal cellars.[51] Those living in flats making an average of less than £250 a year had the cost of a communal shelter borne by the government; those making more had to subsidize their own. Many had shelters in their basements, under-stairs cupboards, or the basements of workplaces.

Many people refused to shelter at all. The ultimate assertion of good morale was to continue with everyday life. Ignoring the raids as a form of resistance was the rationale for many Londoners' refusal to go to shelters. In a November 24, 1940 letter to a friend in Canada, Isabelle Granger defended her decision to stop using shelters: 'It is impossible to live in a constant state of emergency. One of the things Nazism is up against is a normal way of living; I intend to cling to it. It is possible to disregard the raids up to a point, we have learned to do it, to lead a normally happy life and see a lot of our friends.'[52] Fears of being buried alive also kept some from shelters. Rose Macaulay wrote to her sister: 'I am getting a burying-phobia, result of having seen so many houses and blocks of flats reduced to piles of ruins from which the people can't be extracted in time to live, and feel I would rather sleep in the street, but I know I mustn't do this.'[53] Harold Nicolson also wrote: 'I do not mind being blown up. What I dread is being buried under huge piles of masonry and hearing the water drip slowly, smelling the gas creeping towards me and hearing the faint cries of colleagues condemned to a slow and ungainly death.'[54] For some, not using the shelters became a point of pride, tied to good morale and continued production. Frank Lewey, the Mayor of Stepney, recalled with civic pride: 'Some left the district, others went into the Tube or other large shelters outside the parish. But such people were in the minority, for they are workers here, and could not – and *would* not – spend hours standing in shelter queues.'[55]

The extent to which these feelings affected the actions of Londoners is reflected in the low numbers of those taking any shelter at night during the Blitz.

Class Geography of Raids

Air warfare's attacks on civilians seem to imply universality. As Tom Harrisson wrote: '[it] looks like a manifestly "democratic" way of distributing destruction to rich and poor'.[56] Official media reports were careful to emphasize the universality of raids on London's geography. On September 9, 1940, Lawrence Wilkinson of the *Daily Express* told the story of an East End man bombed out of his home and showing off his ruined piano, a traditional symbol of working class respectability. He and his friends laughed at the twisted wreckage, as being bombed gave him a new measure of respect, of being 'in it'.[57] The following day Hilde Marchant reported on the £8 a week 'neat and expensive, but small' flat, now wide open to the street: 'they left all manners of things, for their one idea now was to get a cup and saucer, and a bed'. The raids reduced the middle classes to the simpler needs of the working classes. On September 11, the headline read '£50 a week homes can take it', and 'Big house and cottage face bombs the same way', and on September 12, the headline quoted the Queen as saying: 'My home, too, was bombed', after minor damage was done to Buckingham Palace. The government was also careful to assert the indiscriminate nature of the bombing. On September 9, the Ministry of Home Security released a bulletin that gave minor details of London's biggest raid to date. They asserted that bombing in the later part of the raid was widespread and 'appeared to be indiscriminate'.[58]

But there was a class geography of bombing raids.[59] Especially in September, they were concentrated on the docklands and the East End area, particularly West and East Ham, Stepney and Silvertown, hemmed in by the Thames, the river Lea and the docks. These areas also had fewer social provisions for raids, partly because of lack of organization and will on the part of local authorities and the London

County Council. Bombs also had more impact on the social geography of East and South London due to a working class culture that lived mainly in the street and public institutions such as pubs.[60] Assertions of the commonality of raids glided over the 'stubbornness' and class feeling of East Enders, who in early September marched to Epping Forest to protest the lack of amenities.

Ritchie Calder, a journalist for the *Daily Herald*, was one of the few contemporary observers to publish an account of the differences in conditions between the East and West Ends. He spent a night in an East End shelter in early September, where he observed the high spirits of Cockneys despite the lack of facilities. The next night he spent in a West End luxury hotel:

> The majority of people there were homeless. They too, had undergone the ordeal of bombs. Their houses in the fashionable squares were in ruins. To that extent they were 'in it' with the people of East London. I spoke with some of them. There was nothing wrong with their morale either. But there was a world of difference in the way their morale was being maintained, and in the treatment money could buy for them. For instance, a wealthy merchant from one of the fashionable squares told how he and his wife were dug out of their basement by the rescue squad, how a warden got them a taxi while some warm clothes were salvaged for them. Then they drove to the hotel, where they were welcomed as old clients. The hotel staff wrapped them up in blankets and took them down to the spacious, well-heated shelters in the vaults. There they were given brandy and sal volatile. There were comfortable settees on which to sleep, and hot-water bottles. Next morning there was a lavish breakfast, and it had now been arranged that they should go to a quiet country hotel. All the technical details had been turned over to the family solicitor.[61]

The result of these visible class differences (despite talk of being 'all in it together') was not lower morale among the East Enders, according to Calder, but an excess of it: 'not panic but a rising flood of indignation'.[62]

Public shelters were not the social arena in which classes mixed during the Blitz. Luxury hotels, restaurants and, to a lesser extent, clubs, were the contested spaces where the battles of entitlement were fought. Hotels especially were the scenes of Communist demonstrations, of social mixing of the respectable and less-so in their restaurants, and the setting for a class relationship of service between the staff and the guests. These public/private spaces questioned the wartime emphasis on universality: luxury hotels, restaurants and private clubs were border spaces within London, where the tensions subsumed in the rhetoric of solidarity erupted.

High-level bureaucratic action went on in these hotels, clubs and expensive restaurants. Charles Graves wrote in the preface of his wartime diary that spending time in luxury settings was necessary for his work as a journalist:

> Much of the Diary is naïve. Looking through it, I seem to spend far too much time at smart hotels and restaurants (when I am not doing my Home Guard duties). It must be realized, however, that for three-quarters of the time during which this *Off the Record* Diary has been kept I was a newspaper columnist, and experience has taught me that certain hotels and restaurants, like the Savoy, the Dorchester and Grosvenor House, provide far greater likelihood of casually encountering Cabinet Ministers and others useful to me in my newspaper work.[63]

Dining and living in clubs, restaurants and hotels relieved the wartime pressures of finding accommodation and food. Diana Cooper stayed on the eighth floor of the Dorchester with her father during the Blitz. Here they took their meals and sheltered in the Turkish baths:

> At 11, a little lulled by Chianti but utterly unexhilarated, we walk down to the Turkish bath, stepping over hundreds of

hotel mates dossed down on mattresses, some with dogs that
bark as you go past, some snoring, some reading with a torch.
The Turkish bath is not safe, as it's not under the main building, but it has cubicle-privacy, a cot, blankets not sheets, a light
apiece, and above all deadened noise. ... The cleaners arrive at
dawn, and with dawn the All Clear, so one trudges up to one's
proper bedroom and it all begins again.[64]

The relative comforts Cooper described were not always appreciated
by hotel guests. In October Alexander Cadogan recorded with
dismay his evacuation to a hotel:

October 21, 1940: In the present circumstances of our squalid
existence in a hotel [the Carleton], I can't keep up this diary. I
don't remember what happened this day. There was a Cabinet
meeting at No. 10 at 5. P.M. away and nothing v. interesting.
We dined with the H.'s at the Dorchester to meet Philip
Lothian. The Dorchester is the worst spot on earth to live in.
We dined on the 6th Floor, to an accompaniment of 4.5" guns,
which knock the glasses off the table, tear your eyebrows out
and snap your braces. Poor Dorothy is evidently completely
rattled, but H.'s deafness, I suppose, stands him in good
stead.[65]

Compared to the communal shelters and Tube shelters elsewhere in
London, conditions at the Carleton were hardly 'squalid'. Like
Cadogan, Cecil Beaton found the Dorchester Hotel almost intolerable, because of the mix of classes in the restaurant: 'Cabinet
Ministers and their self-consciously respectable wives; hatchet-jawed,
iron grey brigadiers; calf-like airmen off duty; tarts on duty; actresses
(also), déclassé society people, cheap musicians and motor-car agents.
It could not be more ugly and vile and yet I have not the strength of
character to remain, like Harold Acton, with a book.'[66] For one used
to the circles of highest society, the mix of customers was debase-
ment of the highest order.

The Savoy Hotel, where many others, including the ubiquitous Diana Cooper, entertained, also had a strange wartime mixture of people:

A great deal of our welcoming took place at the Savoy Hotel where we had decided to perch until I could divest my house of its battle dress. The Savoy was selected because now more than ever is the Grill the one place in London. Without music and apparently without closing time, you are certain to always find bits of the Cabinet there. ... Workers off their shifts, actors, writers, the Press, Mayfair's hostesses who have abandoned their private houses and still want to entertain – they are all grazing at the Savoy Grill. ... By living in this great hotel one need never wrestle with the blackout, which is blacker than ever.[67]

Cooper described the hotel as a communal shelter imbued with glamour. Yet the shelter was hardly public. On September 15, 1940, a group of Communist party activists led by Phil Piratin, communist party organizer in Stepney, decided to storm the Savoy, closest of the luxury hotels to the East End, and the home of many American journalists, in order to highlight the differences in shelter conditions for rich and poor. A party of seventy people presented themselves at the door of the Savoy, asking to be admitted. Phil Piratin's memoir presents the action in a heroic light, describing the group's courageous entrance into the shelters, followed by the women and children. His account contrasts with Constantine Fitzgibbon's description, in which Communists push a woman in late pregnancy in front of them, playing on the gender privilege of safety.[68] The basement shelters of the Savoy were undoubtedly luxurious:

In the early days of 1940 the Abraham Lincoln Room and the adjoining Pink and Green Rooms were converted into air-raid shelters and gradually arranged for sleeping accommodation. Here about two hundred beds were installed in separate curtained bays. Special compartments were set aside for the conferences of important individuals, and there was even a compartment for snorers. The air-conditioned, gas-proof and sound-proof dormitory was equipped with its own maids and valets and waiters, with a room for coffee and a small bar one floor up.[69]

And Piratin depicted the reaction of the East End shelterers as awed:

'Shelters', they said, 'why we'd love to live in such places!' Structurally, the lower ground floor had been strengthened with steel girders and by other means. But the appearance of the place! Each section was decorated a different colour, pink, blue and green. All the bedding, all the linen, was, of course, the same uniform colour. Armchairs and deck chairs were strewn around. There were several 'nurses' – you could easily recognize them.[70]

The storming of the shelters was not the only Communist agitation at the Savoy. Stanley Jackson described how a group of Communist women staged a demonstration during a visit by Wendell Wilkie: 'Some opened their fur coats to reveal incongruous banners proclaiming, "Our Children Are Starving" and "Ration the Rich," and a number had even arrived in taxis to storm the barricades.' The women then sat down, 'screaming abuse or demanding to be served with food', tying themselves to chairs or pillars in a vain effort not to be removed. The police arrived and refused to get involved, but eventually the Head Porter convinced the women to leave, and Wendell Wilkie apparently remarked that at the Waldorf Astoria they would have been dislodged with a riot squad and tear gas.[71] Though written over twenty years after the event, Jackson's account is brimming with anger and suppressed violence, calling on stereotypes of suffragettes and the brash 'munionette' in the fur coat of the First World War, reviling the women who behaved so disrespectfully in a reputable restaurant. In descriptions of hotels and shelters, solidarity is within social classes, not between them.

The destruction of social and cultural sites of privilege garnered more public attention in the press, as well as the public imagination. The Café de Paris nightclub bombing, for example, received more press coverage than less glamorous hits. The transformation from glamour to horror caught the public imagination. Phyllis Warner expressed her shock at the news of the bombing the next day in her diary. March 3, 1941: 'Most of the band and the dancers were killed, whilst the people in the balcony generally escaped. What a ghastly scene for that luxury setting. One always feels so frail and defenceless in evening dress anyway. I am glad none of my friends was rich enough to take me there last night; the band was playing "Oh Johnny how can you love" so I'd certainly have been on the floor.'[72]

John Lehmann had a similar reaction on hearing that his club had been hit: 'It was with a shocked sense that this time the Nazis had gone too far, that I arrived at the Athenaeum to find liveried staff sweeping away debris while disconcerted Bishops stepped as delicately as cats over the litter of broken glass.'[73] For the male members of the privileged classes, clubs provided material comfort and the psychic comforts of sociability. At Pratt's Club in Park Place, Alex Waugh and Harold Nicolson found enjoyment in the vintage port and good talk.[74] John Lehmann had sought refuge at his club when he was bombed-out on September 11, 1940:

When the evacuation order came, the first place I went to was the Athenaeum, asked for a bath and then breakfast. Soon it was round the club that I had been bombed out, and so many waiters and other Club servants came to condole with me that I was surprised and moved. Air Marshal Joubert passed by on his way to breakfast, looking very preoccupied. I telephoned to a great many friends, sent off some letters and telegrams dealing with the problems of the Hogarth Press, then went down to A.'s flat in Bayswater as he had suggested.[75]

The Club provided the amenities which allowed him to get on with the business of running the Hogarth Press. It also gave Lehmann an arena for physical comfort (a bath and breakfast), emotional support that surprised him from staff and servants, and the reassurance that military needs were being looked after, as evinced by the preoccupied Air Marshal Joubert. The bombing of the Carlton Club on October 14, 1940 destroyed the building but left 250 members and staff uninjured. Churchill remembered an unnamed Labour MP's comments: 'The devil looks after his own.'[76] Harold Butler, upon emerging from the wreckage, went first to Henry Channon's house, for 'a bath, champagne and succour, and we gave him all three'.[77]

The nature of restaurants and the individual service they provided also undermined ideals of universalism. Jane Gordon described dining with her husband Charles Graves in the basement shelter of Grosvenor House. Graves saw Lady Eleanor Smith, and asked the waiter to take over a note to her:

> As the man looked rather vacant he added, 'Do you know what she looks like?'

> 'No,' said the waiter, 'and I don't give a damn.' His voice was quite polite, which made the remark even more astonishing. 'Are you usually so outspoken with the guests?' asked Charles with great interest. 'No, but my house was bombed last night and I have lost everything.' Charles said: 'I am very sorry – it must be awful for you; but now if you can bring yourself to it, I would still like you to take that note for me.'[78]

The sympathy expressed on both sides, by Lehmann's club staff and by Graves towards the waiter, did not disrupt the hierarchical pattern of class.

Restaurants not only offered protection from raids and the more unpleasant aspects of public shelters, but they also allowed diners to eat 'off the ration' and enjoy a quality of food that could not be bought in the shops with rationed points. Quentin Reynolds recorded a birthday dinner with fellow journalists and its sumptuous menu:

> October 1, 1940. Our restaurant is below street level and you can only hear bombs that drop very close. You hardly hear the guns at all. We went down and had a good dinner. Low knows his way around a wine list. He had gotten some Nuits St Georges, 1923, the last bottles left in London, he told us proudly. We had lobster cocktails first and iced aquavit with that. ... We had partridge and bread sauce and all kinds of vegetables and a salad, and Mansell, our pet captain in the restaurant, had gotten us a birthday cake with one candle in it.[79]

Though Stanley Jackson described the restrictions placed on the chef at the Savoy, who invented the Woolton vegetable pie and shouted at the waiters, 'Tell them it's steak or ships!', restaurants still provided more luxurious servings of the most precious wartime commodity: food.

Rationing: 'The Cubic Inch of Cheese'

Compared to the dramatic punctuation of raids, food rationing affected daily life in London through consistent privation. At the outbreak of war, the government had assumed responsibility for the supply and distribution of staple foods. Consumers were asked in November 1939 to register with retailers for butter, bacon and sugar, and rationing was introduced for these commodities in January 1940 and for meat in March 1940. Government subsidies helped to keep prices low.[80] After the fall of France in the spring of 1940, food supplies were in danger of falling dangerously low, and the government implemented an extension of rationing. Margarine was rationed in July 1940, preserves in March 1941 and cheese in May 1941. Increasing food shortages necessitated the implementation of a coupon-replacement scheme for foods in December 1941, at first for canned goods and eventually extending to many other food items. The National Government also instituted a scheme of workplace canteens, in which meals were provided for workers off the ration. The National Milk Scheme was introduced in July 1940, which provided free or subsidized milk to expectant mothers and young children. Robert Boothby, Parliamentary Secretary to the Ministry of Food in 1940, asserted in his 1947 memoir that this scheme had already had a beneficial effect on the population and would stand the test of time.[81] In addition, local authorities helped set up communal feeding centers and communal kitchens. The London County Council, which had experience in social welfare feeding services, set up the first field kitchen in the Isle of Dogs on September 15, 1940. Two weeks later, the Council was operating 27 feeding centers, and 242 cafeterias by May 1943. Canteen meals were designed to supplement rations, and patrons were expected to pay cash for meals, which in September were 10d for a set meal – still affordable compared to private restaurants and canteens. The canteens throughout London helped to sustain local communities, and subsidized local shops, where they obtained up to 60 per cent of their food supplies.[82]

Rationing and subsidies helped to maintain a level of consumer expenditure on food consistent with pre-war levels.[83] But the types of food eaten changed. The pre-war urban working-class diet rich in fats, eggs and sugar gave way to grains, potatoes, dairy products and vegetables, which showed dietary increases of up to 22 per cent by early 1941.[84] The change in consumption habits occasioned by rationing, along with fluctuating availability of foodstuffs, was the focus of the propaganda campaigns of the Ministry of Food, the only Ministry to control its own propaganda. Rationing was billed as one of the major ways that civilians' wartime sacrifices contributed to the war effort. Ministry of Food policy and propaganda emphasized the egalitarianism of rationing, and the doctrine of 'fair shares'.

Yet the public responses to rationing were complex, and varied according to social group and particular policy initiatives. Experiences of rationing were fundamental to morale during the war. While civilians understood the need for rationing, they often felt that the privation was not equally shared. The principle of fair shares was also overlooked in obtaining goods 'off the ration' or on the black-market, which civilians saw as a testament to their ingenuity, rather than an unpatriotic act or misdemeanor. The black market in food and other scarce goods, defined as 'widespread infringement of the regulations by producers, distributors and retailers, ultimately sustained by public demand', was extensive during the war, and marked the limits of public acceptance of rationing.[85]

While rationing levels maintained pre-war average caloric intakes at approximately 2,300 calories a day, this did not always provide for the increased energy requirements of workers.[86] Manual laborers and miners received extra rations, but other heavy work was not accounted for.[87] Mrs M. Morris, a nurse, described being hungry all day because of the physical nature of her work:

> October 1, 1940. We dash about all day and I am always hungry. There are times particularly in the fore-noon when I feel so faint from hunger that it is impossible to carry out my innumerable duties. Our food ration is totally inadequate – 1 oz cheese, 2 oz butter per week and one egg each fortnight, and of course our one orange each month. ... Serving the patients lunches is a painful experience. It is exquisite agony to have to serve their food when one is so hungry.[88]

Women's work was perceived as less physical, and they generally received extra rations only when pregnant. In most cases, privation was perceived chiefly as a problem of variety, since the availability of familiar foods was limited during the war. G. W. King wrote on December 3, 1940: 'Tonight there has been a talk by the Lord Woolton, the Minister of Food. He has plainly told us that we have done very well in the way of foodstuffs up to the present, but there are a good many things we have to do without, and live more plainly, like we used to do when I was a boy.'[89] Rationing also limited hospitality, as hosts and hostesses could not afford to be as generous.

A housewife from Brockley complained in her diary in October 1940 about an acquaintance who dropped in for a meal while his wife was out of town: 'I'm afraid I shan't make him as welcome if he doesn't bring his rations.'[90]

Rationing on the coupon system also made shopping more complicated. Shoppers had to register their ration books with a specific retailer, which limited choice and mobility. The majority of British women, even at the height of mobilization, were housewives and bore the brunt of the added complexities of shopping and menu-planning. This altered their perceptions of wartime austerity and rationing, making them more critical of the idea of 'fair shares'. For those who worked long shifts, the extra hours of queuing and traveling to different shops was a burden. But for Florence Speed, who gave up her job to take care of the meal preparation for her brother and sisters, the complexity of shopping under rationing made it more of a challenge and therefore more enjoyable:

> November 23, 1940. I think I may get to like shopping now it ceases to be a dash in and out during a lunch hour. The colour and foreign smells are pleasant. Norah bought Parmesan Cheese – 'The last you will get' she was told. I suggested we should be getting the 'American Parmesan' and the assistant sniffed. 'It's pastures [pasteurized]' he said. 'As well make Cheddar cheese in America. It would be just as bad. You *can't* make Parmesan in America'. But I read that they are making it in America! And that it is so good an imitation that the enormous export trade Italy had with America will be lost for ever. And after all that Norah left the cheese behind! I couldn't get it so someone must have picked it up.[91]

Shopping was not only a new hobby, but an overtly political act, as Speed celebrated America the rising superpower through its imitation Parmesan. The political importance of cheese was also proclaimed in graffiti chalked on a wall in South London in the spring of 1941: 'Cheese not Churchill'. George Orwell, who recorded this slogan, found it summed up the 'psychological ignorance' of the 'communist or blackshirt' who did not realize that 'whereas some people would die for Churchill, nobody will die for cheese.'[92]

Registering at a particular shop meant that one's relationship with the proprietor could affect the quantity and quality of one's food. Those who were kind to their grocer or butcher often received a little extra. Vere Hodgson received some cheese this way:

> February 22, 1941. Went for my bacon ration yesterday and while he was cutting it had a word with the man about the Cubic Inch of Cheese. He got rid of the other customers and then whispered, 'Wait a mo'.' I found half a pound of cheese being thrust into my bag with great secrecy and speed! Then going to the dairy for my butter ration I was given four eggs and a quarter of cheese! Had no compunction in taking it, for I went straight to the Mercury Café and gave it to them ... they said they did not think they could open the next day as they had no meat and only a morsel of cheese. I could not resist, when I got it, cutting off a hunk of my piece and eating it then and there.[93]

Hodgson had no compunction about taking her illicit cheese, because she shared it. But anyone who could manage to get extra food did so, and there is no evidence of pangs of guilt for those who would have to go cheeseless or be otherwise restricted as a result.

Civilian diaries asserted again and again the right to an adequate and familiar diet over which they could maintain control. Writers and the Ministry of Food presented individual choice in food preparation and in food choices as central to morale. Communal kitchens were unpopular, as Naomi Mitchison found in a discussion of communal cooking with a man and his wife. The man disagreed with sharing any kind of housework in order to release women into factory work: 'February 14, 1941. He said if she has a nice home and a good wage and plenty to eat that's what a woman wants. We then went for one another, and his girl sat silently eating and looking blank. God knows, she wouldn't want anything else. ... He thinks I'm just

barmy, that of course no real woman would believe any of that
nonsense. He says of course if you'd ever been a working class
wife...'[94] The unnamed man questioned Mitchison's authority to
prescribe solutions for the difficulties of food preparation, just as
many civilians resented the prescriptions of the Ministry of Food. A
twenty-eight-year-old widow who volunteered at a canteen wrote of
the boredom of the Blitz's winter diet:

> February 3, 1941. Today, seeking desperately for inspiration
> for the week's catering, I took down from the shelf for the first
> time in many months a cookbook published just after rationing
> first came in, entitled 'A Kitchen Goes to War' and purporting
> to be a collection of recipes suitable to wartime conditions. I
> remembered this vaguely as being a selection of poverty-
> stricken sort of dishes of uninspiring drabness. But very much
> on the contrary, I was bewildered by a rich lavishness and
> variety mostly quite unattainable, by present-day standards,
> beyond one's wildest gastronomic dreams![95]

She then named dishes that seemed sumptuous to her, as onions,
tomatoes, rabbit, prunes, were all now scarce. It was not even the
restrictions in diet she minded so much, she wrote a few days later,
as the heavy-handed propaganda of the Ministry of Food:

> February 18, 1941. I find it hard to tolerate this incessant
> nagging, these endless exhortations and scoldings, those
> pompous official lectures from Lord Woolton – whose
> utterances, far from encouraging us to endure our monotonous
> and restricted diets with good grace, infuriate us and are
> anything but conducive to the maintenance of good morale. If
> carrots and potatoes are the only things we can get to eat, all
> right we'll eat them; but it really is *too much* to be lectured all
> the time about the excellence of carrots and potatoes, and
> scolded for not having eaten more of them before, and nagged
> at for having eaten too much of other things...[96]

Resentment of prescriptive propaganda added to the strains of a restricted diet and complex shopping routines. Admonitions about food preparation in particular represented to civilians the small-minded bureaucracy targeted by J. B. Priestley:

> Sometimes I feel that you and I – all of us ordinary people – are on one side of a high fence, and on the other side of this fence under a buzzing cloud of secretaries, are the official and important personages: the pundits and mandarins of the Fifth Button! And now and then a head appears above the fence and tells us to carry our gas masks, look to our blackouts, do this and attend that.[97]

The official insistence on making life more drab than it needed to be was a current running through Priestley's broadcasts, and reflected in the comments and complaints of civilian diaries. Londoners knew that rationing was essentially fair, that it provided a minimum level of nutrition for everyone and rectified the dietary inadequacies of much of the working poor, but they hated to be told what to do. While the argument for fair shares was apparent during the war, more stringent postwar restrictions undermined popular support for the egalitarian principle rationing represented.[98] While rationing seemed to offer arguments for a wider acceptance of universalism, the resentment of authority and the debates over entitlement continued beneath the surface.

Please Get Killed Quietly

London during the Blitz was stratified not only along class lines, but also by gender. Raids, rationing and conscription were promoted in a language of universality that contradicted traditional notions of male heroism and the sanctity of the home. The equalization of danger, therefore, eroded the ideal of male chivalry, and helped create a new demand for male civilians to be protected as well as women. Since men could not protect women from the dangers of bombs, placing themselves in danger became meaningless, and the concern for the safety of women over men galling. Resentments expressed in gendered language were also cross-cut and exacerbated by class divisions, all centering on the twinned ideas of wartime participation and the attendant right to be protected from wartime dangers.

The historical association of masculinity with chivalry and protectiveness made the presence of men in the shelter seem incongruous. Isabelle Granger, in a letter dated December 12, 1940, pointed out that the tradition of male protection only added to men's inability to cope with raids:

> The raids seem to be more upsetting to men, on the whole, than to women. Don't think I am indulging in a bout of feminism please, but whether it is generations of protecting weeping women while they work, or some quite other reason, they seem to take it more heavily. They speculate on the origin of every sound, impute the most sinister origin to a slammed door or to a cock's crowing – everything is a bomb … or a flare or a land mine or a shrapnel.[99]

One man in their shelter insisted on silence when he heard a plane's engine so he could locate its position, while another flung himself to the floor at intervals: 'Nancy summed him up by saying he dropped faster than the bombs.'

The official perception that women needed protection from the bombs more than men did was expressed in signs that the government posted in Tube stations asking men to give up their places of safety to women and children. The *Daily Express* echoed this request on September 27, 1940, and its writer reported: 'One man who curtly announced that he was a pacifist threatened to punch me in the nose because I asked him why he was in the shelter. He did not carry out his threat.'[100] The public perception that women deserved more protection angered some men. A forty-year-old man in Muswell Hill expressed his resentment at this presumption:

Sept 30, 1940. I see the underground now has notices appealing to able-bodied men to stop away from tubes. What a damnable notice. Are able-bodied men less likely to be killed if a bomb hits them? Is the loss of the breadwinner of such minor importance to a home? The poster raises two questions in reply 1) Where do these able-bodied men go? And 2) Why haven't women and children and old people been evacuated? It would have been more honest to put a notice 'His Majesty's Government through incompetence, inefficiency and selfishness have been quite unable to provide shelters. Please get killed quietly.'[101]

His reaction called into question the possibility of male heroism or sacrifice in the face of indiscriminate death through bombing. He also argued that men had a right to protection due to their families' dependence on their wages. Thus he reversed the traditional role of the male protector, while maintaining the privileges of the bread-winner and the citizen. Ironically, his own wife did not leave London until October, and he recorded: 'I feel lonely this week as my wife has left. Raids got too much for her and she has gone home – at any rate for two weeks.'[102]

Equal participation in the war effort was central to debates over protection, and over shared resources. Women resented being told they were not entitled to equal shares of scarce consumer goods. A twenty-nine-year-old volunteer canteen driver and worker recorded her angry reaction to being told that women should give up smoking to free tobacco supplies for men:

April 9, 1940. Then one of our RAF customers had the rind to suggest that 'you women ought to give up smoking for the duration you know'. *This*, when they have the alternative of smoking pipes which is not open to us, when not only do they get first pick of available supplies at their private [military] sources which are not available to us, but also their uniform gives them the advantage over us at our own general sources of supply [for the canteen]...[103]

Her sense of injustice demonstrated how the ideal of the heroic
soldier had been undercut by her participation on the home front.
The fact that soldiers could more easily get supplies from the canteen
in which she volunteered was supremely unfair. As the RAF soldier
implied, women were expected to do without. Working-class May
Rainer did when she gave up sugar for the duration. At a canteen,
Rainer ordered two teas, one with sugar and one without: 'The man
came to the table with the tray, said "no sugar I bet that is for the
Lady." Obviously he had got used to the idea that the women were
the ones who went without.'[104]Although he could have been
suggesting self-deprivation for the sake of vanity, Rainer used his
comment to underline her own self-denial.

In men's diaries, the complaints about women were based less on
concepts of 'fair shares' and more on women's unfitness for the
serious demands of a population at war. A thirty-four-year-old single
man wrote in his diary on September 14, 1940: 'More and more
women are crying for peace. They say they don't care what ensues as
long as the bombing ceases. They have been too much molly-coddled
and flattered these last few years [so] that they have no reserve of
self-reliance in this crisis.'[105] He did not specify the basis for this
observation. Though it was true that people were more anxious in
the first two weeks of raids, the fact that he would make this a
gendered observation instead of a class one is telling. The diarist's
complaints expressed resentment of women's supposed elevated
status as protected beings, unfit for the serious demands of a
bombarded population.

Both the concept and the public representation of rationing
schemes and bombing raids appealed to ideals of universality. Yet, as
the diaries and memoirs of Londoners show, the civilian response to
both experience and official exhortation was often critical. Bombing
raids revealed differences in amenities and attitudes. James Lansdale
Hodson, a writer and journalist, wrote: 'I find I dislike the notion of
being bombed when all of London is being bombed, more than I did
when it was a new experience in France – an amusing sidelight on
human nature. When everybody's somebody...'[106] Public shelters

were not only the cheerful rooms of people singing 'Roll out the Barrel', but places of tension, fear, wakefulness, annoyances, and most seriously, thefts and violence. B. Garman described many instances of arguments and physical fights in his warden's log.[107] Many returned to bombed-out homes only to find them looted, sometimes, allegedly, by firemen or civil defense workers.[108] Although rarely punished, the penalties could be serious, as two Portsmouth policemen found when they were given sentences of ten years penal servitude for looting in December 1940.[109] Getting food off the ration also undermined ideals of universalism implicit and explicit in discussions of rationing and bombing. Even those not affected recognized the unfairness of raids. Miss V. Bawtree, a devout Christian, read of a hit on a shelter which killed many people, and made her question her faith in God: 'I've come up to my room all dazed and tearful.' By the next day she felt better:

> I got more normal by tea time. I think that possibly God allowed such horrors, including the insecurity of shelters, so that men and women should realize to the full that this sort of thing should be abolished for all time and that no amount of deep digging will make people immune from the peril. Only, why is not more horror and destruction allowed to happen to the homes of those in high places, who are far more responsible for allowing bombers to be created than are the poor people of the East End?[110]

Even when bombing targets were spread more evenly over London, raids were only egalitarian in concept.

As the raids slackened in the spring of 1941, few people felt they had cause for celebration or even relief. A twenty-eight-year-old widow wrote in February, 1941:

> I'm afraid I seem to be completely and horribly demoralized altogether these days. I've never felt so completely cowardly and gloomy and fed-up at any time during the war as in the last

ten days or so. It's partly the waiting I suppose, the 'coward dies many deaths' business, and partly, perhaps, a natural reaction to a period of slackness following one of extreme tension, but it's also largely a sort of despairing rage and general browned-offness and loss of confidence at finding that the previous terrific ordeal by Blitz was not, as we'd been allowed to suppose, either final or unsurpassable – that we'd been encouraged to congratulate ourselves on coming through the worst only to discover the worst still lies ahead...[111]

Not until they had faded after the war could the difficulties and fears of the experiences of raids and rationing be recalled as steps towards victory. Shelters as symbols of the Blitz and rationing as the symbol of the civilian war effort generally did emerge in debates over postwar social and political planning, but the symbols often obscured the complexity of actual experiences. The opaque insistence on the shelters and rationing as evidence for a breakdown in social barriers denies the historical experience of Londoners, the very people on whose behalf claims for more universal social programs were and are made.

Looking beneath the veneer of public descriptions of civilian morale and steadfast national identity reveals the complexity of civilian reactions to the experiences of war and the government policies set in place to deal with them, and the notions of morale and national identity themselves. In wartime public narratives and postwar memoirs, the ideals of British valor and the insistence on the dramatic and heroic aspects of raids helped to validate simplistic notions of 'morale'. As we will see in the following chapters, exhortations to maintain good morale sought to ensure civilian acceptance of the status quo, rather than the promise of future entitlements in a postwar Britain.

3

WORKERS AND CIVIL DEFENCE

Everywhere there was the sound of broken glass being swept off the streets, the sound of hammers. The city was dazed, but it was working. ... They had to keep the city going and at the same time fight a battle. ... The civilians had become an army, London was depending on the civil defence – on the people.[1]

I'm all for sending unemployed miners [to clear London bomb sites] and keeping them busy, but as for whatever soldiers can be spared for our own defence, I'd personally far sooner see them sent to Libya and Syria than London.[2]

American journalist Ben Robertson's passage described the heroism of London's workforce after the second night of bombing. But under the veneer of praise for London workers, as the second extract from a Mass Observation diary shows, the legacy of the 1930s and its questions of entitlement and unemployment lingered. Work had an increased visibility in wartime London and centered around civil defense, the civil service and light industry rather than heavy industrial production. The period of the Blitz, between September 1940 and May 1941, also marked the transition between voluntarism in civil defense and women's labor, and the beginning of conscription in these areas.

The wartime need for increased production in addition to military service made the worker the new hero of 1940 and the subsequent war years. The fortitude shown by workers who labored long hours under stressful conditions and the temporary cessation of trade union rights created the public image of a 'People's War', in which workers ostensibly showed their patriotism and good morale through high levels of industrial output and, especially on the days after heavy raids, attendance at work. The increased national importance of work during the war and workers' patriotic motives have been used as an argument for the expansion of workers' postwar material and social rights and a lessening of social barriers between classes in the face of this new national unity. However, the two routes by which most workers came to war work, voluntarism and conscription, as well as the reasons people gave in diaries and memoirs for their wartime work, show that motives were seldom purely patriotic, and that changes in work were perceived as temporary.

The extent to which wartime changes to work unified Britain hinge on conceptions of class. Class relationships in Britain were not confined to the factions of organized labor and middle- and upper-class ownership that had fought so bitterly in London during the General Strike in 1926. Social class also encompassed a variety of social relationships related to paid work and to other aspects of everyday life such as food, family and sexuality. Class is best understood as defining a group of people who share a set of opportunities and restraints based on their common economic situation.[3] Thus descriptions of resistance (in this case related to work) in diaries and memoirs are implicitly related to class, as are the experiences of unemployment and underemployment. While wartime policies and the experience of full employment may have lessened the material effects of social inequality, those effects persisted. 'Ordinary people', as historians have suggested, kept the war effort going, but there is no direct and causal connection between their work and a new sense of social and political entitlement leading to a more egalitarian postwar society.[4] Indeed, as studies of affluent workers in the 1950s and 1960s suggest, a higher level of income does not usually correlate with a change in class identification or traditional political allegiance.[5]

War Work

In the 1930s, London's industrial make-up began to diverge from the rest of Britain. At this time, only one percent of London's manual laborers worked in coal, shipbuilding, cotton, wool or iron and steel, which helped insulate the city from the problems of interwar unemployment concentrated in these industries.[6] Instead, London's industries and services were aimed at the growing domestic consumer market providing services such as hotels, transportation, manufacturing domestic goods and construction.[7] London had the advantage of being the largest consumer market in Britain, with its large middle class working in the civil services, the professions and commerce. London also enjoyed prosperity though the testing and application of new technology and as the centre of finance, marketing, warehousing and distributive services. Of the 614 new factories which sprang up in Britain between 1932 and 1938, 518 (over 80 per cent) of them were in London.[8] Poverty and unemployment still existed in London, but it was less tied to industrial decline than in other regions.

The declaration of war in September 1939 had a drastic effect on employment in London. The production of luxury goods was curtailed and many people left London for safer areas, which in turn deflated the building, service and hotel industries. Unemployment rates, a million and a half at the outbreak of war, rose over the winter and did not begin to decline until March, and by June 1940 still stood at over one million.[9] Britain had cut its defense spending in the 1920s, and only slowly were factories converted to military manufacturing to restock the armory and equip the army. The slowness of military production and the resultant ill-equipped army led to the loss of Norway in May 1940 and was compounded by the loss of arms and equipment left behind at the evacuation at Dunkirk in June 1940.

The production crisis of 1940 emphasized the drastic need for increased output from Britain's factories. Instead of taking over

control of the individual factories, the Government controlled
production through the physical allocation of raw materials, machine
tools and labor, and by using its position as the dominant purchaser
to fix contract prices. The allocation of materials for labor fit into a
larger pattern of macroeconomic fiscal ideology. The physical
planning of industry was complemented by a high level of taxation
that reduced the demand for consumer goods, preventing inflation
and encouraging production for war needs instead of consumers.
The new approach to budgetary policy was formally set out in John
Maynard Keynes' 1939 article in *The Times* and in his 1940 pamphlet
titled 'How to Pay for the War'. The budget of 1941 enshrined the
Keynesian arithmetic of total demands versus total resources, and
would affect subsequent budgetary policy for years to come.[10] The
Central Statistical Office, created as part of the War Cabinet in 1941,
provided 'scientific' statistical data on the materials of goods and
labor.

The government also encouraged workers to increase production
though official slogans such as Herbert Morrison, Minister of
Supply's 'Go To It!'[11] Factories began to work 24 hours a day, and
the Whitsun and August bank holidays were cancelled.[12] Yet the
increased effort did not yield a leap in production; industrial output
increased steadily, but slowly. In December 1940, Sir William
Beveridge produced in secret a Report of the Manpower
Requirements Committee which estimated the needs of the three
Services and Civil Defence at 1,750,000 men and 84,000 women
between September 1940 and the end of 1941.[13] To equip these new
forces, the munitions industry also needed one and a half million
more workers above the three and a half million they currently
employed. This meant that, in addition to releasing more men from
protected industries, women had to be recruited to work on a
massive scale, and skilled men had to be available to supervise their
work.

In March 1941, the Board of Trade organized 'concentration'
schemes to shut down or convert factories in less essential industries,
reducing consumer output to the minimum thought necessary to

maintain civilian morale.[14] Ernest Bevin, Minister of Labour, began to supplement his policy of voluntarism with the direction of labor. His Essential Works Order No. 302, which became law on March 5, 1940, meant that any war work could be declared 'essential', and thus workers could neither leave nor be fired from essential jobs. The *Daily Express* headline's *double entendre* – '100,000 Women Wanted in Two Weeks: Bevin Calls' – was a humorous foreshadowing of the Registration of Employment Order of March 1941, which required men over 41 and women between the ages of 20 and 31 to register so that they could be directed into essential war work. While during the course of the war only 200,000 women were formally directed into industry and 2067 were prosecuted for failing to take up war work, the threat of compulsion once registered pushed many women into taking up war work voluntarily. Bevin's insistence that all workers would enjoy adequate wages and conditions of work helped to temper the unpopularity of direction.

While direction helped to increase the contribution of women, more work was needed. Women had been exempt from the National Services Act of September 2, 1939, to which Civil Defence had been added in April 1941, but on December 10, 1941, the controversial National Service Act No. 2 became law, marking the first conscription of women between the ages of 20 and 31 into the Armed Services. The Women's Services became part of the Armed Forces of the Crown and thus subject to military discipline and conscription. Herbert Morrison also put forward an act that made the Auxiliary Fire Services, the Police War Reserves and the Civil Defence Reserve parts of the Civil Defence Forces, and in April they were also made subject to direction and conscription. Thus the Blitz spanned the period of the voluntary worker, and the beginning of conscription, when 'what might be called the "amateur" war was coming to an end'.[15]

The increasing regulation of labor and production helped to increase the numbers of the Civil Service. As government expenditure increased six-fold, from £1 billion in 1938–1939 to £6.2 billion in 1944–45, civil and military defense grew to 83 percent of the budget. The expansion of government policies to cover war supplies, the direction of food and labor and even, after 1942, the design of 'Utility' furniture and goods necessitated a leap in Civil Service workers from 388,000 in 1939 to 705,000 by 1945.[16]

The historical debates surrounding the war's effect on labor hinged on the experience of, and governmental response to, pre-war unemployment versus the worker's experience of full employment and the government's need for high levels of production. In this sense, the two nations of capital and labor, divided by the General Strike, were brought together by the workers' efforts to increase production and win the war and the government's concern for their social welfare. The efforts of industrial workers, especially after 1941, were the coin of promised postwar rewards. Sir William Jowitt, The Paymaster-General, stated on December 1, 1942 in the House of Commons that 'I myself suggest that the objective we ought to aim at is the maximum employment of our people.'[17] Hugh Dalton, President of the Board of Trade, went farther in a Parliamentary Speech on January 12, 1943: 'Who will stand up and deny that full employment is a practical possibility? Only those whose minds are paralysed by the dull disgrace, for which we must all accept our share of responsibility, of mass unemployment in the interwar years.'[18]

Dalton's statement underlined the unintentional irony of statements concerning the heroic and patriotic nature of industrial work in wartime. Although work conditions in factories during the war were difficult, workers were only doing what they had asked to do in the strikes in the 1920s and the hunger marches of the 1930s: to work. A letter written by Dorothy Mainwaring on November 24, 1940 pointed to the hypocrisy of pronouncements on worker's morale:

> In the badly bombed places, mostly working class districts, the courage of these people has been marvelous. These same people in my opinion have always shown courage, courage to face unemployment, courage to face bad conditions, sickness,

and all the other evils it has been their lot to bear. It makes me sick to hear the people who now talk so glibly about the wonderful morale of workers. In peace time these same people can only see the workers as something quite beneath their notice, or if they do say anything about them at all it is to their detriment. ... I hope that when this is all over we shall see to it that the workers get a fair deal as they deserve.[19]

For Mainwaring, workers had always been heroic, and the surprise that underlay praise for the morale and efficiency of workers was not only unflattering but unjustified.

Vera Douie also noted the gratified surprise in the official praise of women's war work: 'The astonishment of their capacity implied in this applause cannot, after all, be regarded as an unmixed compliment.'[20] Indeed, the assumption that paid employment was a new experience for most women, evident in such government pamphlets as *Eve in Overalls*, ignored the five million women already employed in industry, commerce and the armed forces in 1939. By 1943 their number had increased by 2,250,000, which meant that only 31 per cent of the 1943 total could have been new employees.[21] One of the few public references to the history of women's work in Britain was in the newspaper *The Jewish Chronicle*, which traced not only women's entry into the workforce in 1914–1918, but also pressed for a national system of organized training for women and a widespread system of nurseries. The *Chronicle* held up as an example the Jewish women of Palestine who set up a system of skills training to help acclimatize women to their new surroundings in a semi-tropical land. Mainstream newspapers and other forms of popular culture projected a deeply ambivalent attitude towards women workers, which also permeated government policy.[22]

War Work and Morale in London

Because civil defense, women's work and most industrial labor depended on voluntarism at the beginning of the raids, continuing

with work became the ultimate symbol of civilian morale in the face
of danger. Work represented the continuing belief in possible victory
and the justness of Britain's cause, and, for many, this faith ennobled
workers. J. B. Priestley asserted in a *Sunday Express* newspaper
column in September 1940 that the industrial workers had been the
backbone of England since the Industrial Revolution:

> It was these people who, toiling from the dark of early morn-
> ing into the dark of late evening, produced the great wealth
> that this country accumulated in the nineteenth century. ...
> Fortunately, instead of disappearing from it, the industrial
> workers have been making greater and greater appearances in
> this war...They are doing a grand job, away from the limelight,
> and without uniforms, medals or the hope of special leave. ...
> They know that this is their war.[23]

Not only production but business of all kinds were posited as central
to the waging of the war. Ben Robertson saw high levels of civilian
morale in every aspect of the continued life of the city:

> All over London signs went up: 'Business as usual'. Everyone
> realized this was a production war: that the factories must be
> kept going, that the stores and restaurants that supplied the
> factory workers must stay open – it was total war at last, with
> everyone a member of the civil army. The girl who sold coats
> at Selfridges' store now could feel she was as important to her
> country as the soldier behind the gun in Hyde Park – she was
> working under fire just as he was; bombs came down on
> Selfridges' just as they fell by the battery off the Marble Arch.
> There was resolution and determination – London now
> depended on the people, and the people knew it.[24]

Populist references to the 'people' of the 'People's War' implicitly
presented a unified social ideal. Ritchie Calder, for instance, wrote
that war work was bringing people closer together:

> Old reticences, old inhibitions, old selfishness, and old ideas have been cast off, and just as some have put on the visible uniforms of the Services, there is also the invisible uniform of service. After the war this is the one uniform we must not discard. In a thousand ways, for a thousand common objects, people have learned to work together, to appreciate each other's values…[25]

The most common symbol of the 'invisible uniform of service' was the Civil Defence. Here, social classes mixed under the rubric of patriotic service, as Stephen Spender wrote:

> Civil defence, as I hope to show, is a very good starting point for a study of our wartime behaviour. In common with the other services, it provides its personnel with experience, such as camaraderie and living for a common cause, which will be necessary if we are to win the peace. Moreover, it shows us how the mixing of social classes, the social work done by Civil Defence, need not be necessarily confined to war. … One such experience is the breakdown of social barriers among neighbours, the discovery that at the warden's post, or the depot, or the fire station, men and women leading entirely different lives can become friends and respect each other.[26]

Spender was not talking about breakdown of class barriers, but an increased friendliness among neighbors. His description of the relationships within civil defense posts makes clear that relationships between classes had not changed:

> After training, in the stations themselves, the officers are on terms almost of equality with their men. … The relationship between station officer or Chief Warden and the men and women underneath him, is a parental one, and the more important officers who may interrupt the life of a station by coming in sometimes from outside are regarded as rather

superior hoity-toity relatives who have to be treated more respectfully than seriously.[27]

Although Spender leans towards arguing for equality in the station, he immediately qualifies it with the word 'almost'. He then moves entirely away from equality with his familial metaphors of Chief Warden as a parent, and other officers as relatives who must be 'respected', emphasizing both the duty and deference characteristic of hierarchical models of society.

Spender was not the only one to attach such importance to civil defense. As the bureaucratic and organizational centre of Britain, London had to continue to work. As the first fears that the populace would riot under bombardment faded, and as the threat of invasion receded by October 1940, the prime public concern was to maintain London services for the city's population and workers. The bureaucratic system created to organize emergency services in Britain arose at first from the Civil Emergency Organisation, which was created after World War One, used in the General Strike, and whose framework was maintained until 1938.

The Air-Raid Precautions Act (ARP) of 1938 required local authorities to plan schemes for neutralizing, reducing or repairing the effects of enemy action against the civilian population. The London County Council set up an ARP Sub-Committee to organize and supervise arrangements for fire and ambulance services, evacuation of children, and structural concerns such as drainage.[28] In February 1939, Sir Harold Scott was appointed the Chief Administrative Officer of the London Region. It was then his responsibility, as he described in his memoir, to coordinate the ARP plans of London's services, which existed under 95 different authorities, and whose numbers were swollen by thousands of volunteers.[29] He began by dividing the County of London and surrounding areas of Surrey, Essex and Kent into groups that contained a number of local authorities. Regional Chiefs were created for each of the services; for example, Sir Pierson Frank, the London County Council Chief Engineer, was chosen to coordinate the Repair Service. The Chiefs supervised training in each of the groups and kept track of the needs of each service. The London region had two Regional Commissioners and a Senior Regional Commissioner, who, along with Scott, worked out of London's Regional Headquarters housed in the Geographical Survey Office and Museum in Exhibition Road, in South Kensington. Heading each borough or district was an ARP Controller, usually the Town Clerk or Mayor, who was responsible for all the ARP services in his district. The Control Room of each borough's ARP services was linked by telephone to the individual wardens' posts, ambulance stations, first aids posts and fire services. When a bomb dropped, the local warden completed a report form, and telephoned its contents into the Control Room. There, telephonists received the reports, pinned the area of each bomb on a large map of the borough, and sent out the requested services.[30] The Fire Service had a similar, originally separate control system, but was amalgamated with the ARP under the title of Civil Defence in September 1941.

The lack of a central authority for civil defense made Scott's organizational job more difficult. Services were organized through local authorities under the responsibility of the relevant ministry; assistance to the injured and care of the dead, for example, was the responsibility of the Ministry of Health, as were water and sewer repairs. The feeding of those who had lost their houses or gas was the responsibility of the Ministry of Food, while salvaging furniture and clearing up debris were under the care of the Ministry of Home Security. Supplementing local authorities were the Assistance Board Area Officers who handled distress schemes and injury claims, local gas and electric companies who were in charge of repairs, the Employment Exchange Officers and the local military commanders who were often in charge of unexploded bombs.

It was the responsibility of each local authority to organize their ARP services, and organization was often delayed by disputes over which section of government should pay. Scott's system of control encouraged the appointment of the Town Clerk as the ARP Controller, so the organization of each borough was dependant on its local government. Thus the highly organized Poplar region, under the direction of Alderman William Key (who had led the famous Poplar rates strike in the 1920s) created an efficient system which resulted in the lowest death toll per weight of bombs dropped in the East End.[31] In contrast to Poplar's efficiency, the borough of West Ham delayed setting up an ARP Committee until they discovered how much the central government would contribute, and then stinted on spending because they felt the cost should be entirely covered. Four successive failures at finding an effective ARP Controller and a threat from the Regional Commissioners to impose a direct order finally led to the appointment of the very effective Reverend Wilson Paton, but only after the worst of the bombing was over.[32]

Wardens also felt the confusion surrounding ARP responsibilities. S. M. S. (Stephen) Woodcock described the disputes among the ARP services on January 30, 1941:

> It seems that the incendiary bomb last night burnt out the First Aid Post at Lancaster Road baths. The bombs were seen by our Wardens from St John's Hill but they assumed that the nearer Wardens would see it. They didn't! Nor did the F.A.P.! Incendiaries also fell in Portobello Road and there were apparently many scuffles between people dealing with the same bomb and accusing each other of 'pinching my bomb'.[33]

Many wardens, like those who fought over the bomb, no doubt enjoyed the new authority and power their role gave them, especially after the derisions of the period preceding the Blitz. Gladys Langford wrote in her diary on September 15, 1940 that her local wardens relished their fleeting power, though wardens' diaries and memoirs are more matter-of-fact and emphasize their responsibilities.[34]

The concern over the cost of the civil defense of London was reflected in the pre-Blitz debates over the cost of maintaining an ARP system. In December 1939, London had over nine thousand paid wardens (averaging nine to a post), ten thousand full-time stretcher bearers and twelve thousand paid workers in the rescue service. These were supplemented by many more part-time volunteers, particularly among the wardens. The continuing 'leakage' of people to industry and the armed services forced the government to introduce a measure of direction. In June 1940, police and firemen were ordered to continue in their jobs, while civil defense was offered as an alternative to men between thirty and fifty volunteering for military service. In September 1940, when the raids began, London wardens were ordered to stay in their jobs as well. The direct conscription into the civil defense was not enacted until the worst of the raids were almost over, in April 1941. Yet even when people began to be conscripted, the mix between volunteers and paid wardens in the civil defense system created problems for the discipline of offenses. While pre-existing services had their own sanction, including fines or loss of rank, these could not be applied to such a heterogeneous group and the only recourse was dismissal.

The main figure in civil defense was the warden. In the year before the bombing raids wardens were mainly responsible for ensuring that the black-out was kept and imposing fines if it was not, a task that earned them the public's dislike. When the raids began, they had a dual role: to report all incidents to the Control Centre, ensuring the dispatch of services, and to be a 'good neighbour' – helping the bombed-out get to the shelter or rest-centre, directing the emergency services if necessary and ensuring good morale in their neighborhood. Wardens were the most visible link between civilians and the Civil Defence, and they were also the most temporary of war workers, with no peace-time equivalent to their duties.

Of the diarists and memoirists in this study, five out of one hundred women acted as wardens, and seven out of eighty-three men. Many of their diaries were logbooks, describing incidents in their area and sometimes their own personal reactions. B. Garman's ARP logbook was an hour-by-hour commentary of the days he spent on duty. November 23, 1940 was an average day:

5:30 Police call ambulance for man who fell over outside.
5:40 Ambulance arrived.
6:30 Action sirens.
7:00 Raiders passes [sic].
8:00 Abulance [sic] sent for by PC 106 for Mrs G. Samuels
suffering from pregency [sic].
8:15 Ambulance arrived.[35]

Wardens performed an important role in organizing responses to
bombing raids, maintaining shelters and ensuring order was kept in
their neighborhoods, but the temporary nature of their wartime work
could not have much postwar effect on work in London.

While wartime work in the civil defense was presented as an
assertion of patriotism and morale, civil defense workers did not
always believe everything they said. William Regan, a rescue worker
in the Isle of Dogs, made contact with the injured and uninjured in
his surveys of bombed neighborhoods. He wrote in his diary on
September 12, 1940:

> To Plevna St, we found no casualties, but visited all shelters
> down one side of the street, by walking through the first house
> we found open, into the back garden, then climbing over the
> low walls, and down to the end of the street. Most of the
> shelters were empty, those we found occupied had nobody
> hurt, so we soft-soaped them with the assurance that bombs
> never dropped twice in the same place; I knew differently but
> they took some comfort from it.[36]

Reassurances were intended to shore up the morale of people in the
district, and were not necessarily a reflection of the civil defense
workers' own morale or work motives.

Firemen were in a more anomalous position than wardens. During
the war, their units were a mix of professional and amateur firemen.
Furthermore, the physical dangers of firefighting made firemen more
akin to soldiers risking their lives than other positions within the civil

defense. Cyril Demarne, a professional fireman who trained auxiliary firemen during the war, did not consider firemen civilians, who produced the equipment for war and protected the family unit.[37] But neither were they soldiers, as evinced by their anger at being targeted by the machine gun of a *Messerschmidt* on September 5, 1940: 'Harold Marriott, a veteran of the First World War, was highly indignant. "What the bleedin' hell do they think they're doing," he yelled. "We're firemen, not bleedin' soldiers."'[38]

Of diarists and memoirists, one was a Regular in the Fire Services and three were Auxiliary Fire Service (AFS) volunteers. F. W. Hurd was a twenty-four-year-old man who joined the AFS in April 1939 and was called up in September 1939. His diary revealed how he treated raids as a game, emphasizing in his accounts the sense of adventure, challenge and male camaraderie. September 7, 1940:

> We entered our shelter (a room on the ground floor) and settled down to await the all clear and supper, which would be served around 6.30. We were getting a bit fed up with this sort of thing [nuisance raids] and I think a few of us (I know I did) half-hoped for something to happen and then felt ashamed for letting the monotony 'get us down'. Then suddenly it came! The alarm bell rang at 6.15. All pumps (2 heavy units and four trailer pumps) were ordered to Kingsland Rd. Station to 'stand-by'.[39]

Hurd was killed in the December 29, 1940 fires.

Nicolas Bentley, an illustrator, was a wartime volunteer for the AFS. In his memoir, he wrote that although the regulars must have distrusted the volunteers' lack of experience and shorter training, they welcomed them with generosity and friendship:

> Whether it was the circumstances of our trade and the common risk of easy annihilation that seemed to draw us all together, I don't know, but certainly there was a feeling of fraternity among us that was unlike anything I have known to

exist between other groups of men. I daresay it was not exceptional and that the spirit ran through all the services, but for me it was a new and comforting sensation, and at times a very moving one.[40]

This camaraderie, however, was exclusively male. The women who joined the AFS did not share this fellowship as they were not permitted to perform active firefighting duties. Instead they made the tea, cooked the meals and drove the vans; they worked in conditions of danger, but theirs was not the active bravery of firemen. They were also paid £2 a week in contrast the men's £3. Yvonne Green, a firewatcher in Chelsea, downplayed her active role in a letter to her mother on October 8, 1940:

Do not let your soul fill with horror thinking of me firefighting like a ruddy heroine – I've been in the service over two years now, and I haven't yet seen a fire, so set your mind at rest. I am not leading a very perilous existence and it would be more to the point if you prayed for the safety of our men who are such nice fellows and doing a superb job of work.[41]

Though the intention of her letter was to reassure her mother, the danger she faced was real. Green was killed on April 16, 1941 in Chelsea Old Church. For the AFS members, dangers were universal even if camaraderie was not.

Women performed a variety of jobs in Civil Defence in London. One in six of the approximately 90,000 London wardens during the Blitz were women. In contrast to the heroic language used to describe men, the nurturing aspect of their role was emphasized. A 1942 pamphlet titled *Front Line* described women wardens as maternal: 'they had their own touch with the nervous or the restless, while their reports lacked nothing in balanced accuracy'.[42] This was not the language of patriotism or national unity.

Women also participated in voluntary organizations and Medical Services. The YMCA, the Salvation Army, the Friends Ambulance

Unit and the Red Cross supplemented local authority schemes, and the Women's Voluntary Service also organized rest centers, canteens and clothing depots. Medical Services were an organized part of civil defense. First Aid parties, usually four men and a driver, were dispatched to scenes of bombing. First Aid posts, doctors, nurses and other nursing auxiliaries made up London's medical services. Ambulance drivers, usually women, evacuated hospitals and rest homes, and transported the injured from bombed sites to hospitals or between hospitals. Because ambulance drivers were often female, in the tradition of female drivers in World War One, they were publicly characterized during the war as some of the most incongruous defense workers:

> She had volunteered because she had been used to driving her own car, most likely, or the family's. 'Civil Occupation: Housewife' she had written on the application form: or 'Typist', or occasionally 'None' – what they called a Bright Young Thing. She had shuddered at a dead bird on the footpath, and now she was going out to deal with death and mutilations in forms as horrible as any battlefield had ever seen.[43]

This passage emphasized the privileged class position of women drivers, who all supposedly had their own cars before the war, in order to make their war work both incongruous and less threatening, since driving for wages was an unlikely postwar prospect for upper- and middle-class women.

Although women made up a significant part of the civil defense system, their contribution was not considered as heroic. Vera Douie, in her 1949 history of women's work done during the war, stated that the work of women could not be compared 'either in terms of value or in terms of sacrifice, with the work of the men in the Fighting Services and Merchant Navy, or with that of firemen or rescue men in the civil defence Service'. Yet the work done by women was enough to earn them the praise that 'they showed themselves good citizens, and are entitled to hold up their heads'.[44]

The desire to 'hold up their heads' and to be involved in the national effort motivated some wartime volunteers. Elizabeth Watson, an artist turned ambulance driver, wrote in 1941: 'Back home I wondered what I should do. Should artists be detached commentators or combatants? Could they record such events accurately from the outside? I felt sure I wanted to be involved somehow, to join in.'[45] She joined an all-women's section of the City of London Ambulance Brigade.

The desire for excitement, adventure and personal usefulness coexisted with patriotic motives for involvement in the war effort. The Blitz and their work in it was a high point in many lives. Jo Oakman, a warden in Chelsea, was described by a contemporary as one such person:

> She was indefatigable: always ready for an emergency, always at hand with a tea-pot or a hot-water-bottle, always even tempered, and of course immensely courageous during raids. She was one of those people who came into their own during the war; when it was over, frankly she was lonely. But she was much loved, *and* admired.[46]

War work provided Jo Oakman with excitement and a sense of purpose. She so cherished the memories of her work that she preserved her ARP logbooks and passed them on to her nephew, who attempted to have them published.

People also volunteered for war work because their peace-time work was no longer possible. A. S. G. Butler was an architect, and his private practice was, of necessity, suspended during the war. During the Blitz he acted as a ruin-recorder for the borough of Chelsea, 'a sort of a brass-hat among the demolition gangs', recording the damage to property in the Borough.[47] War work could also provide material benefits other than a wage. S. G. Champion's house was partly destroyed by a bomb on September 21, 1940, so he volunteered for roof spotting (looking for approaching bombers to warn employees to go to the shelters) and fire duty at his firm so he could have a place to sleep.[48]

Work also provided a distraction from fear and worry, as John Lehmann wrote:

> The scientists tell us that during this period we were all doped with self-secreted adrenalin, that marvelously helped us to endure things that appeared totally unendurable in prospect. For me, and for many of my friends still carrying on professionally or assimilated into the war bureaucracy, I think work was the real adrenalin. To have to answer letters, to have to go on reading manuscripts, to have to go on making one's business plans and calculations, whether bombs were falling in the distance or not, prevented the imagination from straying too far and steadied the nerve quite remarkably. Actors and dancers found, I believe the same; in fact if the sirens went, it was more difficult to remain unconcerned when one was a spectator in front than while one was performing on stage...[49]

Work was the real adrenalin because it offered a sense of personal usefulness and a distraction from uncontrollable wartime events.

The motives for war work expressed by diarists and memoirists were patriotic, but there were always more personal motivations as well. Workers were influenced by the need for money, distraction, excitement, company, but these effects, like much war work, were temporary.

Dangers of Work

War workers in London were heroic because their work put them in danger, though newspapers and published books during the war were careful to downplay the actual physical danger of working through the Blitz. Charles Graves claimed in his 1941 published diary: 'Another interesting statistic was that of the 200 dead omnibus drivers of the LPTB [London Public Transport Board], 125 were killed sheltering and 75 while on duty. So it is all a matter of luck.'[50] The public concern with praising the morale of workers had a

subtext about the difficulties of work in wartime. The social
conditions of London during the Blitz – the sustained tensions of
living under threat of bombardment, the long hours spent in office
shelters with workmates, the shifting and evacuation of offices and
the difficulties of travel – added to the burdens of workers. Florence
Speed, in a shelter at work, wrote on September 16, 1940: 'Am
beginning to hate the monotony of our shelter and its dull gloom,
Miss Davies' harsh voice and Mrs Wetherwalls' perpetual giggling.
Martha never stops talking. Each piles horror upon horror. Perhaps
it is because I have a brutal headache that I notice it more this morning.'[51] Likely the desire to avoid prolonged contact with workmates
was one factor which led to the virtual abandonment of going to
shelters after warning sirens unless the roof spotters saw real danger
approaching.

The geographical size of London also made continuing its work
life difficult. The concern that many felt for their loved ones' safety
added to the work of communications workers in London. Nellie
Carver, who worked for the Central Telegraph Office, bemoaned the
raids that interrupted the Office's Tube Service and Phone Service
on September 12, 1940: 'Hand Service is taking the bulk of London
work and is it busy! If only our City wasn't so large! Everyone is
wiring and asking if their folk are safe, then when the answers
eventually come back these are piled up with the rest and we started
with three days delay!'[52] Getting to and from work was also increasingly difficult. The rationing of petrol limited the use of private cars
and public transportation could be frustrating as well as frightening
in raids. Transport was disrupted for days after by the damage
inflicted on roadways and Tube stations by bombs, as Canon J. H.
Rumens found: 'It is awful trying to get from one place to another in
the city. The bombs have done so much damage that a very devious
route has to be taken.'[53] The emergency bus service, described by a
young civil servant, was an unmarked lorry crowded with people, in
which she had to sit on a newspaper in the middle of the floor,
unsure of the lorry's destination and unable to see out the windows.[54]
Regular public transportation was supplemented during the Blitz by a

regular boat service from Greenwich Pier to ferry workers to the City and West End.[55] Those who worked in a variety of locales, like G. W. King, who transcribed law proceedings, found the difficulties of travel even more frustrating.[56]

The evacuation of offices from London to rural areas also created difficulties for workers and their families. George Beardsmore's section of the BBC was evacuated. He wrote in his diary how he and his wife expressed reservations about following his job out of London on October 7, 1940:

> But I must confess that whereas with Jean not leaving home is the whole reason, with me it's only part. The excitement of London under bombardment is one thing but rural Worcester-shire is another. The job itself is chiefly copying orders in triplicate and making the relative entries in the ledger, plus the high excitement of being in charge of the stationary cupboard. Is this all I can do in a time of war? Good God! ... Why can't I make people my business instead of ledgers?[57]

Despite these misgivings, by the end of the conversation Beardsmore decided to stay with his job at the BBC, comparing it to a 'tram I can't get off'. Workers dissatisfied with their jobs nevertheless stuck with them, in part because of lack of physical mobility.

Beardsmore's diary also revealed the common frustration of workers absorbed into the wartime bureaucracy. This was especially true of writers who worked for the Ministry of Information during the Blitz. Alfred 'Duff' Cooper, the Ministry's Director in 1940–41, wrote in his memoir: 'The main defect is that there were too few ordinary civil servants in it, and too many brilliant amateurs. The word I got most used to hearing and most to dislike was "frustration."'[58] Temporary officials, who were unused to being thwarted by the bureaucratic machine, came to him tendering their resignations again and again, trapped in wartime bureaucracy.

Peter Quennell was one such Ministry of Information temporary bureaucrat. His brother volunteered for a Territorial Regiment, but as London was expected to be bombarded, Quennell felt he could take a civilian job without undue discredit:

> Thus I added my name to a list of middle-aged, or nearly middle-aged men, writers, editors, journalists, artists and executives, who believed that their training qualified them for some pacific kind of war service, and presently found myself a hard-worked press censor at the Ministry of Information. There I remained through the long-awaited Blitz, seated in an immense but overcrowded room, behind a wooden office-desk, applying the point of a worn-down pencil to countless slips of flimsy paper.[59]

The strains of bureaucratic work during the Blitz were not only those of unrecognized genius. Anthony Weymouth described in his diary how he had become a 'troglodyte', working 14-hour work days at the BBC organizing speakers and writing scripts, and sleeping in the communal shelter in the basement where the staff repaired at night: 'In the dim light which comes only from the illuminated "Exit" notices over the doors you can just make out a sea of mattresses – on the stage and on the steeply rising floor from which the tip-up chairs have been removed. Our ration is one mattress, one pillow and two rugs, and very welcome even this "bed" after some fourteen hours of work.'[60] Portland Place, the broadcasting house of the BBC, was bombed on October 16, 1940, resulting in the deaths of four employees, a fireman and a civil defense worker. The building was not evacuated and work carried on, though a bomb had crashed through the News Room, the fourth and fifth floors of the building were gone, and the lower floors were awash in a sea of paper.

After the City was ravaged by fires on the night of December 29, 1940, in part because of inadequate supervision of buildings, Herbert Morrison ordered in January 1941 that office buildings be protected by mandatory fire watches. The organization of office workers to fill the rotas added to the burdens of workers and was so resented that two thirds of those called up claimed exemption. Phyllis Warner, who worked in a newspaper office in the City, wrote on January 29, 1941:

> At a staff meeting this afternoon we were told that we must start a regular fire watch. The fact that you are already doing it at home makes no difference because by the law the place of work takes precedence over the home. Of course the law doesn't apply to women, but we're so short of men that we shall all have to volunteer to make things work. So it's going to mean spending one whole night a week and one whole weekend a month on the job. What a ruddy nuisance. It's funny how a mere irritation like this brings war home much more effectively than anything you read in the papers, even than air raids. The food situation has the same effect – it gives the daily routine a jolt.[61]

Marie Laurence was also annoyed at hearing that fire-watching was compulsory, even for women. After her boss read the duty roster she said, 'it will mean an average of 27 hours per week'. He replied that she had better find out where she could sleep while on duty. She then called a higher-up, Mr Piper, with whom she discussed the long hours and the difficulty of sharing the burden equally among employees. In the afternoon she decided to confront her boss when she saw that the staff would be paid only two shillings a night for being on duty:

> 'Well' he said 'You will be on tonight, have you done anything about it and rung the Library.' I said 'no I am not on I have told the T. C. I am not doing it.' He nearly passed out, glared at me, then thought it over. When I said Mr Piper had been interviewed he said 'Oh well of course the hours are too long and of course you could not be expected to do it.' I passed out to my room and thought pot hooks to you.[62]

Marie Laurence's showdown with her boss was no doubt one of many.

Nellie Carver reported to work on December 30, 1940, only to find her office building had been burned down by incendiary bombs during December 29 raids: 'We have often groused about our office, most of us, in fact, at one time or another, but today many were in tears, realizing that we had seen the last of the old building and that one chapter in our daily lives was closed.'[63] Nellie Carver's office work continued in a new building, but others were not so lucky. Isabelle Granger wrote on April 17, 1941 that she found it difficult to keep employment during the Blitz. She had been fired from the Ministry of Housing for giving too much money to applicants, and then earned a meager living working long hours in a law office.[64] Gladys Langford was unemployed because she was a teacher who did not evacuate with her school.[65] One Londoner, as a decorator, could not find work during the Blitz, and could not sign up for war work as he was a Conscientious Objector.[66] S. G. Champion's factory had been bombed out in the December 29 raids, and he joined the RAF in January 1941. Max Cohen, a carpenter, had left London to seek work, but his union, the Amalgamated Society of Woodworkers, sent out a call for carpenters to go to London to repair bomb damage and he returned in December 1940. When he went to the Labour Exchange to sign on, the effect on the clerk was electric: 'Hey, whaddye think!' he called jubilantly to his fellow-clerks. 'Here's a carpenter! *A carpenter!* Come to London to work on bomb damage!'[67] He was told there were thousands of jobs waiting for him, but the only job he could get was repairing a damaged railway bridge, about which he knew nothing. He hated the cold, the dirt and noise:

In the meantime there was the bridge as well as the blitz. It was a moot point whether the blitz affected my attitude towards the bridge, or the bridge diminished my capacity to endure the blitz with the requisite amount of *sang-froid*. What was certain was that with every passing day I found work on that bridge more intolerable.[68]

Though Cohen found another job working on the construction of an

Aerodrome, it was not until the spring and the end of the bombing raids that had made his work on the bridge so hard to bear.

The order for mandatory fire watches reflected the danger of factories and offices being destroyed or burnt-out in the bombing raids. Phyllis Damonte showed up for work after the first night of the bombing only to find the factory in which she had sewn dresses was gone: 'Next morning in a daze of bewilderment and sleeplessness I left for work as usual. I didn't know what to do. … It was then I saw my factory workshop a burnt-out wreck. A burnt piece of wood looking like a gibbet jutted out into the sky. I turned away sick with apprehension at what was now in store for us all.'[69] The image of the gibbet may have overdramatized her feelings of helplessness, but with the destruction of her physical place of work she no longer had an income and could not collect her wages. Her other job had been to entertain Civil Defence workers, but after the raids began and the wardens were kept busy her theatrical work was no longer needed.

Towards the end of the war, voluntary and conscripted wartime labor became a symbol for national unity. In these arguments, workers' relinquishing of trade union rights under dilution and conscription was a social contract that should be rewarded with the rights of material citizenship in the form of postwar full employment.[70] Though the experience of full employment and welfare in the wartime industrial factory is almost impossible to link to a change in the working classes' sense of entitlement, the link between work and citizenship was enshrined in the 1942 Beveridge Report's plan for contributory employment insurance, and its less respectable, less well-paid and means-tested national assistance program.[71] Work was promoted as central to the rights of citizenship, and to the health and the wealth of the nation.

A 1945 pamphlet published by the Ministry of Information on Trade Unions inverted the Marxian axiom to argue that 'Labour is not a commodity.'[72] The author asserted that 'Workers cannot be treated as merchandise. They are citizens with homes and families, rights and responsibilities, likes and dislikes, thoughts and feelings.' The patriotism of workers, expressed through their production and acquiescence to directed labor, gave them expanded material rights. Workers in London, through their civil defense work and attendance throughout the Blitz, earned a heroic legacy. Reginald Bell, a journalist, wrote in 1943:

> When the war is done ... none will have a prouder boast than those who can quietly say: 'I was a City Fireman', 'I, a Poplar warden', 'I was a special in Holborn,' 'I drove an ambulance in Stepney', or just 'I went to my shelter each night in Bethnal Green, *and* never missed a day's work after.' With the rescue man in Shoreditch, the Finsbury repair worker, the stretcher bearer from Hackney, and indeed every Londoner, in the services and out of them, who bore a hand through the agony and trial they may at last realize that, all unconsciously in that dark hour, they were touched and illuminated by a shaft of glory.[73]

Such high-flown sentiment may well have sought to reward workers for their fortitude, but instead concealed the continuities of conflicted relationships between social classes in the arena of work. Heroic metaphors had the opposite effect, by making work done well seem anomalous, and by papering over the continuing inequalities and struggles in the workplaces of London.

The public concern with civilian morale under the pressure of bombing raids and privations also extended to work done during the war. Work in London centered on the organization and the maintenance of the city, and workers' efforts to ensure the continued civil life of London was a powerful symbol of morale and patriotism. The motives for war work expressed by diarists and memoirists complicate the conception of war work as a direct manifestation of good morale and reveal the difficulties workers had in trying to maintain their jobs during the Blitz. Their descriptions of the social relationships in the workplace also call into question the extent to which class differences were subsumed in larger patriotic motivations for work. These subjective factors, combined with an analysis of the conscription, compulsion and the lack of mobility between jobs, reveals a more complex picture of work in London than the image of the 'People's War' has allowed.

4

CHILDREN AND THE FAMILY

As the bombs stirred the ground and the shrapnel clattered down the road, we fought a quiet battle of cunning for the bedclothes. Feet touched faces, arms slung across chests, elbows elbowed; snores bubbled and spluttered to be silenced by ostensibly accidental blows; fragments of wild dream talk escaped from the depths of our private lives. Enmity was closer to the surface during those caged nights than at any other time in our well-mannered lives.[1]

Derek Lambert's memories of sharing a small Morrison shelter with his parents during the Blitz reveal the strain of enforced togetherness. Whether confined in shelters, separated by the evacuation of children or a father overseas, or moved to new surroundings, the conditions of the Blitz put great stress on the family. Evacuation, billeting and public shelters also made the private lives of families visible to observers in an unprecedented way. This new visibility, combined with public concerns for civilian morale, national unity and the future social fabric of Britain, gave the family a new importance in public debates and in social policy. Yet social provisions designed to help safeguard the moral and physical health of the family were not the outpouring of a new public and state benevolence, nor were they based on conceptions of universal entitlement to a minimum level of subsistence, any more than were increased social provisions for workers. Public concern for the family relied on an ideal of family life that reflected middle-class values and concerns. Thus while first-person narratives reveal the ways in which all families learned new strategies to cope with the difficult emotional and material conditions of the Blitz, public concern instead focused on normative pre-scriptions for social and moral hygiene. Underneath prescribed 'remedies' for the family were deeper concerns about maintaining the nuclear family and safeguarding children from psychological and physical traumas of family separation and the destruction of the Blitz.

The contrast between how family members described their experiences and how observers depicted families during the Blitz reflects wider anxieties about contemporary family life.[2] Like the labor crises, the changes in domestic dynamics and ideologies in interwar Britain revolved around the idea of 'problem' or deviant family. Increased public concern led to the proliferation of middle-class observers of working class families in urban centers, including district nurses, doctors, school inspectors, Poor Law wardens, and school board officers. Spectators of the family often converted cultural and class differences into pathologies, and the sanitization of the working class urban household was a preoccupation of many voluntary associations and local authorities.[3]

Migration to and within cities was one of the major social changes in the interwar period. London was a popular destination for international, Irish and regional immigration. Increased physical mobility through better public transportation, the increase in motor cars and the growth of housing estates in areas outside of London allowed for more population movement into London suburbs. This increased mobility and immigration allowed people to shed existing familial and community relationships for new ones, or none. Carolyn Steedman, in *Landscape for a Good Woman* (1986), related the story of her parents' flight from the North to start a new life in London:

My parents were immigrants. Strangers to a metropolis during the great depression, they left a northern country, impossible stories left behind them: a wife and child abandoned. In London they created a new set of impossibilities, the matter of terrible secrets.[4]

After the First World War, local councils became responsible for housing for the first time, in the hopes that council housing for the lower classes would lead to an improvement in their childrearing and general habits. Local authorities in Britain also forcibly removed four million people from slum housing between 1930 and 1939.[5] Despite these changes, the social and familial geography of London maintained a certain level of consistency, in the privileged enclaves of the West End and the working class areas to the North, South and East, where most members of the London working classes had been born.[6]

The interwar period also saw a drastic drop in the national birth rate. The year 1933 was a nadir in the fertility rate, which dropped to 1.72, a level unmatched for the next 45 years. In the 1930s, fears of future underpopulation and of 'race suicide' were widely debated in academic and some political circles in Britain. The fact that fertility of middle-class couples was falling more rapidly gave the discussion added bite.[7]

The first years of the war separated London families. Beginning in September 1939, four million people were evacuated and five million members of the armed services were posted.[8] Beginning in 1940, housing shortages and the mobilization of women into the workforce added to family divisions. Increased wartime mobility is evident in the sixty million household address changes during the war, in a civilian population of approximately 38 million.[9] The increasing responsibility of the state in creating and regulating these separations added to public concerns with social and marital morality and reproduction.[10] Wartime propaganda began not only to promote the family as the key institution that would enable the British to surmount the crises of war, but also to represent Britain as 'one big family', overcoming the social divisions of the 1930s. Herbert Morrison, Home Secretary, declared in December 1942 that unfortunate citizens must be cared for by the state as: 'cautious, niggling, worldly wisdom and counting chances while children go hungry would be a miserable foundation for our future life together as a family'.[11]

Yet negative images of the family, particularly the working class family, abounded in public narratives and in social policy. Wartime governmental responsibilities underlined the State's increasing conception of itself as the parent, and foreshadowed the familial social policies of the postwar welfare state.[12] The increased role of the State in postwar reconstruction, especially in the clearance of 'slum neighbourhoods' to suburban housing estates, undermined family and kinship relations and the working-class communities on which they were based.

The family was important not only as the object of social policy during the Blitz. Family relationships were vital to how daily life was experienced. The family also affected diarists by influencing who kept wartime diaries, for what motive, and whether the diaries were preserved. Parents of young children, who were arguably the most affected by war's strictures and dangers, seldom had time to write. One who did was William Regan, who kept a diary not only for historical purposes, but to pass on to his family: 'In the beginning my interest was to keep an account of my activities during the war against Hitler's Germany; then in the event of my death or that of my dear wife, the writings would reveal something of ourselves to our two daughters who might derive some comfort from this.'[13] He conceived his perceptions of the war as his daughters' birthright. Miss G. T. Thomas, a nurse at Highgate hospital, also envisioned passing on her diary to her heirs: 'I often wonder if I shall be spared to the end of the war to finish this diary. If not, I would like my mother to have this book, and then after her days, my little niece, Margaret – it may help her a little in her History. It's been great fun writing this, and a great relaxation.'[14] Even Quentin Reynolds, an American war correspondent in London, published his impressions of wartime London in the form of letters to his father in Brooklyn.[15] Mass Observation diaries, read and archived in monthly installments, were intended as a more communal inheritance, though many used their MO diaries to express their frustrations and other feelings about their family to an unimplicated source. Family frictions could also affect diaries themselves: Vivienne Hall's mother, for example, found and destroyed her diary, leaving only fragments.[16] The effects of family relationships on first person narrative sources are a reminder of how authors writing about their lives do so in the context of their relationships, and of the importance of such relationships to the social experiences of the Blitz.

Looking at Families

The visibility of London family life was not new to the Blitz. Histories of working-class and poorer districts show that much of family life was public, lived in the streets or in sight and hearing of the neighbors.[17] However, the Blitz did make the urban working class family visible to a new class of official and private observers. From the nineteenth century, working class families were visible only to middle-class observers coming into their homes, usually with punitive or philanthropic aims. During the war, evacuation, billeting and public shelters increased the visibility of families throughout London. The war also brought new officials into homes: ARP wardens to enforce the blackout regulations or to investigate bombs, as well as firemen, rescue workers and medical personnel. Rest centers, public shelters and Tube stations made families visible not only to official workers but also to passers-by, official observers and those seeking entertainment.[18] While many of these conditions persisted throughout the war, the sustained bombing raids and controversies over the evacuation of children and families from London created the first sustained debate over the family before the Beveridge Report in 1942.

People bombed out of the East End were sometimes evacuated to the West End, and voluntary and paid labor schemes brought middle class individuals into poorer areas of London, which broadened the range of observers. Witnesses recorded the pathos of those hurt in the Blitz, focusing on the most vulnerable victims. Nicolas Bentley,

who worked as a fireman during the Blitz, was called to an unfamiliar
locale in Whitechapel. He described seeing an old woman crying
amidst the ruins of her house, with a half-buried Anderson shelter in
the yard. Crying like a child, she refused to go to a shelter, and
'presently we were ordered on. The last I saw of the old woman she
was creeping away towards her shelter, still crying. During the whole
of the Blitz I saw nothing crueller than the act of fate which allowed
her to survive.'[19] To Bentley, the woman was anachronistic, dressed
in a traditional costume of dolman and slippers, and bemoaning the
calamitous end to the 44 years she had lived in her home. He foresaw
no future for her, and could conceive of no help other than to
suggest that she go down to the Tube shelter. The evacuation of the
elderly was particularly poignant because of the break with the past it
represented. Elizabeth Watson, the artist turned ambulance driver,
helped to evacuate the elderly: 'Some of the old women wept bitterly,
and it was difficult to drive through my own tears. Their sobs were
so heartfelt at the separation from their homes and families. They
were leaving them for the last time probably for ever, to live in an
unknown place among strangers.'[20] They would probably not live to
return.

Most observers were concerned with young families, particularly
mothers and children, as markers of the future of the nation. Peter
Conway recorded his own impressions, and those of two other men,
of shelters during three periods of the Blitz. Commenting on the mix
of classes in a Tube shelter, he described a permed and be-ringed
woman under a fur coat, reading a magazine and smoking. Just down
the platform lay a family group:

There was a small family, consisting of a thin, deathly pale,
work-worn woman and a couple of small girls, huddled in a
corner, trying to snatch some sleep on a pile of rags that might
have once been blankets. She held the smaller girl close to her,
hugging it to her body to give the child the warmth of which
her frail body must have had all too little. The group seemed
barely human. I could not help thinking, as I looked at them,

of a monkey mother with her young; and there was nothing disparaging in the thought. It was, I think, the pathetic suggestion of near-humanity and protection.[21]

He asserted that only in wartime could these two different women be brought together, and that the sight of the poor mother would hopefully have an ennobling effect on the wealthier woman. Yet he represented the family's poverty as animalism, calling the child 'it' and making the poor mother providing animal warmth to her child an object of pity whose ennobling effects transformed only the viewer.

Conway was not alone in comparing the poor and working poor of London to animals. A Mass Observation diarist described Londoners as 'a colony of ants who build again and continue their life as they build'.[22] John Lehmann also wrote of the 'exhausted ants who still lived and worked in London'.[23] The animalistic nature of the working classes rendered them objects of scorn rather than pity. When Sefton Delmer heard the courage of Londoners praised, he 'thought with shame of those able-bodied proletarians absenting themselves from their workshops while they lay on their mattresses in the Underground, publicly copulating on the platforms and blocking up the stations for those who had to go to work'.[24] Devoid of even the limited compassion of the previous account, Delmer drew on older conceptions of the working class as overly sexualized, immodest, lazy and shirking. George Orwell portrayed Londoners in September 1940 as animalistic in their lack of daytime fear: 'Never seeming to think about the coming night, like animals which are unable to foresee the future so long as they have a bit of food and a place in the sun.'[25] Yet in October, he wrote in seeming contradiction: 'I am virtually certain it is a fact, though one mustn't mention it – that working class people are more frightened than middle class', characterizing them as more timorous.[26] As Geoffrey Field argues, concerns about the stability of the family were most often illustrated by negative class-freighted images.[27] Critiques of Londoners and the working-class evaluated the appropriateness of their behavior, to indicate their morale and ensure their continued respectability.

Family Ties

The collapsing of the boundaries between the public and private lives of families not only evinced middle class voyeuristic disdain, but also created tension and frustration within families. The strain of shelter conditions, added to the increased domestic responsibilities of finding and providing provisions, often exacerbated or created family friction. Conflicts were sharper within family groups because of a shared family economy, familiarity and isolation during the Blitz. The war also created a new military and political language of family conflict, with overbearing siblings or children compared to dictators or 'Little Hitlers'.

Families shared a variety of shelters, but all were confining. Within a single family shelter, the enforced intimacy could help to cement family bonds. A single twenty-nine-year-old social worker described an evening in the shelter with her family:

October 20, 1940: I have dinner on reaching home at 6:45 (if I'm lucky), wash up, wash myself, clean my teeth, do my hair and walk out to the shelter. Then the evening is divided into three phases. I: 7:45-9, occupied in reading daily papers, letters which have arrived during the day, talking over methods of traveling up and down to town ... and listening to accounts of mother's experiences during the day's warnings. II. At 9 p.m. my sister usually goes indoors to listen to the news; I put on the electric fire in the shelter and write letters (which have become an essential part of my life now that friends in other suburbs are inaccessible practically[)]. Doreen returns at about 9:30 with news of the day's aeroplane returns and anything else of interest. III. At 10 p.m. promptly we drink coffee brought out at 7:30 by my mother, from 10 to 11 we smoke one cigarette each and read aloud. I like reading aloud while the others knit ... I think this bit of the evening is quite valuable and has a definite effect on the relationships in my family. A household of mother and two grown-up daughters still in process of adjusting itself to lack of a father (who died a year ago) is not always an easy thing to run. To create similar interests between these grownups is a valuable aid to smooth working and reading books together helps us to do this.[28]

The shared time and space of the family helped to create new interests and new solicitudes among the three women. However, the lack of space also caused tempers to flare. In September 1940, a nineteen-year-old civil servant shared a shelter bed with his parents under a table in the living room:

What a night. Since we had been pretty comfortable the night before Pa decided to shift into another room under another table. Three of us under it lengthways. Talk about a crush. Father was on the outside because his kidneys are getting weak. Then came Ma and me squashed up against the wall. Of course it was not too bad for Pa – he could spread out one way if not the other, but Ma and I were crushed. And of course Pa did all the moaning. First he got cramp in his thigh. Then a headache! And so on. After about two hours of fitful dozing I got fed up with it and wriggled down so that my head was level with Ma's knees and my legs were stuck out miles in front. That was better as regards room – Ma shifted over and we were comfy – till Pa woke up and found out why we had so much room. More moaning! 'If the ceiling comes down you'll be fixed!' 'Don't be silly there's a good boy' etc. etc. And to allay his moans I crawled back up between Ma and Pa. That was worse – I couldn't budge an inch – neither could Ma so after half an hour I wriggled down again and told Pa that if he still persisted in wanting us all under the table he could go against the wall. He moaned a bit and then subsided and we spent a more or less comfortable night.[29]

During the Blitz the position of the father as head of the family revealed a tension between the privileges of his comfort and his duty to protect the family. Although the tension between family members over shelters was usually due to limited resources, this was not always the case. Diana Cooper, staying with her father in the Dorchester Hotel, argued over the advisability of going down to the basement shelter on September 9, 1940:

> There was a big row tonight between Papa and me undressing and in different stages of nudity. Our gun was banging away outside and the thuds were hideous to hear, and I said that we *must* go down to the basement. I had meant to all that day, and taken precautions to stop argument such as 'I haven't got a suitable dressing gown' by buying him a very suitable shade of blue alpaca with dark red pipings. 'I think you're too unkind', I'd say, pulling off a stocking. 'We *can't* go down; I'm too tired. Besides it doesn't make any difference where you are.' I was beginning to cry and to give in when the guns gave a particularly violent salvo and the look-out man popped his tin-hatted head in at the door saying excitedly, 'You are advised to take cover.' This was a break for me and it settled Papa, who then donned his Tarnhelm outfit with the slowness of a tortoise and down we went.[30]

These frictions were also evident in working-class families. Doris Pierce's father's drinking indirectly compromised his family's safety:

> Dad had always liked to spend evenings in the pub, a few drinks over the odds and he would be the happy clown, singing and fooling about. Just one or two more and he would become argumentative and abusive. This behaviour caused the rest of us much embarrassment in the shelter and finally he was banned from going there. Of course it was unthinkable that we should go without him, so there we were back home again.[31]

Such uncritical loyalty was not always the case. A twenty-four-year-old civil servant lived with her parents, a chronically unemployed brother and a sister. Tempers had begun to flare in October, beginning with her father saying she looked like a barmaid with a scarf around her head: 'I'd had just about enough of those two as I could stand, with their eternal squabblings and stupidities and no compensations. Why on earth couldn't I live with someone I liked? Etc. Then it suddenly occurred to me that 1) I must be suffering with war nerves and 2) I really did look rather frightful now.'[32] After a particularly bad raid in November, she recalled: 'I awoke to hear a roar and thundering to feel that horrible "got you" thud of a heavy bomb and the feel half the world raining down on us.' The whole family was screaming and her mother was particularly hysterical:

I was yelling at them all, beseeching them to stop, but it didn't help. Dad turned on me, said I should show more respect to my father. I said I didn't show respect to anyone unless they had earned it. He said I should have to answer for all 'these things' to God one day (these are all favorite remarks of his!). I told him that was my affair and I shouldn't have to answer to him anyway so shut up!

Family tensions undoubtedly pre-dated the Blitz, but the strains of war exacerbated them and the rhetoric of war gave them a new language. Florence Speed lived with her brother and four sisters in 1940, and conflict between the siblings was frequent. She confided in her diary that her sister Bertha refused to contribute to the family economy: 'She paid less into the house and demanded more than anyone. Only two days ago she said. "I'll be glad to get away from the lot of you" but now it has come to the point, she begins to realize the comforts she had.'[33] After Bertha moved to Glasgow to do war work, the conflict turned to another sister, Norah, and focused on the shared family shelter. On December 29, Florence recorded a fight over Norah wanting to listen to the wireless in the shelter when everyone else wanted to sleep. Since the radio was next to her bed, it blared in Florence's ear. Florence eventually lost her temper: 'I do not lose my temper very often and after I have, hate myself for having done so, but the atmosphere in the house is wearing.'

For Florence, this incident provided proof of Norah's despotic personality: 'Norah wants to be a little Hitler. To rule us like children, on old-fashioned lines. She is unhappy herself because she is kicking against the pricks all the time. Will not adapt herself to the conditions war has imposed upon us all. And she is making everyone else unhappy too.'[34] Authoritarianism in a parent was more accept- able than in a sibling, because the apparent equality of siblings called on a democratic ideal rather than political despotism.

Competition within the family for supremacy and for scarce resources is part of the social reality of working class families but as an aspect of family life is rarely discussed. Carolyn Steedman used the example of her life and her mother's to reveal the impact of competition on her family: 'Personal interpretations of past time – the stories that people tell themselves in order to explain how they got to the place they currently inhabit – are often in deep and ambiguous conflict with the official interpretive devices of a culture.'[35] The conventional language of the family, like Derek Lambert's description of his plucky mother, one of a 'loyal, fussing army of mothers [who] fought the Hun', elides the psychological and social complexity of relationships and identities within families.[36] War increased tensions by rendering space, time and food more scarce, in addition to the emotional strains of familial separation. Mrs H. Faber remembered in her memoir her parents' struggle during the war to find accommodation outside London, while her father stayed and worked in London:

About every fortnight he would make a difficult journey by bus to come and visit us, and I can still remember how he and mother would fall into each other's arms and just hold each other and cry, while my brothers and I looked on. I asked one of my brothers recently if he remembered all this but he said 'no'. I am thankful for the fact that he was four years younger than me, and missed this traumatic experience.[37]

The strain of worry was also felt by children for their parents and siblings. Roy Ridgway, a conscientious objector, recorded his feelings of worry for his family:

> November 10, 1940. The wholesale slaughter of innocent people makes me think that man is doomed to perish, that life is without purpose, and that there is no God. If I lost Mother and Dad, I would not want to go on living. Why should they suffer? They didn't want this war, and neither did hundreds of other innocent people who are losing their homes, their dear ones, all the things that make life worth living. ... When I left Foscote Road this morning, Mother gave me a black tie and said: 'You may need this.' I will never be happy again until Mother, Dad and Joyce have left Hendon.[38]

Worries for the safety of family members was undoubtedly one of the greatest emotional strains of the Blitz.

Looking at Children

Personal and public concerns met in debates over the safety and health of children. The public concern for children brought together two disparate strands of wartime debates: concern for the public health, manners and morality of Britain's 'plastic, impressionable, imitative children, mirrors of every breath of national trouble', and the effect of the strains of the war on the psyche, especially the vulnerable psyches of children.[39]

The public concern over Britain's declining birthrate in the 1920s and 1930s, as well as the increased emotional investment in children resulting from smaller family sizes, increased worry about the separation of children from their families and the condition of evacuated children.[40] The evacuation of urban children to rural areas in the first year of the war had unintended effects. It revealed flaws in the government's planning and provision for evacuation, and it focused middle-class attention on the poverty of urban working-class children.[41] During the war and after, analysts saw evacuation as 'the most important subject in the social history of war because it revealed to the whole people the black spots in its social life'.[42] But contemporary sources and autobiographies of evacuated children reveal not an awakening of social responsibility, but censorious disapproval of the children's dress, diet, manners and morality, and parents.

Public reaction to the first wave of evacuation was collected through various voluntary and official bodies.[43] The National Federation of Women's Institutes sent a questionnaire to their 1,700 member institutes, published as *Town Children Through Country Eyes*. The members thought the report to be of such value to public health that they encouraged its wider publication, so that 'these conditions should be ventilated and corrected. In spite of all that the Public Health Authorities have done and are doing, the neglect of the parents is astonishing.'[44] The Federation reported with distaste the large number of verminous children and those afflicted with sores and skin diseases, and remarked that the children were not used to nourishing meals eaten at the table, and were underdressed, ill-mannered and dirty. The widespread bedwetting that afflicted many evacuated children was seen by the respondents as the 'lack of home training' instead of a response to anxiety or distress.[45]

The terrible conditions of the first wave of evacuated children was rarely discussed in contemporary literature. The *Daily Mirror* on September 25 trumpeted that 'All Open Homes to Children', quoting offers of homes to evacuated children, but in actuality many evacuees met with hostile anti-Semitism, Social Darwinist attitudes and the mutual suspicion of class. Even the often-critical journalist Ritchie Calder wrote that 'all that early talk of "lousy slum children" is long since forgotten. To the country folks, "*those* children" have become "our children".'[46] Yet conflicts persisted throughout the war, and improvements in the reception of urban children was largely due to the placement of the second wave of evacuees, from 1940 to 1941, into working-class homes. The second wave of evacuation also included a wider range of children, evacuated because their homes had been destroyed or they had no caregiver. Evacuation increasingly became a social welfare scheme and a safety valve for bombed urban areas.[47]

Memoirs written by evacuated children, as well as memoirs collected in popular histories recall varied experiences of evacuation.[48] Some children were met with kindness and experienced pastoral pleasures for the first time. Others recalled the fear, loneliness and sometimes cruelty of their experiences. Even those with pleasant memories, such as Edward Dorking, felt themselves to be the exception:

> Later in the war I had other foster parents whom I came to love and still remember with great affection, whereas many evacuees led very unhappy lives with foster parents who were spiteful and mean. Perhaps we were fortunate because some evacuees were selected [from the town halls] for their appearance, which must have been heartbreaking for those who were rejected, and in some cases the new foster parents insisted on only taking one child, which meant that brothers and sisters became separated. Nobody asked the children what they wanted or how they felt and a great deal of distress was caused by many unthinking and uncaring adults.[49]

Penny Elaine Starns and Martin L. Parsons have detailed some of the abuses and deprivations that children faced as evacuees, using oral history testimonies, but a thorough academic history of children's experiences of evacuation in the Second World remains to be written.[50]

After the first wave of evacuation, even during the bombing raids of the Blitz, many families decided to stay together. Michael Reynolds recalled that he wrote his parents telling them he did not want to become an orphan and they brought him home.[51] By November 1940, almost as many children were returning to London as were being evacuated, despite government exhortations.[52] Part of the reluctance of the poorer urban families to evacuate their children was due to the cost of maintaining evacuated children. The government expected parents to pay the billeting allowance of 6s., unless they could prove they were unable to do. This emphasized social differences within the national scheme rather than diminishing them.[53]

By the start of the bombing raids there were many children still in London, those who had returned from evacuation or had never been sent. This gave children, already the focus of ideological and social concern, an increased visibility within the public spaces of streets, shelters and Rest centers during the Blitz. Older children, whose schools had not been evacuated, sheltered at school during daytime raids, while younger children shared shelter spaces with adults. There they were the focus of much adult attention, as in one Londoner's diary: 'Two raids. Had dinner in shelter. So did neighbours. Their little girl is a cheerful child. Apparently the raids don't affect her. Encouraged by her parents she treats it all as great fun!'[54] An incident in Liverpool in which several women used their shoes to beat the suspected molester of a three-year old girl in a shelter reveals a darker side to the increased visibility of children in shared spaces.[55]

Children also faced the same dangers as adults. The death of children in raids was rarely mentioned in public commentary, though in 1938 the activist J. B. S. Haldane used visceral images of children killed by raids in his lectures and book to emphasize the need for more effective and organized air raid precautions: 'Air raids are not only wrong. They are loathsome and disgusting. If you had ever seen a child smashed by a bomb into something like a mixture of dirty rags and cat's meat you would realize this fact as intensely as I do.'[56] The death of children was especially poignant for observers. Mrs C. Eustace recorded in her diary on December 12, 1940 that a young boy from her Scout troop had been killed by a direct hit from a bomb: 'Of all the family, only Malcolm's arm was found, and at least we can be thankful that death must have been instantaneous and they suffered nothing. We were reading a story when they told me of his death and I still don't really believe it. He was so very, very vital and alive, so happy and full of promise that I am selfish enough to grieve at his passing, even while I know that ... he was passed to higher service. I *must* get hold of a photo, though.'[57]

Children who were not martyred were not as idealized. A fifty-three-year-old woman, suspected by her neighbors of having pacifist beliefs and questioned by the police, described a three-year-old child, who had bitten another child, as a dictator:

> Billy was the stuff that Dictators are made of ... I have never seen a more odious child of three, and think a long line of heredity must have gone into his making, for a defective environment of itself could not have produced his caste of face. He ought to be segregated and dealt with as a problem child, but I should not be surprised to learn he was hopeless and nothing but a lethal chamber could rid the world of his odious presence![58]

Apparently the irony of comparing the child to a dictator and then proposing a lethal gas chamber as the only solution for his inherited traits was lost on the peace-loving woman. Her words demonstrated not only callousness, but also the belief in the inherent and inherited negative traits of certain sectors of the population, whose 'defective environment' alone did not account for the child's 'caste of face'.

Marie Paneth put forward a similar eugenic argument in her sociological study of the children of Branch Street in London. She described a welfare centre that had arisen from ARP volunteers' concerns at the wildness and poverty of the children in air raid shelters. Paneth and a group of other volunteers tried to establish a Play Centre for children, where they could profit from adult attention and toys, and in doing so lose their coarse, dirty, violent and thieving ways. Paneth remarked that the children were ill-tended but fiercely protected by their mothers, and behaved badly because they were 'hurt people'.[59] Her attempts to help them, though she felt she had failed, were of vital political importance:

We should also remember that the horde which Hitler employed to carry out his first acts of aggression – murdering and torturing peaceful citizens – were recruited mainly from desperate Branch Street youth, and that to help the individual means helping Democracy as well.[60]

Paneth did not use the language of universal rights or communality, but the language of dictatorship. Clearly she felt her calls for compassion would be best received if couched in the language of danger, and thus described the poor children of Branch Street as 'other' to the civilized and democratic British community.

Parents

Just as children became more visible in the Blitz, so observers were more aware of parents – how they cared for their children and the strains and losses they faced. The death of children, as Mrs Eustace wrote, was particularly heartbreaking and difficult to understand, but it was the parents' grief that remained visible. Harry Walters described how a direct hit on a block of flats in Essex Road killed and wounded many people. Particularly sad were the images of parents:

'Has anyone found a girl in a red dressing gown? She is wear-ing a red dressing gown.' A pitiful parent searched for his young daughter. One poor mother who was trapped between two doors beneath the debris clung to her baby for hours, still believing it to be alive. When she was rescued her arms had to be encased in wire cradles in the position that she had held her child. She walked about for many weeks in this position, a con-stant reminder of the terrible ordeal that she had gone through. And the look of fear and remorse on her face no-one who saw her will ever forget.[61]

The trauma of the mother was written on her body in an excruciat-ingly poignant way.

Mothers came under the closest scrutiny during the Blitz, not only out of compassion, but also to judge their fitness. As in discussions of the family, many of the judgments rested on the appropriateness of their maternal emotions. Wanting to be close to one's children was considered inappropriate when it inconvenienced others. Elizabeth Watson complained about the new mothers in the maternity ward who insisted on being paired with their own babies before being evacuated after a hit. Mothers who kept their children in London or in shelters when evacuation was possible were also seen as selfish. James Lansdale Hodson wrote that working-class mothers who wanted to keep the family together were failing to consider the needs of children: 'One wonders in such odd moments whether we are always wise to allow parents so much liberty to decide these matters. The question arises again now when families shrink from being separated and mothers won't have their children even two doors away during an air raid.'[62] The 'we' in his statement could be the public to whom he is addressing his book, published in 1941, or could be the middle-class person, who supposedly understood the needs of children better than the superstitious or selfish working-class mothers.

Middle-class observers often commented on the poor mothers they saw in the shelters. Florence Speed commented on the cruelty of keeping children in the fuggy atmosphere of the shelters:

Among the 'all-nighters' at the Oval today, with a baby of 5 weeks. It was the sweetest little thing possible, like a big doll. So little and lovable. It was asleep on a cushion. How cruel it is that it should have to sleep in so foul an atmosphere. The mother, poor soul, already looked weary and jaded. She had an outside position, where there is nothing to rest the back. She smiled warmly when we took notice and asked her baby's age.[63]

Although Speed was less critical than some, her compassion was tinged with the moralizing undertones implicit in the word 'jaded', with its connotations of the loss of innocence and lack of caring.

East End families using West End shelters also prompted com-
mentaries on poor mothers. Stephen Woodcock worked as an ARP
warden in a shelter in Kensington, where some refugees from the
East End were billeted. On the night of 13 September, 1940, he
noted that he had 15 aliens and 20 East Enders in the basement
shelter:

> All went well until a worn-out girl asleep on a bench dropped
> her baby on the stone floor and pandemonium ensued, with
> the baby's screams and all evacuees complaining of a lack of
> comfort ... I heated some milk (adding sugar and water as I
> heard babies needed) and we fed the baby who lapped it up
> eagerly, being obviously famished. The mother went to sleep
> wrapped up with the baby to everyone's joy in the shelter.
> Later I found her off the narrow bench and lying on the stone
> floor but couldn't wake her and had to leave her in danger of
> catching a chill![64]

The mother was obviously exhausted. Like Conway's 'monkey'
mother, she is portrayed as passive even in her gratitude:

> When dawn came Miss Bushell and I led the shivering girl and
> the dirty baby to the First Aid Post at Zion Convent where
> they washed the baby and put the mother to rest – on a deck
> chair! The mother was grateful in a quiet pathetic way. Next
> day I sent her a parcel (at Gwen's [Woodcock's wife] sugges-
> tion) containing a blanket, large towel and two bits of soap. We
> hoped the mother would not think the soap an insult but it was
> badly needed.

The Woodcocks were prepared to risk a potential insult in their
reminder to the mother to perform her duty to her child.

Yet in the context of nurseries and women's work, the separation
of women from their children was seen less positively. The large
number of children's nurseries, which increased from fourteen to

1,345, with places for 62,000 children by the end of the war, created anxiety about mother and child relationships.[65] John Bowlby of the Tavistock Clinic argued from his wartime observations of residential nurseries that children were damaged by separation from the mother or mother-substitute: 'There is a high degree of association therefore between the affectionless character [of a juvenile thief] and a history of mother-child separation.'[66] His link between juvenile offenders and working mothers was widely used to discourage governmental commitment to nurseries and women's postwar work outside the home.

Middle-class parents themselves were also very concerned about the effects of the war on children, and how to cope with the challenges of parenting. Many upper and middle-class parents who could afford it, such as Vera Brittain, evacuated their children overseas.[67] Vera Brittain wrote a very short diary entry about sending children to be evacuated on June 26, 1940: 'Children sailed from Liverpool.' This entry was followed nine days later on July 4, 1940: 'Heard Children's boat had arrived.'[68] The curtness of the entries reveals the extent to which she found the parting painful, as did her November 5 description of her attempts to intervene in the mistreatment of a child on the street. Henry 'Chips' Channon, concerned for his son's safety, was relieved both by his son's safe arrival in Montreal, and the assurance of his own immortality: 'Now I care less what happens; my life is over, the rest is residue. I can live on in my dauphin who looks, acts, re-acts, and thinks, just like me.'[69]

Children who remained in London were a worry as well as a source of comfort. An MO diarist recorded the trouble of putting a child to bed in a shelter: 'I've thoroughly had the blues today and Michael has been so tiresome tonight in the cellar. He gets too excited when he plays with her [neighbor's] eight year old. Of course, he should be going to bed in his own quiet dim-lit bedroom instead of being in a brightly lit room with adults talking and laughing at his antics.'[70] The freedom of older children also worried parents, as Anthony Weymouth wrote in his diary:

September 8, 1940. This is a terrible time for us all – it is an awful time for those of us that have children. What is best to be done? On the one hand, we must do all that is possible to ensure their safety; on the other, we must avoid instilling fear into their impressionable minds. I have told Hod that he can go out on his bicycle, provided he promises me to stay where he is when the sirens sounds or to go into a public shelter if he hears them when he is in the streets.[71]

The conditions of the Blitz also made pregnancy, labor and out-fitting a newborn more difficult, though giving birth was tinged with a patriotic heroism. Verily Anderson gave birth during a raid, with her share of what she described as 'Churchill's blood, tears and sweat', and the *Daily Mirror* reported a dramatic birth during a raid in the East End, in which a warden delivered a baby in the dark in a bombed-out house, with water only available from a horse trough.[72] Paradoxically the war made the adoption of children easier, as 'war babies' and babies whose parents were unable to care for them were put up for adoption. May Hobbs described how her father, dressed in a RAF uniform, came to collect her from her evacuation billet, only to tell her he and her mother could not care for her and she would go to a foster home.[73] Adoption rates climbed during the war to reach a height of 21,000 in 1946, in addition to extra-legal adoptions.[74] Edith Evans adopted an eight-week-old baby girl whose mother was married, but whose husband had deserted her. Grace Foakes also wrote of adopting a child whose father was in the Air Force and whose mother 'never came to visit him'.[75]

Children

The public was acutely concerned about the psychological effects on children of family separation, interruption in schooling and witness-ing the raids. Their resilience was judged according the national situation. During the Blitz: 'when they were sheltering from the bombs, roaming adventurously though the littered streets, or traveling to the country as evacuees, they were regarded as important and honourable young citizens'.[76] The heroism and pluckiness of children who ran messages, put out incendiaries, spotted planes or otherwise contributed to the war effort during the Blitz was extolled by public individuals such as Frank Lewey, Mayor of Stepney, and in a pamphlet produced by the Ministry of Home Security, which described the children in London as 'very expert shelterers and Blitz citizens', whose playgrounds were demolished homes and bomb sites.[77] J. R. Sweetland, R. W. Hill and George Pluckwell were among the memoirists to recall their amusements with debris and craters during the Blitz, and games feature prominently in John Boorman's autobiographical film *Hope and Glory* (1987).

But as the war wore on, public concerns about juvenile delinquency and the long-term effects of wartime freedoms grew.[78] The *Jewish Chronicle* anticipated the political comments of Marie Paneth and was one of the first newspapers to assert the need for the discipline of children in war conditions. The editors argued that laxity could result in a morally impoverished generation susceptible to 'evil leadership', as were the children of Central Europe after the last war.[79] A similar controversial argument was made by Peter Loewenberg in 1971, when he asserted that, 'The war and postwar experiences of the small children and youth of World War I explicitly conditioned the nature and success of National Socialism [in Germany].'[80] While psychohistory has been criticized for its emphasis on unconscious motivations, Loewenberg's argument does draw attention to the negative impact of childhood deprivation, separation and fear on the adult individual.

Psychologists and psychiatrists during the Second World War shared fears of the effects of evacuation and bombing on children. Psychiatrists set out to study the effects of war on children: Edward Glover in a War Emergency Clinic in Gloucester Place, set up by the London Clinic of Psychoanalysis, Anna Freud in the Hampstead Nurseries, and Melanie Klein in an individual case study of a ten-year old boy obsessed by war.[81] They generally concluded that in addition to their realistic fears of death or injury, children were vulnerable to psychic anxiety regarding their own destructive and aggressive impulses which they had only recently learned to control.[82] Yet their conclusions about the function of psychological anxiety in the face of the external threats of the war were based on case studies of individual children rather than on larger samples. Observations of the effects of bombing on children were impressionistic, as in Jane Gordon's observation that the Convalescent Home in which she worked re-opened during the Blitz to 'treat children whose nerves had definitely suffered from continual bombardment. Some of the children whom we sent to the Convalescent Home were very pathetic. When they heard distant gunfire they would sit up in bed and whimper like puppies.'[83] Gordon's animalistic metaphor echoes that of writers observing working-class people in shelters, and commenting that they had weaker nerves. Only children who had developed emotional or psychological disturbances were assessed by professionals, skewing the results towards the perception of mass psychological trauma in children, in a reversal of the No-Neurosis myth for adults.

Children's experiences were seldom recorded in histories of the Blitz, a dearth that characterizes most historical periods.[84] Sometimes their reactions were preserved in the diaries of others, if they were particularly endearing or humorous. For example, Frances Partridge recorded the reactions of her son John: 'May 11, 1941: B. [John] suggests writing to Hitler: "Nasty Hitler! Stop this horrible war and go right away altogether." "And then," he said slyly, "I should sign it "Love from John".'[85]

Although children wrote diaries during the war, they were for the most part psychologically and historically un-illuminating records of times and durations of raids and daily activities. Joyce Smith, who was 11 years old in 1941, recorded in her diary daily activities, such as going to school, going to the allotment and having a day's holiday. Reports of a bomb were written in almost the same tone. April 20, 1941: 'At 2:30 a.m. a *bomb* fell at the top of our road. People from Number four house who were in the public shelter came in our house. We gave them a cup of tea. Mrs and Mr Hawkins, Mrs Ott, and Jean and Audrey Ott, Mr Boreham and us all had a cup of tea.'[86]

Yet diaries written by young adults between the ages of 13 and 18 were much more dramatic, describing in detail what they saw and experienced. Young adults usually still lived at home with their parents, were finishing school or beginning to work. They had both the energy and the time to record their experiences of war, as well as their relationships with their parents, their friends, the opposite sex, and their leisure pursuits. Adolescents were very often passionate observers, anxious to capture and record the drama and excitement of the war. Geoffrey Dellar, who was 15 in 1940, entitled his diary after the war a 'Precise record of Timing and Duration of air raids and air raid warnings experienced by Geoffrey Dellar while living in Croydon, until he joined the RAF in 1944'.[87] Fifteen-year-old C. Brownbill gave play-by-play accounts of raids in his diary which read like sports announcements: September 6, 1940, 5:55 p.m. 'Hallo, sounds like another formation coming over yes there they are, twelve of them travelling towards London. There is a huge column of smoke riding from the Thames haven, they must have set the oil tanks on fire again.'[88] In his breathless excitement, Brownbill eschewed punctuation.

The most passionate observer was Colin Perry, whose extensive diary from 1940 was published in 1972. He recorded the raids and other events he witnessed with a passion for detail and a feverish excitement. He described a scene he witnessed from the top of a hill on September 7, 1940:

As I stood on the neat grass verge of the row of suburban houses, transfixed, I saw one fighter (I very much fear ours) rush earthwards. With ever-increasing speed it fell, silently, to its last resting ground, amongst the green of Surrey. I had no time to dwell upon the fate of that man – I could not look up – I just stood, and machine after machine rushed frantically, screaming, it seemed, at me. I had no cover, I held my glasses; I don't know what I felt, but I was proving my theory – that in danger one knows no fear, only a supreme feeling, indescribable. I would not disown those minutes of Life itself.

Zooommmmmm, eeeoooohhhhhooooowwww, rurururururururr
– engine after engine, machine gun after machine-gun, boump
after boump, and I could scarcely see a thing so hazy was the
sky, so brilliant the sun.[89]

Instead of taking cover he went to look for a better vantage point to
overlook the Croydon airport. His narrative combined vivid poetic
description, onomatopoeia and childish excitement, with a dash of
extreme patriotism thrown in. Like the self-styled 'war correspondents' who reported on the state of London, he was very much aware
of witnessing history, and wanted to be *the* witness.

The diary accounts of children not only give insight into their
daily activities during the war, including how schools were affected
by raids and evacuation, but also show how they perceived the
dangers and anxieties around them. Thirteen-year-old Mary Comyns
described in her diary the changes in school shelter arrangements. At
first, the whole school trooped down to shelters, but in January the
rules were changed so that they only left their desks if there were any
warning whistles from the 'roof-spotter':

Jan 10, 1941. So far nothing has happened in school hours but
we had a practice of getting under our desks, which is most
awkward except for little Cicely Cook, and we are longing to
do it in reality, except for large Effy, who just doesn't fit.[90]

Children tended to perceive the change in routine offered by raids as
exciting, rather than dangerous or frightening. A letter written by a
six-year-old child from a shelter, in the archived papers of Ronald
Weir, detailed the games the child played. The letter began 'Dear
Nan, This letter is from Corporal Ronald Weir. Mum has made me 2
stripes and I've got three medals and a homeguard band on my right
arm and one of the boy scouts of the office has given me an air gun.'
The child drew a picture of himself playacting, and described the
exciting atmosphere of the shelter: 'During the day [I] play draughts
with Curly, Bert, Piper and Dad. Mum does knitting all day long.

Most tenants bring their typewriters down and make a machine-gunning noise. We've got the wireless down the shelter ... and we've got the electric fire down here too. There are several bangs going on while I'm writing [sic] this letter, they may be bombs they may be guns we don't know what it is anyway we hope we will be safe in our shelter.'[91] Other children found the shelters less exciting. P. M. Donald, a thirteen-year-old girl, described in her diary how the constant interruptions of the raids took their toll on her and the adults around her. Her six-year-old brother was being naughty in the shelter. The adult supervisor, who was irritated by lack of sleep, hit and shook him out of anger and frustration.[92]

Almost every child and young adult described his or her tiredness. Colin Perry wrote on August 28, 1940: 'I have not had a peaceful sleep since Friday. I am past fatigue. One cannot even settle down to sleep in a warning for the continuous drone of enemy planes overhead makes it distracting and disturbing.'[93] Tiredness and strain led to emotional outbursts, such as that described by Mary Comyns: 'The day after we broke up [school for Christmas holidays] I dropped a card in Miss Jones' door (my French teacher, a neighbour) and on Xmas Eve she dropped one in for me. It was so unexpected, and the card, in black and yellow showing a little boy with a candle creeping upstairs, that I burst into wild, mirthless laughter, automatic laughter; thank goodness no one heard me for it was the nearest I have ever got to hysteria.'[94]

Although children, like adults, felt the wartime strains of sleeplessness and disruption, as adults they tended to remember their fear most vividly. As Carolyn Steedman argues, all children experience a first loss, a move from innocence to experience, and often lives are shaped around this exclusion. Mnemonic studies show that adults remember most clearly the events in their childhood and adolescence that were perceived as times of change.[95] Adults remembering their experiences as children in the raids thus pointed to the importance of fear to their experience of the war. Memories of fear during raids assert the writers' participation in the historic events of the war and challenge the nostalgic portrayals of war. Bernard Kops described his fear as a fifteen-year-old boy in the East End:

I heard sirens. And sirens and sirens. Early in the morning, in the afternoon and in the evening. And we went underground to get away from the sirens and the bombs. Yet they followed me and I heard sirens and the world became a siren. One endless cry of torture. It penetrated right into the core of my being, night and day was one long night, one long nightmare, one long siren, one long wail of despair. Some people feel a certain nostalgia for those days, recall a poetic dream about the blitz. They talk about those days as if they were a time of true communal spirit. Not to me. It was the beginning of an era of utter terror, of fear and horror. I stopped being a child and came face to face with a new reality of the world.[96]

Kops also identified his fears as the beginning of his initiation into adulthood, with a new awareness of the cruelty and complexity of the world. Part of the initiation into adulthood was the realization of personal danger. Bryan Forbes remembered this moment: 'I felt curiously, irrationally secure in the fetid darkness of the small shelter', until he heard Lord Haw Haw on the wireless saying that the Germans would be dropping disinfectant on Earlham Grove, the Jewish Quarter of Forest Gate, his own neighborhood: 'In repeating the remark here I am not trying to perpetuate that distant, vicious smear, I merely wish to record the absolute amazement and fear I felt at hearing my own locality mentioned by the remote voice of the enemy. For the first time I had a premonition of my own death, and I was very afraid.'[97]

Children experienced bereavement through the raids of the Blitz, but few records of their reactions exist. The letters of Mervyn (Merv) Haisman and L. E. (Bill) Snellgrove, twelve-year-old boys who wrote to each other in 1940 and 1941, are an exception. Mervyn described the reactions of his classmates when a friend of theirs was killed.[98] Bill told Merv about the death of his grandmother, whose house received a direct hit. In a letter dated August 31, 1940, Bill wrote:

Dear Merv,

I'm afraid I've got some very bad news. My grandmother was killed in an air raid a few days ago. Her house at Welling received a direct hit during the night from a 'hit and run' raider. The first that I knew that anything was wrong, was when I heard shouting and crying very early one morning. It was only just dawn. I ran downstairs to find a policemen standing in the living room. Mum had collapsed with a slight heart attack and dad was sitting in the chair crying like a baby. I'd never seen him cry before so I knew it was something bad. When the policeman told me, I burst into tears too! I cuddled Dad, the first time since I was a child...

His dad wouldn't let him go with him to identify the body, so instead Bill cycled over to the remains of her house:

The house was a complete wreck. Naturally I am used to wreckage, but this one was different. It was a house I'd known all my life. Walls, pictures, curtains, lamps, ornaments, which I could remember since I was a baby, were all smashed or thrown about. ... The Wardens told me she had died instantly. I think they were being kind. After all, how could they know for certain?

As I cycled home I still couldn't believe it had really happened. You never think these things are going to happen to you or your relatives. All through the Blitz I never thought that we, the family that is, were in any danger. Only other people get killed. I know it's daft, but that's how I felt. Now it had happened and I just couldn't stop crying every time I thought of it.

His distress was visible at home and at school, and Headmaster Haggar, with whom he previously had an adversarial relationship, called him into his office. Haggar lit a cigarette, and told Bill how he had lost eight friends who had fought beside him in the First World War, as well as his mother when he was overseas:

> He said he knew how much I liked writing and advised me to write down how I felt. Don't show it to anybody, just write it for yourself, he said. For a mathematician, I thought that was quite clever. It would help me relieve my feelings. Whether Miss Wilcox had told him I keep a diary I don't know. He told me he still had letters he had written in the trenches; letters so personal he had never shown them to his wife. They were his sad secrets, he told me. They had stopped him from going mad.[99]

Bill's story demonstrated the traumatic impact of a death in the Blitz, the suddenness, the destruction of their familiar home and possessions. His narrative also revealed how the loss initiated him into the world of adulthood, as his Headmaster spoke to him as an equal, signified by the cigarettes and personal revelations. The Headmaster's advice also made explicit the link between the trauma of the First World War and London during the Blitz, with the same feelings of helplessness, which could be released through diary writing, a frequent motive for diarists of the Blitz.

The narratives of children mirror those of adults in their voyeuristic excitement of the Blitz and their increased awareness of danger and loss. The impact of war on the child's psyche, widely debated by contemporaries, did not in many cases lead to pathology, as was feared. Instead their experiences led to a privileging of their Blitz memories in their life narratives, and to the formation of their adult identities. The centrality of Blitz memories to the generation who were children during the war is another reason for the continued emphasis placed on the Blitz in memoirs and autobiographies.

The accounts written by children also suggest that concerns of the social disruptions of the Blitz on children and families might be exaggerated. In fact, public concerns of the war's effect on children and families were less related to understanding the complex interrelationships and strains on the family than with imposing standards of respectability, conduct and hygiene on 'problem families'. Public concern with families as 'cases' or 'problems' influenced social work during the war, and the proposals for family benefits begun by the Beveridge Report of 1942. Wartime and postwar social welfare policies, aimed at the family and propagated as universal, actually revealed a continued anxiety concerning the respectability and moral fitness of the working classes and the poor.

5

LOVE IN THE BLITZ

As soon as the bombs started to fall, the city became like a
paved double bed. Voices whispered to you suggestively as you
walked along; hands reached out to you if you stood still and in
dimly lit trains people carried on as they had once behaved
only in taxis.[1]

In his memoir, Quentin Crisp, homosexual, artist's model and café
habitué, maps London during the Blitz as a geography of newly
liberated sexuality. In the predominant literary depiction of London
during the war, Crisp and other writers described a city of combined
tension and torpor punctuated by raids, in which sexual morality and
mores were suspended for the duration. They perceived a playground
of sexual pleasure: the combination of the black-out, public shelters,
the popularity of underground clubs and restaurants, chance
encounters, dropping bombs and the possibility of death heightened
the sense of urgency of romantic relations and moved expressions of
sexual desire into the public sphere. The sexual atmosphere of
London during the Blitz is captured most memorably in three
wartime novels: Elizabeth Bowen's *The Heat of the Day* (1949),
Graham Greene's *The End of the Affair* (1951) and Henry Green's
Caught (1943). Bowen's novel traces two stories of betrayal – Stella
Rodney's lover Robert's betrayal of his country, and young bride
Louie's betrayal of her soldier husband – neither of which has

straightforward moral consequences. Greene explores the extra-marital affair between Maurice Bendrix and the married Sarah Miles. When a Blitz bomb falls on Maurice, Sarah makes a pact with God to give up Maurice if God will spare him. Maurice is only unconscious, it turns out, and Sarah breaks off the affair. The Blitz was both the apex of their affair and the literal cause of its end. Henry Green's novel delves into the relationship between Richard Roe and Albert Pye, who work in the Auxiliary Fire Service. In the tense atmosphere of first waiting for the Blitz and then fighting its fires, each man pursues half-hearted sexual relationships born of guilt or loneliness. Pye traces his present troubles back to a sexual escapade in his youth, which he comes to believe was with his own sister, and he commits suicide. Each of these novels presents London during the Blitz as a city in which the strange geography, the fears and anxieties of raids and privations, the separations of families and the lapse in community supervision created greater possibilities for sexual relationships outside the boundaries of love, affection and marriage.

Other contemporary written sources from the war bemoan the lack of sexual morality in the metropolis. As in the First World War, the dangers of the uncontrolled sexual behavior of young girls was of paramount concern, not necessarily because of their vulnerability, but because of their enthusiasm for soldiers.[2] Author George Ryley Scott blamed much of the moral and physical dangers of the unlicensed sexuality of the Second World War on the 'emancipation' of women in the First.[3] He cited as evidence a memoir written by a female ambulance driver at the Front, which detailed both her sexual knowledge and her sexual experience, gained from billeting with men in close quarters and becoming familiar with the men's bodies through her war work as an ambulance driver and medic.[4] In the Second World War, the zones of contact between men and women moved from the battle front to the home front, and to London in particular.

Throughout the war, sexuality was indissolubly linked to civilian morale and national unity. Concerns with sexual control and propriety helped to delineate national boundaries and distinguish citizenship status.[5] Maintaining faithfulness and adhering to pre-war sexual morality also implied a belief in ultimate victory and a return to 'normality' in the postwar future. Wives were expected to remain faithful to husbands overseas, and women workers to focus on productivity, not reproductivity. Propaganda and the press linked uncontrolled sexuality to venereal disease and illegitimate pregnancy, and warned of its effects on military and civilian morale and productivity. The new visibility of family life and the social upheavals caused by the Blitz, as well as family separations and their perceived negative effects on married women and adolescent girls, created public concern over new sexual dangers in the city. Admonitory, as well as celebratory, narratives linked perceived wartime changes in sexuality to the urban place and space of London, where the mix of people, relative anonymity and blackout made sexual encounters easier.

The topic of sexuality is compelling to historians today, but for different reasons. In the past ten years, ground-breaking works have explored the concept of sexuality in historical context. Historical studies of sexuality have focused on urban geographies, examining the ways in which 'cities and sexualities both shape and are shaped by the dynamics of human social life'.[6] Recent work on sexual geography has examined homosexual culture and activity in London as well as American urban centers such as Philadelphia, San Francisco and New York, and cultural representations of sexuality in cities such as Berlin. The topics of heterosexuality, bisexuality, fetishistic sex and fluid sexualities which reject notions of a shared identity are largely still to be tackled.[7] The Second World War has also been the focus of recent histories of sexuality, which for the most part trace the activities of and attitudes towards American soldiers, whether heterosexual or homosexual.[8] Yet the constraints of the historical portrayal of Allied soldiers as liberating heroes, as well the strictures of writing about events in living memory, has meant that J. Robert Lilly's study of American GIs, which details the 17,000 rapes they committed in England, France and Germany between 1942 and 1945, has yet to find a North American or British publisher.[9]

Despite the difficulties which face this relatively new area
of research, new methodological criteria have been established
for historical geographies of sexuality. A successful study must
combine an assessment of an overall pattern of sexual experiences
and understandings and situate them within the historical
production of categories of sexual identity and deviance. As Matt
Houlbrook argues, 'The challenge for a historical geography of
sexuality is thus two-fold. First, it must situate geographies of sexual
encounter, identity and experience within wider urban social
relations. Second, it must bridge the division between discourse and
practice by relating the experience of sexual subjects to their
representation as marginal, and vice-versa.'[10] This chapter
accomplishes the first challenge by relating sexual relationships in
London between 1940 and 1941 to the wider social relationships
described elsewhere in this book, such as gender, class and age. But
how can we fulfill the second challenge within the boundaries of this
study, which requires substantiation of the narration of sexual
experiences described in first-person sources with external evidence?
Criminalized or violent sexual activity, such as homosexuality and
sexual violence, has left historical traces in criminal and military
records. But sexual identities and sexual practices not considered
marginal are more difficult to trace. Birth rates, evidence of venereal
disease treatments, arrests and prosecutions for abortion or
infanticide and testimony from postwar divorce cases can be
combed for information on heterosexual practices. But in many
ways, these sources are not evidence of sexual activity, but
incomplete echoes, especially with increasing knowledge about
contraception in the 1930s. Sexual experiences remain – unlike
family ties, work experience and material conditions – largely
unverifiable, since so much of what constitutes sexuality happens
inside the head. While historians, following Foucault, want to
analyze sexuality as a historical construct, it is popularly seen as a
private 'essence' which transcends history and culture, and as the
core of individual identity, which people may be reluctant to
divulge.[11] To get beyond individual silences and social histories

which focus on repression, Foucault suggests examining sexual discourses; that is, the practices, objects and languages surrounding sexuality. In our case, we will examine the practices and objects detailed in the discourses of diaries and memoirs, as well as the language used to describe them. Another aspect of sexuality difficult to quantify historically in personal narratives is the dates of relationships. While narrators' evocation of historical events can be checked against a set timeline with a fair degree of accuracy, their personal lives adhere to no such pattern. I have tried to date the events mentioned within the eight months under discussion, but these dates are unverifiable.

Though they create only a partial historical geography of sexuality, first-person sources reveal a set of complex and competing constructions about sexuality in London during the Blitz. Diarists' attitudes can be divided into two groups. The first wrote about their pleasure in danger. They had access to London's commercial and leisure activities that persisted in wartime, and access to safety that made the raids more a nuisance than a threat. This group consists mostly of male writers, who explored a non-procreative sexuality, whether homosexual or heterosexual. Their writings were published, some during the war but most afterwards, and were intended for the consumption of others in the public realm rather than to be kept private.

The second group consists of those who feared the dangerous consequences of pleasure, whether of an unchecked and voracious female sexuality, or of the strains of war on existing marriages. Writers who expressed these attitudes generally wrote in more private sources such as diaries, and were more often women than men.

Yet diaries, although personal, are not really private, since they are meant to be reread at some point, if only by the writer. It is no coincidence that the most frank detailing of sexual desire was in Mass Observation [MO] diaries, which were solicited from 1939, read in monthly installment by a panel, and then archived. MO's founding aim was to observe the working classes objectively and anthropologically, without an overt consideration of material or social divisions. Sexuality formed an important part of these observations, as, for example, observers in working-class 'resorts' such as Blackpool tried to assess the libidinousness of male and female workers on holiday.[12]

In their MO diaries, women diarists wrote of the physical manifestations of desire, and of their sexual relationships with their partners. A young civil servant's diary frankly detailed her sexual feelings: October 7, 1940, 'Awoke from a luxurious sexual dream to Isabel trying frantically to switch off the alarm.' She linked her surge in sexual desire to the war: November 28, 1940: 'Must confess that this afternoon I felt a strong desire to be alone with Sam – a strong desire. ... Doubtless something to do with the war, though I believe it has always been common enough.'[13] Her association of her feelings with the wider social sphere of the war shows her awareness of the MO audience panel, though she deflates their expectations in her dismissal of the historical and sociological implications of her sexual desire.

Analyzing how people represented their sexual feelings, experiences and identities permits an assessment of whether diarists see the Blitz as an occasion of sexual change in the same way they see the Blitz as a moment of historical change. Contemporaries could not agree on the extent to which the Blitz changed existing sexual values and expressions, whether they feared such changes or embraced them. Analyzing sexual experiences and feelings narrated in memoirs demonstrates to what extent sexuality disappeared in published remembrances of the London Blitz. My task is to understand why.

A Sexual Geography of Wartime London

Previous chapters have described the geographical, material and social conditions of London during the Blitz. The most important effect of these changes on sexuality was an easing of social barriers and an influx of new people. The movement of troops from Canada, other Commonwealth nations, Poland after 1940 and the United States after 1941 created a new mix of people throughout Britain, and especially in London. After the fearful first few weeks of war, Londoners returned to public places of entertainment and pleasure. Dance halls reached new heights of popularity, with line dances such as the Palais Glide and the Oomps-a-Daisy, and the scarcity of liquor available for purchase meant people increasingly sought out pubs and nightclubs.[14]

The social intensity of life during the Blitz reversed the twentieth-century trend towards more formalized courtships by creating unique informal opportunities for flirtation.[15] This was especially true among young, unmarried working and lower-class people, who were more likely to be working together and sharing air-raid shelters. The shelter created not just physical proximity, but also the intimacy of seeing – and of feeling – the physical vulnerabilities of others asleep. S. Mogridge ran a bookshop in London. In his 1942 memoir, he described his increasing infatuation with a woman who shared his shelter. He saw the Blitz as the cause of the acceleration of his feelings:

> Going to bed was not a complicated process, it only meant lying on our mattresses instead of sitting on them, and trying to roll up in a blanket. Miss B. had gone away, but Ann, of the sparkling eyes, was very much present. Our friendship made rapid progress, the blitz was a hothouse for such delicate plants as friendship and love.[16]

A single female ambulance driver slept in a shelter with other women who were either single or whose husbands were absent. They often took in passers-by during raids, and on September 27, 1940, she described an impromptu couples party in the shelter with the two young Home Guards across the way. The Home Guard men offered beer, then they all drank coffee and schnapps and told jokes and stories.[17] Not knowing if there would be a raid meant that evening sociability often stretched until the next morning. The American journalist Quentin Reynolds wrote: 'On a bad night, such as tonight, when you invite someone to sleep with you, nothing but a night's sleep is implied. Girls often go to dinner in slacks these nights never knowing whether or not they'll be able to reach home. Slacks come in handy if you have to sleep in a cellar or a damp shelter. Usually you sleep where you dine.'[18] Reynolds was careful to downplay to his American audience any suggestions of lasciviousness associated with girls going to dinner in 'slacks'.

The increased familiarity among coworkers, who spent longer hours and nights fire-watching together, made their courtship more public than usual. Compulsory workplace fire-watching after January 1940 obscured the boundaries between workplace and home, and many offices established sleeping rooms for those on duty and for use as shelters during raids. Olivia Cockett described the ease with which she was able to socialize with men from work: December 1, 1940:

Have just been out with one of the men and had 2½ pints of beer – am feeling unwontedly cheerful in consequence. Have walked up Whitehall and down again in the pitch black out, feeling rather a devil and listening to his account of his wife's nerves. Stood on Westminster Bridge for a few minutes and giggled away at his vague advances, thinking sententious thoughts about the Thames being the same in spite of war – except for the strands of coloured lights of peace.[19]

In February she became friendly with another middle-aged and married man from work: February 2, 1941: 'Cheered up the dull evenings with a mild flirtation, my first for ages. Have let him kiss me but didn't enjoy it much so shall not repeat, anyway, I've had enough heartaches from married men!'[20] Along with communal shelters, civilian organizations such as the ARP also brought neighbors together.

The relaxation of the boundaries of sociability was not always condoned. A letter from a mother to her daughter told the story of an 'awful scandel [sic]' in an undated letter. Elsie, a younger friend or relative, was working at a canteen, where a Canadian soldier washed up for her all evening. He was escorting her home when they got caught in a raid. They went into a shelter that housed two other women, who shared their bed with Elsie, while the soldier slept on the floor. Around 6:30 the couple left the shelter, but she parted from him without revealing where she lived. 'So please be MUM about it, as it does sound bad, but we both laughed. He is only 23 and has 5 days leave but she took care not to let him know where she lives, although he said he would be waiting for her at the station to take her to business. Of course she went in at another entrance, so as to miss him.'21 Her family was worried about what others in the neighborhood might think, even though the couple had been chaperoned. Even those who did not share it acknowledged potential social disapproval. Joan Johnston wrote in a letter: 'Billy [a neighbor] shared our shelter one night, as May gets very worried about him sleeping in the house. I had to smile when I woke up once and could feel his knees in my back. What would our grandmothers have said? Wonderful how our sense of values changes in an emergency.'22 Yet Johnstone described not a change in a sense of values, but in a sense of propriety. Sharing a sleeping space did not challenge values of pre-marital continence, marriage and fidelity, though it did seem to stretch acceptable boundaries of sociability between unmarried couples. Her only physical contact with Billy seemed to be the touch of his knees, and there could be little secret sexual transgression in the cramped space of a shared shelter.

Pleasure in Danger

To understand the extent to which London's new sociability led to increased sexual activity, we must examine the sexual geography of London before the war. London, as the largest and most cosmopolitan city in Britain, had been since the nineteenth century host to the largest sexual subcultures of prostitution and homosexuality. In the nineteenth century, there were as many as 55,000 prostitutes in

London, living mostly in the East End and South London, though many went to work in the West End.[23] Indeed, the marginal expression of sexuality spread across London from East to West. In contrast to New York, homosexual culture in London did not emerge solely in working class areas, but also in West End private clubs and bars.[24] What was feared and celebrated during the Blitz was that the immorality of the traditional, if marginal, sexual subcultures of prostitution and homosexuality would spread to the wider population, specifically the middle classes. Through a greater anonymity and the excitement and danger of air raids, the Blitz provided new social opportunities for carnal adventure. It also presented a symbol of the dangers of sexual license – as George Ryley Scott bemoaned, when death was near, morals tended to go out the window.[25]

While sexual subcultures spread from East to West, access to safety during the bombing raids did not. German bombing strategy concentrated on the Docks and the poorer East End. While in October and November 1940 the *Luftwaffe* increased its bombing range to include all areas of London, the East End had been hit first and hardest, and had the fewest amenities with which to handle the physical and material consequences of raids. Thus the narrative of danger and excitement written by diarists and memoirists was not merely nuanced according to class and neighborhood, but substantively different as well. The pleasure in danger that many diarists and memoirists describe was partly a relief in being safe amidst danger. Literary Blitz narratives almost always articulated feelings of people insulated by class and geography from the worst effects of the bombing raids.

Their cultural geography also determined how Londoners experienced and wrote about their sexuality. During the war, rough-and-tumble Fitzrovia replaced genteel Bloomsbury as the new artistic circle of influence, gaining authenticity during the Blitz for its vision of an art which thrived on 'the fear of sudden death and the snatch at urgent life'.[26] Unlike the more refined Bloomsbury circle, the Fitzrovians, including Dylan Thomas, Julian Maclaren-Ross and Nina

Hammett, were publicly hard-drinking and open about their sexual proclivities. Joan Wyndham's memoir of the war, *Love Lessons* (1985), openly described her social and sexual encounters with many of the Fitzrovians.[27] While the sexual lives of other public figures of the time were somewhat well-known, such as Harold Nicolson's affairs with young men, his public Whitehall role in the war inhibited acknowledgment of his sexuality in his and others' writing.[28] Similarly, John Lehmann, editor and owner of the Hogarth Press with Virginia and Leonard Woolf, did not write openly about his homosexuality, but in his autobiography spoke in generalities without a gendered pronoun. In his autobiography, *I am my brother: Autobiography II* (1960), he wrote that at the time of the Blitz he had a transformative emotional and spiritual crisis, which consisted of three elements: 'an unhappy love-affair, an entirely new sense of death as nothingness in the midst of life and an almost unendurable anxiety about a younger friend who had gone to sea in a state, I knew, of despair.'[29] The only memoirist who spoke frankly about his homosexuality was Quentin Crisp, a fixture in the bohemian cafes and pubs of Soho and Fitzrovia. In contrast to the club members of the Bloosmbury elite, Crisp's openness about his sexuality and his habit of cross-dressing already made him a social pariah.[30] He not only had less to lose by his frankness, but the salaciousness of his writing would only increase the shock value of his memoir and his cultural status. Lehmann and Nicolson, ensconced in Bloomsbury and Whitehall respectively, had to be more discreet. Yet even their links to Bloomsbury artistic circles made their homosexuality acceptable in a way not possible in the context of the wider public sphere.

Historians and geographers have described the Western city's sexuality as an eroticization of many of the characteristics of modern urban life: anonymity, voyeurism, exhibitionism, consumption, authority (and challenges to it), tactility, motion, danger, power navigation and restlessness, all of which were exacerbated in wartime.[31] The excitement generated by the twin poles of danger and pleasure during the Blitz found outlets in the chance meetings, the blacked-out streets and the improvised shelters.[32] While descriptions of personal sexual experiences during the Blitz were few, one writer, Peter Quennell, described how the raids spurred his and his girlfriend Astrid's sexual passion:

> Astrid's house was an old and fragile building; but that night fear and pleasure combined to provoke a mood of wild exhilaration. The impact of a bomb a few hundred yards away only sharpened pleasure's edge; and next day we wandered, agreeably bemused, around the shattered streets of Mayfair, crunching underfoot green glaciers of broken glass strewn ankle deep upon the pavements.[33]

The darkness and anonymity of blacked-out London not only enhanced sexual pleasure but allowed its previously marginalized expression to become more public. Quentin Crisp savored his memories of sexual experiences in the Blitz: 'By heterosexuals the life after death is imagined as a world of light, where there is no parting. If there is a heaven for homosexuals, which doesn't seem very likely, it will be very poorly lit and full of people they are pretty confident they will never meet again. ... During the war ... the whole of London was one long towpath, one vast movie house.'[34] Such anonymity, writers hinted, also benefited 'naughty girls', as the dangers of the streets during raids also paradoxically lessened the supervisory capacities of authoritative parents and policemen:

> [The war] was God's gift to naughty girls, for from the moment the sirens went, they were not expected to get home until morning when the 'all-clear' sounded. In fact, they were urged to stay where they were. Certain restaurants, such as Hatchett's and the Hungaria, and all hotels provided bed for their customers. Girls went out for dinner with their night attire, toothbrushes and make-up.[35]

Unfortunately, no 'naughty girls' left behind diaries or memoirs, perhaps because of such hectic schedules.

No one exemplified the hard work of naughty girls more than the showgirls of the Windmill Club, which declared proudly that it had never closed during the war. In their 'bravery' and steadfastness, the management and the dancers personified patriotism and good morale. Charles Graves interviewed the showgirls for his published wartime diary, and rated each according to her voice, looks and acting ability, as well as their lack of 'nerves' and heroism:

> Two other girls gave first aid to a number of dying people; in one instance a dead man, twenty minutes before doctors arrived. I have told Van Damm that he can make a packet by sending these girls out to America as the London Blitz Girls. The United States seems to admire this country so much, particularly London, that the only chorus girls to work right through the air raids would get a very big hand.[36]

Graves' passage was an odd ode to the women's heroism, since presumably first aid to the dead had little redemptive effect. Like Reynolds, he was keen to present a sexy and patriotic vision of heroic London women for an American audience, suggesting their propagandic appeal, and perhaps foreshadowing the American Varga pin-ups of the later war years.[37]

Wartime London not only gave unique opportunities to lovers, but also increased anxiety about sexual fidelity. John Lehmann wrote about how the war added to the uncertainties and traumas of jealous love, while giving the unfaithful lover an arena in which to misbehave:

> The partings of lovers during the war were especially hard to bear, because of the danger which lurked everywhere and the fear that every goodbye embrace would be the last; but when suspicion and jealousy suddenly began to play their evil role in the midst of these partings, the naked dependence of one soul on another, which is the extreme of love, made the suffering all but intolerable.[38]

The movement of sexuality into the public arena also increased anxiety for spectators.

In her memoir, *Chelsea Concerto* (1959), Frances Faviell described the love scenes her work as a warden made her privy to: 'The darkness and sandbagged entrances to houses were kind to lovers. Mrs Freeth was seething with indignation one evening when she came upon a couple in what she called a compromising situation in my area amongst the sandbags. But the man was in khaki so she excused him, she said.'[39] The romantic and opportune milieu was enhanced by the man's uniform, probably for the woman he was with as well as for Mrs Freeth.[40]

The most sexually frank postwar autobiographies were written by Alec Waugh and Peter Quennell, two men who shared the attributes of a comfortable middle-class job and income, and a literary penchant. Their autobiographies follow in the tradition of male urban bourgeois writers established in the late nineteenth century. European literary bachelors, such as Arthur Schnitzler, were casual about their sexual affairs, due to both their class background and cultural cachet as artists.[41] In Britain, urban middle-class masculinity was also associated with the consumption of fashion and art, a trend which Frank Mort has traced to the present.[42] Waugh and Quennell combine these traditions in their autobiographies. Both became professional writers, and both wrote poetically in their autobiographies about their wartime consumption of London's cultural amenities, and of wartime romances gone sour. Their narratives of tragic romance echoed Bowen's, Greene's and Green's novels of doomed wartime passion and added legitimacy to their role as artists who had suffered for love. Their failed love affairs provided a literary passage from an innocent past to experience and disillusion, as in a coming-of-age novel, and reflected the assertion of a masculinity tied to worldly experience. Waugh and Quennell both tie the situation of the affair in wartime London and the pain of its conclusion to the historical narrative of the Blitz, to situate themselves not only as part of a wider circle of bourgeois writers, but also to situate themselves in the genre of historical memoirs of the war.

In *The Best Wine Last* (1978), Alec Waugh related the story of his unhappy wartime affair and how it was begun, flavored by, and destroyed by the Blitz. He was married, but his wife and two children evacuated to Australia in 1939. In early 1941 he was posted to London, where his friend Diana was living:

> When I came up to London for my interview I was faced with a personal problem. If I was to be stationed in London, I should need back my flat, but Diana was still living there, and I was by now desperately in love with her, wholeheartedly committed as I had only been once in my life before, with the American Ruth of whom I told the story in *The Early Years of Alec Waugh*...[43]

Waugh decided to move back into his flat, and he and Diana continued their affair at close quarters. Yet the affair was colored by his certainty it was doomed by the constraints of life during the Blitz, especially the spatial difficulties of sharing a small enclosed space, and the social claustrophobia of limited sociability:

> And all the time there was Diana. My absorption in her increased every week. I knew that it was foredoomed. It could not last. As she was not in love with me, she resented the situation in which she found herself. It had been one thing to go down to Chagford for four nights and picnic on the moors. It was quite another to have me about the place all the time. She felt trapped. It had been one thing to have a cubbyhole to retreat to when the bombing was a novelty, but now that bombing had diminished, or rather now that Londoners had gotten used to it, she wanted to live her own life independently. She was a very independent person. She was bored with her employment at the Ministry of Aircraft. She was itching to shake her shoulders and be rid of everything.

Yet although the strain of social conditions during the winter of 1941 affected the affair, the pleasures of safety amidst danger also created a shared happiness:

> And even as it was, the good times were so very good, for me and I think too for her. She has told me that she too, can remember nostalgically evenings in the first winter when we would sit on our return from work, sipping sherry. The sirens would go. The air would be loud with the explosions of anti-aircraft fire. There would be the dull thud of bombs. 'Let's get out of this,' I'd say.

They often went to an underground restaurant, Boulestin's, on the Strand. Underground restaurants and nightclubs were immensely popular because they were considered safe from bombs, until a bomb fell through the floor in the elegant Café de Paris in March 1941. In Boulestin's, Waugh and Diana enjoyed good cooking and a good cellar, and believed themselves to be safe from the dangers of the raids:

> We felt very close to one another as we sat there sipping the cool sweet wine, letting its richness seep along our veins. The bombing earlier in the evening was a bond. We shared if not actual danger, at least the sense of battle. Later on we would have to go back to see what the skies held for us; but at the moment we were deaf, soothed by good food and wine, together. ... Those few hours, scattered over those few months, were as good as anything that life has brought me.[44]

The privileged access to the safety of underground restaurants in the West End allowed Waugh and Diana to experience the excitement of raids with little actual danger. The assumption of safety reduced the bombing to an historically and erotically titillating sound for the underground diners, heightening their intimacy as part of a wider group of 'Londoners'. The end of their affair, when it came, proved sad and slightly humiliating for Waugh. He had wished to be posted away before its ending but was replaced by 'a stranger across a crowded room' whom Diana met at a party.[45]

Alec Waugh's account demonstrated not only the tension between intimacy and irritation created by the conditions of the Blitz, but also the dual importance of memory and narrative in his account of his love affair with Diana. He recounted the affair as part of an auto-biographical and historical narrative of the Blitz.[46] And he described not only his own fond memories of that time, but assured the reader that he had spoken to Diana in the intervening years and she shared these fond memories. Thus he not only imbued his narrative with the authority of his own memory, but also with the authority of her memory integrated into his own narrative, giving it further legitimacy.

Peter Quennell also defined his wartime love affair against the backdrop of wartime London. In *The Wanton Chase* (1980), Quennell described how in 1940 he had tried to escape from his war work at the Ministry of Information by writing a novel, hidden behind the pile of files on his desk, and in a love affair with a woman named Astrid. But in early 1941, he transferred his affections to her friend Julia, with mixed results. According to Quennell, Julia's personality changed according to her geography: 'Julia's character appeared to embody two completely different selves – the hostile self she often revealed in London, and the friendlier, warmer self that unfolded in the country. Yet even in London she could be spontaneously affectionate; among my troubles I had moments of vivid pleasure.'[47] As in Waugh's memoir, London here represented the tension between overcrowding, work and anxiety, and the shared pleasure punctuated by raids. Yet the warmer self Julia revealed in the country was not always directed towards him: 'While I was detained in London, a gallant young soldier had been asked to take my place, I learned, and had naturally accepted.'[48] The local curate, who came to have a book autographed, mistook the soldier Z. for Quennell: 'Z. acted with military promptitude – he had campaigned in the Middle East – accepted the volume, took it into the sitting room, procured pen and ink, and signed my name, succeeded with a flourish and an

appropriately courteous sentence, upon the virgin title page.'[49]
Quennell's resentment focused more on the literary appropriation
than Julia's sexual infidelity: the title page of the book was virgin
even if Julia was not.

In order to underscore the validity of his autobiographical narration of their love affair, Quennell referred almost exclusively to his
wartime diary entries when discussing his feelings for Julia. Quoting
his diary allowed him to recapture the complexity and intensity of his
emotion for her, and to remove his present self from his past
emotions and actions. It also added validity to his narrative, as the
diary gave him literary access to experiences less mediated by
memory. Behind the screen of diary entries, he editorialized his past
self, 'Our conflicts never entirely ceased; they chequer the pages of
my diary. During these clashes, I see, my behavior, I can see now,
was neither sensible nor strong minded.'[50] Though Quennell wrote
poetically and longingly about the beauty of a marble nymph outside
his office at the Ministry of Information, his relationship with the
flesh-and-blood Julia was certainly less idealized: 'Though I was
never as decisive as I should have been, from time to time our rows
were violent, and on February 4th, I wrote that "the bruise on her
nose has spread – giving her a darkly spectacled look that is not
altogether unattractive."' He tried to distance his present self from
the act of violence he had inflicted on Julia by quoting the passage
from the diary, instead of integrating the event into his main
autobiographical narrative. He apparently continued to view his
violence as desirably decisive: 'Early the next day, after a night spent
fire-watching at the Ministry, I found that Julia had vanished; felt
oddly calm – almost relieved … a load seemed to have dropped off.
Independence. Clarity. More good resolutions…' The load could
have been the responsibility of having inflicted violence, and his
ellipses helped to hide Quennell's conflicting emotions. Violence as
an appropriate male response was also publicly expressed during the
war in the *Daily Mirror* on November 11, in response to a letter
written by a woman describing her and her husband's continuing
flirtations. An anonymous man wrote in declaring that the previous

writer was 'a disgrace to her sex and an enemy to the sanctity of marriage', and that when he found his wife holding hands with another man he whipped her with his belt, and that his wife was later glad of it.[51] Whether Julia was 'glad of it' or not, their relationship wound to a close: 'Not until mid-March did I finally decide that "a continuous record has become too depressing"; and from that point, so far as its principal subject is my relationship with Julia, I can put away my diary. This I am glad to do; it is an unedifying document.'[52] Once Quennell had finished with the painful memories of Julia, he was able to put away the diary, unedifying in its unflattering revelations as much as in its lack of further insight.

Waugh and Quennell's narratives illustrate the conditions of increased tension and increased intimacy in the geography of wartime London. The two men explore the pain and pleasure they felt through their affairs in the historical context of the Blitz, using their unhappy affairs both to enhance the literary legitimacy of their narratives and to underline their positions as artists. Their accounts also reveal their pleasure in perceived danger, though each was insulated from the worst effects of the raids – Waugh in underground restaurants and Quennell in the country cottage. Their narratives also reveal the complexity of drawing on memory in the subjective arena of love. Each drew upon an external source – Waugh on Diana's memories and Quennell on his diary – in order to validate his narrative. Their detailed descriptions of sexual relationships made them unique among Blitz diaries and memoirs. In comparison, the reticence and silences of other first-person sources do not reveal great changes in sexual expression or knowledge.

Danger in Pleasure

In contrast to those insulated from the dangers of the Blitz, the raids were especially hard for those who worked outside at night, such as prostitutes. The empty streets and the threat of bombs not only caused anxiety but curtailed business, though it could also be used to appeal to potential customers, as Harold Nicolson recorded:

September 12, 1940: 'I have to walk back to the Ministry through a deserted London. I have no tin hat and do not enjoy it. When things get very hot, I crouch in a doorway. In one of them I find a prostitute. "I have been drinking", she says: "I am frightened. Please take care of me." Poor little trull.'[53] Keith Monro also described his encounter with a young woman he took to be a prostitute outside the entrance to his shelter. Monro wrote that the incident was part of the 'avid desires' created by the Blitz and shelter life, though he described himself as 'far from a passionate man'.[54] Though he gave her a pound on their first encounter, and kissed her on their second, they did not consummate the liaison.[55] Indeed, he later discovered she was the wife of another shelterer, who threatened violence against her and any man caught with her. For those without the protection of underground restaurants, there was less pleasure in danger.

The dangers of sexuality during the Blitz encompassed more than those faced by prostitutes. Sexuality was linked to long-standing twentieth-century debates on marriage, as well as wartime concerns over the threat of uncontrolled sexuality to waging the war and to maintaining national security. Uncontrolled sexuality and its effects of illegitimacy, venereal disease and failed marriages were considered as a threat to both these aims, and to a unified and healthy postwar Britain. Though marriage had been linked to debates surrounding population growth and birth rate since Malthus, the marked drop in the birth rate during the 1930s and the separation of couples during the war led to increased anxiety over marital sexuality.[56] The concern over procreative sexuality was enhanced by public concern about the welfare of children evacuated and at home during the war.

During the interwar years, the criminalizing approach to sexuality was overtaken by increased emphasis on 'social hygiene' through sex education writings.[57] Beginning in the 1920s, the framework of domestic ideology began to change, leading to smaller family sizes across the classes, and the increasing conceptualization of marriage as a relationship rather than a contract. The emerging ideal of companionate marriage, with its emphasis on the marital relationship and the different but complementary roles of husband and wife, sought to harmonize marital conflicts, partly through an emphasis on sexuality.[58] The marriage guidance movement addressed the ideas of changing roles in marriage, and used published marriage manuals and organizations like the National Marriage Guidance Council to encourage sexual expression within marriage as a way to both cement the relationship and to address the falling national birthrate. Founded in 1938, the Council aimed to promote the ideal of 'companionate' marriage and family life and to counter the radical views of people like Bertrand Russell. During the war and in the postwar period, they tried to restrict sexual expression to marriage by drawing on contemporary concerns about the disintegration of the family, by arguing that women needed traditional marriage structures, and through the frank discussion of sexuality inside marriage.[59] Marie Stopes' best-selling marriage manuals and treatises on birth control within marriage also increased discussion of sexuality in marriage, especially female sexual pleasure, but circumscribed the expression of sexual pleasure through her insistence on the primacy of marital penetrative coitus.

Yet although the public discussion of marital sexuality seemed to convey an atmosphere of openness, its normative impulse had the effect of silencing or concealing forms of sexuality that were not procreative.[60] This normative impulse emerged in two sex surveys conducted in the 1940s. Moya Woodside and Eliot Slater's 1943 sociological and psychological survey sought to study the marriage relationship among the urban working classes, using two groups of soldiers from London and their wives, a section of men hospitalized for 'neuroses' and a control group hospitalized for other injuries. The authors found that husbands tended to define sex as a conjugal right, or a habit, and they did not expect responsiveness in their wives; many, in fact, mistrusted it. Among wives, 'a puritanical attitude was widespread', which conspired against a 'healthy attitude' towards sexuality.[61] Another sex survey, conducted by Mass Observation in 1949, attempted a random sample of the sexual attitudes and sexual behaviors of people in Britain, with similar results to the Slater-Woodside survey. In both surveys, women's less enthusiastic attitudes towards sex were interpreted as 'puritanical', rather than as a concern about supporting large families.[62] The normative impulses inherent in public discussions of sexuality would not have encouraged discussion of non-procreative or non-marital sexuality, even in diaries.

The wartime strains on marriage, a worry to both the marriage movement and those concerned with Britain's dropping birthrate, created an even more vigorous concern with sexuality and its social control, and a greater desire to contain it within the marital sphere. The social conditions in 1940s Britain, with many husbands absent and foreign troops stationed in Britain, exacerbated twentieth-century risks to sexual morality. Public concern for sexual behavior of young girls, especially working class girls, had been a concern in Britain since the First World War. Worries about 'khaki fever' among young girls shifted sexual agency from the male seducer in Victorian narratives of sexual danger to the active sexuality of young women.[63] The Second World War exacerbated existing concerns about the control of female sexuality, as the supervisory roles of parents diminished, especially among evacuated children, and the 'bad examples' of courting couples became common in the London streets. Although until the 1944 Education Act only one third of schools had made any provisions for sex education, many girls were privy to wartime *ad hoc* 'special lectures'.[64] The typical content of such lectures is documented in the diary of Mary Comyns, a fourteen-year-old schoolgirl in Enfield:

April 9, 1940. Directly after prayers Miss Sharp told all 4th, 5th and 6th form girls to go into the music room and there she gave us a talk on the dangers of lowering morals in wartime, our relations with our boyfriends, and makeup, and the dangers of talking to strange men, soldiers, etc., something like Daddy told me some time ago at the beginning of war. Miss Sharp carried it off very well, I thought, I shouldn't like to have to do it. It was slightly embarrassing, even for me whom it didn't concern in the slightest.[65]

Most public concerns focused, despite laments of American soldiers being 'over-paid, over-sexed and over here', on the dangers of female sexuality. The wartime stereotype of the sexy woman as a threat to national security featured in wartime films and in posters like 'Keep Mum, She's not so Dumb'. Sexy women were also depicted as threats to health. Another memorable poster portrayed a skull in a flower-adorned hat with a caption that read 'The "easy" girlfriend spreads Syphilis and Gonorrhea, which unless properly treated may result in blindness, insanity, paralysis and premature death.' George Ryley Scott, in *Sex Problems and Dangers in Wartime* (1940), linked the dangers of the blackout and the breakup of the family to a rise in all types of venereal disease (VD), of which he provided graphic descriptions.[66] By 1943 the incidence of venereal disease in Britain had risen 139 per cent from 1939 rates, spurring questions in Parliament in 1944 and an intensification of the government's vigorous propaganda campaign against VD.[67] Uncontrolled female sexuality could lead to the loss of the health of fighting forces and the morale of husbands fighting overseas.

Both strands of concern over wartime sexual behaviors focused on the actions of women, whether an encouragement of a procreative marital sexuality, or anxiety about non- or extra-marital female sexuality. No public warnings were issued about the dangers of homosexuality, though military sources show that homosexual activity among soldiers in and near London was not uncommon.[68] Similarly, there was no contemporary reference to lesbianism, and only one mention in a memoir, by a woman in the Women's Auxiliary Air Force who believed that her roommate was a lesbian.[69]

Sexual morality was conceived as not only crucial to morale, but also to questions of national security and postwar social reconstruction.[70] Public concern about the institution of marriage was exacerbated by the difficulties of couples separated in wartime. Psychologists Eliot Slater and Moya Woodside estimated that wives could stand a separation of two years, but in the subsequent years they often 'lapsed', adding to worries about the stability of family life.[71]

As in the First World War, illegitimate births caused great public concern about the institution of the family. That a large proportion of illegitimate babies were born to married women whose husbands were overseas added to social anxiety. The concern over 'war babies' exacerbated the social stigma attached to single motherhood. Mrs Morris described a young woman in hospital with acute 'scalpingitis', most likely due to an illegal abortion: August 23, 1940 'Julie's parents came in this afternoon and are sitting by her bedside. They are so sad and bewildered, as they can see that their beloved daughter is dying. She is semi-conscious now. If only there was not such a stigma attached to being an unmarried mother – Julie would not be in this state.'[72] Julie died later that night. Frances Faviell, who worked as a volunteer nurse in a hospital, also recalled in her memoir how she became friends with a pregnant woman who was 'abnormally sensitive about being unmarried', and who was taunted by the other women in the labor ward.[73] Illegitimate wartime births have been taken as evidence for a change in sexual expression, though in many cases, they were more likely due to the difficulties of legitimizing pregnancies or births with a quick marriage. No first-person sources written by unwed mothers in London in 1940–1941 have been found, though Mass Observation holds a diary written by a Londoner living in Belfast who discovered at the age of 35, in March 1941, that she is pregnant by her married lover, to her pleasure. Her struggles as a single mother of twins and her fight to hold on to her senior job as a tax inspector in the civil service are well-detailed up to 1944, when the diary ends.[74]

Public concerns about sexuality focused attention on the institution of marriage. Two of the social functions of marriage – the regulation of sexual activity, and the pooling of economic resources – were put under stress by the exigencies of war.[75] Due to rationing and conscription, as well as the emotional difficulties of separation, relationships between men and women during the war were often strained. For married couples, new demands placed on women, such as the conscription of married women without children after 1941, as well as new opportunities in volunteer and paid employment, created fissures in middle-class ideals of domesticity. The separation of younger couples exacerbated this trend. The emotional difficulties of wartime separation were poignantly evident in a November 1940 incident. A young mother attempted to push her son towards the edge of the Underground station platform in order to bring attention to her increasing depression brought on by the wartime separation from her husband.[76] The *Daily Express* headlined this incident as the 'Drama of an "over-devoted" wife parted from husband'. The pressures of loneliness combined with the privations of living on a military spousal allowance were difficult to bear.

Diaries and memoirs reflected popular concerns over marriage as a stabilizing societal institution. While some people responded to the dangers and dislocations of the Blitz with a desire for excitement and adventure, others reached out for the illusion of security offered by marriage. Marriage provided the possibility of economic security, and a move away from the parental home, as well as social respectability, especially for women.[77] Wartime marriages expressed the ideal of restoring social harmony, by supplanting the conflict and death of war with the image of harmonious domesticity and the possibility of new life.[78]

Yet marriage as a solution to other social problems was often illusory. As her archived memoir reveals, Mrs P. M. Damonte married a man during the war out of a desire for security. She had lost her job entertaining in a factory shelter when the factory was bombed, so she had no way to support herself:

> The fury of the blitz went on and on, there was no let up. At six-o'clock each night the sirens would wail their warning, night after night. Feeling very despondent and unsure of my future, I accepted a proposal of marriage from the only eligible man I knew of near my own age. We had had a casual relationship for some time. I was nearly twenty, he six years my senior.

I grabbed at his proposal as if it were a lifeline as indeed it was.
In my despair I looked upon the outcome of the liaison with
hope. I didn't love him, and with hindsight, I know he didn't
love me. Young boys and girls were getting married in those
early days of the war, it was the thing to do, death was just
around the corner if not for him then maybe for me.

After the wedding she went to live with her mother-in-law who
disliked her because she wanted her son to marry a former girlfriend
who had borne his baby. Then the couple rented a flat in Ilford: 'I
saw very little of my husband now. I think neither of us felt much
sorrow about this. I was glad to be alone.'[79] Damonte tried to use
marriage as an escape from the economic and social pressures of war.
But by the end of the war, with neither she nor her husband dead,
her situation became intolerable and she joined the Women's Royal
Naval Service (WRENS) to escape her marriage: 'I was running away
from the man I didn't love and had no intention of ever being his
wife again.'[80] In her case, the economic incentive could not overcome
the difficulties within the marriage, and the WRENS offered her a
means to support herself and to leave the country.

Getting married held an extra incentive for women during wartime, as it often exempted them from the Conscription Act of 1941.
Verily Anderson deserted the First Aid Nursing Yeomanry (FANY)
in order to get married during the war. FANY sent her a telegram,
'Return to Duty Immediately or Your Discharge not Considered.'
She did not return, as she said they would only send her on leave,
which 'wasn't war work'. 'And this is?' asked her fiancée Donald. 'We
were lounging on deckchairs in the garden of the inn. "Of course it is
darling," I said emphatically. "If I can make you happy, you'll do
your job at the Ministry better. Then we'll win the war."'[81] Anderson
escaped from what she saw as the insufficiently efficient FANY to
shore up morale through housewifery. She evidently preferred the
garden deck chair to the office.

Married couples faced economic and emotional pressures due to
the separations and disruptions of wartime. Slater and Woodside's

study found that the economic disruptions caused by the husband's absence, a reliance on army pay, worry for the other partner, and a pattern of sexual 'deprivation, opportunity, temptation' led many spouses into infidelity.[82] The effects of war on marriage depended to a large extent on the age and class of the couples. Older couples were less likely to be separated or face the worry of caring for young children in the Blitz, and those living in relatively peaceful areas whose husbands worked from home or did not work were subject to fewer strains. Yet even couples who lived together could be separated by busy schedules, as Hugh Dalton reported in his diary on his wife's schedule of war work for the London County Council Parks Committee, on October 27, 1940: 'Sunday. Ruth and I have lunch together – quite an amazing thing! – at the Lansdowne Club. Usually I only see her at breakfast.'[83] The separation of couples also had a subtext of anxiety. Jane Gordon, whose husband Charles was on Home Guard Duty at a Power Station, worried constantly for his safety:

> When lights flicker, someone says, well now they've got the power station, 'I thought, I won't feel sick. He is all right because I won't let anything happen to him. If I believe he is safe he will be. God Damn those bastards. Why the flaming hell can't they go for marshalling yards or the railways tonight and leave the power stations alone.' When the lights flickered to life again I could hear my voice saying: 'I don't think they really could have hit the power station or the lights wouldn't have come on again so soon,' and at the same time something else inside me was saying, 'Oh Christ, please look after him and don't let me be frightened like that again.'[84]

The concern for partners, like that for family members, could undermine the morale of bearing up under raids. A thirty-year-old engineer wrote about his wife on September 1, 1940: 'The whole terrible futility of it oppresses me. Raids become part of the regular routine now. I am much more concerned with the gnat bites Hilda has on her legs. They are poisonous to her.'[85] He reduced the conflict to micro-level, in his concern with the smallest detail of his wife's health. Harold Nicolson also expressed concern for his wife Vita Sackville-West upon hearing about the death of her friend and former lover Virginia Woolf in November 1940 and left London to be with her.[86] The concern for the other partner's wartime anxieties and dangers brought the couple into closer intimacy.

The strains of war drove other couples into open conflict. In these cases, an adversarial relationship usually pre-dated the war, but the war provided new points of tension and a new militarized language in which to express that tension. A thirty-seven-year-old housewife who kept an MO diary had a tempestuous relationship with her husband. They had been married eighteen years, with no children, and yet it was not until 1940 that her husband changed his will and made her the beneficiary instead of his parents, to her explicit gratitude. One typical fight arose about going to the shelter:

November 16, 1940. I [was] terribly fed up, so much so it was all I could do to keep tears back. Nervy really, and I just could not bear the thought of having to stay cooped up down there for 14 hours. Of course we ultimately rowed. H. nervy himself, finding my gloom and taciturnity too much for his irascibility. It was a ghastly row, too awful to relate. I foolishly said I did not care if I did get bombed. H., perfectly furious, replied what about him then, and I unkindly cut back then he'd have no one to wait on him or words to that effect. After that I was told I could do what I liked, he'd stick it out until after the war, but from now onwards I'd get no affection or consideration from him. He knows how to get me every time. I begged pardon most humbly and H. stormed out into the barrage.[87]

The tension of the air raid and the necessity of staying in the shelter brought to the fore the underlying resentments in the relationship. While war 'nerves' caused the fight, her husband punished her by storming out and deliberately putting himself in danger of the raids, thus playing on her fears and anxieties.[88]

The social restraints that precluded much frank discussion of sexuality in personal narratives also precluded the portrayal of marital intimacy and conflict. These strictures centered upon conceptions of marital and personal privacy. In most memoirs, marriage was presented as a static category rather than an intimate experience. The constraints on portraying intimacy in diaries and memoirs were also due to distance. A person who was a constant presence would become the focus in a diary, as Frances Partridge wrote about her husband: 'He is, of course, the central figure in the years covered by the diary, and for that reason may well remain rather shadowy. We were always together, communicated all our thoughts; he was the focus of my life and I had no need to describe what he was like *to myself*.'[89] Though their symbiotic relationship may have been unusual, the daily interactions of intimacy and friction were glossed over in retrospect. The marital silence of diarists is particularly frustrating when biographical details suggest there was something unusual to write about. For instance, despite the unconventional marriage between Harold Nicolson and Vita Sackville-West, in which the couple shared love, devotion and an intellectual and social affinity but were sexually involved in relationships with their own sex, Nicolson's diary makes no substantial reference to either his marriage or other relationships.[90]

Even fewer diarists wrote about sexuality in the Blitz. Conventions of privacy and the objective of fitting personal narratives into public history limited discussion of private sexuality, as it did discussion of marriage. Beyond Quennell, Crisp and Waugh, who wished to portray themselves as outside of the boundaries of conventional morality and part of a smaller subculture of artists and writers, very few diarists or memoirists wrote about sexuality. The others were all women.

Examining the writings of the tiny minority who wrote about their sexual feelings and experiences reveals the strictures surrounding frank discussion of sexuality. Miss Vivienne Hall was a lonely woman in her thirties infatuated with someone but trying to remain moral and resigned to her unmarried fate. She used her diary as a confidante, writing about her sexual desires and her loneliness:

July 31, 1940. I got home, via the YMCA, where I made enquiries about helping in the canteen at Waterloo, and all evening I tried to quell my stupid body – the night was restless and I determined to stop this once and for all, but it's easier said than done – I liked it! Oh dear, I am not settling into my spinsterhood very smoothly am I?

August 3, 1940. Sunday – a mass of washing to do, still feeling ridiculous – it comes in waves this feeling and you feel exhausted when it is over. I think I must be feeling the death throes of my loveless life – rather like a rabbit that's been shot but still jerks a bit after death![91]

While her sexual feelings were frankly expressed, her sexual behavior did not seem to challenge contemporary morality, as there is no evidence that she acted on her desires. Yet such frankness could be dangerous, as can be inferred by the destruction of other sections of Miss Hall's diary when discovered by her mother, with whom she lived. Diaries may have been intended as private sources, but always held the potential for becoming public, especially in small communal living spaces.

The other two diarists who referred to sexual feelings and experiences were both MO diarists. Because sexuality was part of MO's research mandate, these diarists could feel that they were confiding in a panel of interested readers, and at the same time feel they were adding to a sociological understanding of Britain at war. Both diarists wrote about their sexual experiences with long-term monogamous partners. Olivia Cockett was a single woman with a married lover of long standing who eventually left his wife to move in a few doors down. On August 24, 1940, she described in her diary a sexual encounter: 'Man came home with me this afternoon; after 2 hours of the most heavenly love-making we've had in all our 11 years (10 ½), Mickey [her nephew] arrived and we played with him in the garden, tired but happy.'[92] She was also the only diarist to allude to orgasm. 'Six love makings with Man [in January], only one complete for me.'

She also discussed the release of menstruation from worries about pregnancy, her two abortions and her hopes for children. In March 1941 she wrote: 'Sex? Divorce is the topic of the moment, will she or won't she the angle on the topic; money the balance on which we swing. She insists on half his wages *and pension* (!) and he wonders can we manage children on the rest. Still waiting for the office reply as to whether one or both of us getting the sack. Had two afternoons of pleasant passion, one or two thrilling moments at work.' In contrast to Olivia Cockett's pleasant passion, the thirty-seven-year-old woman's sexual relationship with her husband illustrated the conflicts within their marriage. On November 17, 1940, she wrote: 'We lay down in doors and later I failed H. again. Just did not rise to the occasion which started another argument, that I'd lost all my techniques for lovemaking, did I hate him? Tried to make him understand I was just completely negative after all we had been going through the last few days.'[93] Yet sexual failure was not always the case: December 1, 1940. 'Thoroughly lazy first thing. I went into H.'s bed and we were all amiable and it was jolly and like old times.'[94] Since diaries were meant not only to be read by the Mass Observation panel, but also archived for future study, they stand in a complex position between public and private sources. This is further complicated by the thirty-seven-year-old woman's intense fear of her husband finding out she kept a diary, so that she wrote capitalized admonitions: 'DO NOT ACKNOWLEDGE THIS DIARY' in every missive.[95]

The only explicit mention of sexual expression in a woman's memoir was written by Edith Evans long after the war. She wrote about her own sexual experiences in the context of restricted information about sex and the stigmas attached to premarital sexuality before the advent of the 'permissive society' in 1960s Britain. In her 1982 memoir, Evans recalled how frightened she had been on her wedding night early in the war:

I knew next to nothing about sexual activities or any form of love making. Sex before marriage was considered sinful.

Nobody admitted to it. Girls who 'had' to get married were a real disgrace to their families. ... On this night of nights; my 'first night', my long delayed 'wedding night', I truly wished I were dead!...

Many, many years later in the permissive age, love is not necessary. The satisfaction of sexual desire is first and foremost. But with Stan and I it was not so. ... My first experiences of the true facts of life (at the age of thirty-years and five months!) were extremely enlightening as well as rather distasteful. If this was the performance required for producing a family, I had better learn to like it. But I learned to love my husband, and I was as normal in my desires as any other, I longed for the end of hostilities so we could set up home and family together.[96]

Evans sought to present herself as an example of an older generation, with a stricter sense of morality and procreative marital values than the generation of her grandchildren. While anxious to present herself as normal, she emphasized that her desires were really for peace and domestic comforts, not for sex.

Sexuality was central to postwar social reconstruction, as part of the desire to strengthen family life, after the strains and separations of the war, and to build a future based on the home and harmonious and procreative marriage. The Beveridge Report of 1942 linked sexuality with reconstruction in its fear that 'with its present rate of reproduction the British race cannot continue.'[97] The Welfare State, along with postwar planned housing, revealed a continuing public concern with procreative sexuality, and a more complex state interventionism in order to protect it. A Royal Commission on Population was set up in 1944 and delivered its Report in 1949, warning that if the birth rate continued to decline, the English people could disappear. Linked to concerns about reproduction were fears about the future of marriage. Divorce rates after the end of hostilities were high, rising from 1.6 per cent of marriages ending in divorce in 1937, to 7.1 per cent in 1950.[98] Two-thirds of immediate postwar divorce actions, which numbered 60,000 in 1947, were brought by the husband, many citing female infidelity as a major factor in the dissolution of the marriage.[99] Increased scrutiny of the war's effects on marriage also masked the legal changes in divorce proceedings under the Matrimonial Causes Act of 1937. Under this law the reasons for legally ending a marriage were expanded for men and women to include adultery, desertion for three years, insanity, and confinement for five years, and additional grounds for women for reasons of bestiality, sodomy or rape.[100] The rise in postwar divorces also masked the backlog of divorce cases that fell under the new law, and the couples who were eligible to apply for legal aid to help pay for divorce after the Legal Aid and Advice Act of 1949.

The first-person narratives analyzed here cannot give access to 'real' sexual experiences and attitudes during the London Blitz, which are largely inaccessible to historians. Yet they do show how writers were participants in writing narratives of sexuality, whether as artistic or matrimonial rites of passage. Examining narratives of sexuality shows the fluidity of the diary as a historical source. As a confessional, private document, historians could expect to find details of secret longings and deeds. But diaries, especially in wartime, perform a variety of functions, including the need to record historical experiences for posterity, not only in Britain but more urgently for those imprisoned in prisoner-of-war camps and Jewish ghettoes.[101]

Yet the overall impression of sexuality in diary sources is one of silence. The adolescent girl, the focus of so much wartime worry, left almost no written trace of her Blitz experiences. Time, and the liberalization of sexuality since the 1960s, does not seem to lessen this silence but to deepen it, as even fewer memoirs describe aspects of sexuality. Historians are left to decode the silence, whether of deliberate exclusion or of lost memory.[102] With the presently available sources, it seems that the Blitz did not have the feared or desired effect of making London 'a paved double bed'. Comparing public perceptions of sexuality during the Blitz and the personal experiences detailed in diaries and memoirs demonstrates how the

descriptions of sexual experiences were socially constrained by a
heterosexual and marital morality, by the tensions between spouses
and lovers created by the pressures of the Blitz, and by the public
and private emphasis on procreation. The writers who told stories of
sexual abandon and excitement during the Blitz in their memoirs
were those who had a vested interest in presenting themselves as the
new avant-garde of Blitzed London, living outside the conventional
moralities of British society.

6

REMEMBERING THE BLITZ

I had reached one night the corner of Shoe Lane and Little New Street with the sky lit up and the usual steady droning … when there was a most almighty banging and clattering all around me. This turned out to be a cluster of incendiaries, some of which bounced off the wall while others jumped frenziedly around like Chinese crackers. Each weighed about ten pounds and, dropped from perhaps ten thousand feet, would have gone through one's skull like a bullet through an egg. My main reaction at the time was, 'Would you *mind*!', but I knew I had taken another of the nine lives. I often wonder whether that fellow that dropped them survived the war. If so, he ought to come to London and survey the handsome new office block in Farringdon Avenue, for the destruction of whose rather dingy predecessor, quite apart from endangering my person, his incendiaries were entirely responsible.[1]

In his memoir, *My Life and Soft Times* (1971), Henry Longhurst recounted one of the stock stories of the Blitz: his 'near miss' experience. While his metaphor of a bullet through the egg emphasized the personal danger he had been in, his remembered indignant reaction deflated the menace of the bomb, and emphasized his British *sangfroid*. Longhurst also linked his own survival to that of London, emphasizing his personal and Britain's national victory by inviting the German pilot, whose own survival was questionable, to come examine the postwar urban renewal of London. In this passage, as in most postwar memoirs of the Blitz, the Blitz came to symbolize the participants' fortitude under duress, and the strength of the British national character in general. The bombs, instead of destroying the city and the national fabric, had only made reconstruction and modernization easier.

The previous chapters explored how Londoners wrote about their experiences of bombing raids and rationing in 1940–41, and the impact of the Blitz on work, family and sexual intimacy. In this chapter, I analyze how participants rewrote and remembered their experiences in memoirs. The glimpses into the private worlds of wartime social conditions and personal relationships that diaries and letters written by people living in London during the Blitz reveal tend to be simplified and sanitized in retrospect. The memory of the Blitz, beginning as early as 1942, helped to create a retrospective vision of civilian collectivity. In this vision, the fortitude of Londoners during the bombing raids assured them of victory and a new postwar social contract. The British war victory, and subsequent Labour election victory in 1945, consolidated this hindsight vision.

The Memory of the Blitz and Postwar Politics

The defeat of Churchill in 1945 and the victory of Clement Attlee and the Labour Party by a majority of 149 seats was one of the twentieth century's greatest electoral defeats for the Conservative Party.[2] R. B. MacCallum, in his 1947 study of the election, commented that 'One thing will certainly be said of the election of 1945: it will be called a revolution. Given the suitable and secondary definition of the word, it may be a justifiable expression, but it might be well to avoid it. Revolution is a cant word of the day, and is applied to almost any movement of human affairs.'[3] Certainly the word 'revolution' was used with increasing frequency in the years after the Blitz, as the war wore on and observers saw evidence for a popular leftward swing in political consciousness and loyalty. Observers such as Henry Hamilton Fyfe, a diarist who wrote for the *Reynolds News*, used his diary of the first three years of war as evidence for Britain's wartime revolution 'transferring political and economic power from the Possessing Class. ... My aim in publishing this diary is to mark the steps we have so far taken towards that transfer and the opposition that it arouses, as I noted them day by day.'[4] The experience of civilian fortitude under duress during the Blitz, as well as Britain's 'standing alone' against Hitler before the Americans joined the war effort, were seen as central to a perceived popular leftward swing.

The extent and meaning of Britain's wartime swing to the left is widely debated in historiography and popular politics. Interpretations on both ends of the political spectrum agree that the British electorate's political views changed, but differ over whether the leftward shift occurred from the bottom up as an expression of what the Ministry of Information's Home Intelligence Unit in 1942 called 'home-made socialism', or was imposed from above by intellectuals and planners.[5] The memory of the Blitz, used as evidence for a change in private political beliefs and national political culture, has also been subject to popular political re-interpretation over the course of the last sixty years. As Geoff Eley notes, the memory of the Second World War in Britain is periodically reinterpreted according to the political claims of succeeding generations.[6] In the immediate postwar years, the memory of the war was used to cement the postwar political consensus of the need for social welfare. In the 1960s and 1970s, radicals argued that the revolutionary possibilities of the war experience were muted and subsumed in the deficiencies of the postwar settlement. In the 1980s, the interpretation again shifted, as Margaret Thatcher claimed the legacy of the war was Britain's duty to remain a powerful nation state, and to denounce the pettiness of planning which resulted in 'small shares'. As the events of the war move further in the recesses of living memory, the political and social legacy of the war is once again open for another wave of re-visioning.

The Political Legacy of the First World War

The roots of the leftward swing in the 1945 election were not only to be found in the most recent civilian experiences and social policies of the Second World War, but also in the perceived failure to reconstruct Britain after the First World War. The 1945 rejection of the Prime Minister who had, in the popular imagination, brought Britain through her 'Darkest Hour' to victory, also rejected the interwar government policies that did little to alleviate mass regional unemployment, and that had led Britain unprepared into another war:

> The party of which Churchill was the head – and which had contemptuously rejected him in pre-war days – was hopelessly identified with the England – and the Europe – that had died at Dunkirk, the England of the dole queues and the three million unemployed, the Europe of social democracy's defeat, of the Hoare-Laval Pact on Abyssinia and the craven appeasement of Hitler; the England of 'Trust Me' Baldwin and somnolence in the shires, of Ramsay Macdonald's vain rhetoric and the ratepayer business astigmatism of the latter-day Neville Chamberlain.[7]

In the interwar period, there is little evidence for a popular movement away from the National Government and the politicians who made it. The devastating defeat of Labour and the election of a National Government in 1931 and in 1935 and subsequent by-elections on the eve of war showed no indication of a rejection of the Conservative policy of fiscal restraint, which had set the policy on unemployment and constrained defense spending. But the crises of 1940 demonstrated the limitations of the interwar Conservative policy of appeasement and the failure to rearm, and suggested that the Conservatives were falling out of public favor. *Guilty Men*, a 1940 pamphlet indicting the Conservative leadership in the interwar years, sold a quarter of a million copies by the end of the war, and contributed, at least in the popular imagination, to the downfall of

Churchill and Conservative political leadership.[8] The fact that no election was held for ten years obscured the popular political shifts that made the 1945 election results seem more revolutionary than they were.

Behind the indictments of interwar Conservative politicians lay the memory of the First World War. As the shadow of war lengthened over Europe in the late 1930s, many Britons believed that the failure to create 'a land fit for heroes to live in' after the First World War had tainted the honorable and patriotic ideals which had celebrated the outbreak of war in 1914 and the millions of soldiers' deaths that followed in a war of attrition. London was the site of the increasingly ironic national Armistice Day ceremonies at the Cenotaph in Whitehall. During the Armistice Day ceremony on November 11, 1937, ex-serviceman and escaped mental patient Stanley Story interrupted the two minutes of silence by breaking through the line of soldiers towards the Prime Minister shouting: 'All this hypocrisy!' and after it another phrase which sounded like 'preparing for war!'[9] While Mr Story's approach may have been unorthodox, many shared his opinions. Mass Observation surveys on popular attitudes to Armistice Day in 1937, 1938 and 1939 revealed that the people interviewed predominantly expressed indifference or hostility to Armistice Day as 'too painful', though eighty percent of Mass Observers themselves reported that they had kept the two-minute silence in 1937.[10] At the outbreak of the war in 1939 the government and the Archbishop of Canterbury agreed to cancel Armistice Day ceremonies, though a service was broadcast from Westminster Abbey and Poppy Day continued throughout the war.

Diarists writing on November 11, 1940 noted the incongruity of remembering the sacrifices of soldiers in the First World War in the midst of the Second. Many observed the two minutes of silence privately, as Dr Chave did on November 11, 1940: 'Armistice Day has come around again and we are still at war. There was no silence today, the exigencies of war would not permit it, but poppies were on sale as usual. At 11 o'clock there was an alert on, and I went on the roof and observed my Two Minutes of Remembrance that they shall not be forgotten.'[11] The roof was a particularly symbolic place to remember the dead, as place to witness to the visual and aural spectacle of a nation at war again.

Those who did not choose to continue with remembrance rituals on their own nevertheless marked the day. Sydney Walton wrote to a young friend who was about to join the British forces:

Today November 11th used to be celebrated as Armistice Day, used to be celebrated, as you know so well, with noble ceremonial and beauty of reverence. ... Not outwardly was the remembrance kept in Harrow today ... but inwardly within our thoughts, kept with a pathetic wistfulness, kept with wondering regret that so great a sacrifice seems to have yielded the harvest of still more suffering, death breeding death.

Instead of focusing on the irony of the day, Walton located the reason for a renewal of suffering in Britain's failure to do her duty in maintaining 'righteousness in Europe', insofar as she did not 'take heed of the sternly gracious argument which the Eternal ever speaks to the nations. ... Without righteousness, no peace.'[12]

Other writers reacted against the idea of Armistice Day and the selling of poppies. A twenty-five-year-old postal sorter expressed his anger in his MO diary on November 11, 1940: 'Did *not* buy a poppy – the bloody hypocrisy of us all.'[13] Gladys Langford was sickened: 'What hypocrisy to talk of "our glorious dead" when we're bent on hustling another generation of corpses to join them? I could vomit.'[14] For those who had lost a loved one in the First World War, anger was overridden by sadness and loss. Storm Jameson described a part memory, part fantasy, of her brother, a soldier who died in 1916, coming in to look at her son sleeping in his cot in 1915:

Before I could turn away, I saw my young brother on his last leave. He was looking down at the sleeping child. 'He'll never have to fight,' he said in his young indistinct voice, *'we're* seeing to that.' He turned to me for a second the face of a boy,

smooth, unformed – I saw it with shocking clarity – and asked,
'How old is he now?' 'Twenty-five.' 'I'm nineteen,' he said...[15]

The failure of Britain to safeguard the next young generation seemed
to betray the idealism and youth of the men who had enlisted during
First World War. The solace of perceived vigilance with which many
families had comforted themselves in the aftermath of the war now
evaporated at the beginning of another war – a war, furthermore, in
which civilians as well as soldiers were in danger.

The memory of the First World War was the central pivot to
dreams of postwar reconstruction during the Blitz years. Writers
contrasted the failure of reconstruction policies in the interwar years
with a new vision of Britain after the end of hostilities. S. Mogridge,
writing in 1942, asserted that it was misleading to draw parallels
between the first World War and the second, because the Armistice
and the dreams of a reconstructed Britain would not be futile this
time. He presented the motives behind the 1939 war as more pure
and more practical than those of the First: 'We left Jingoism behind
when the Siegfried Line proved unsuitable for our washing...'[16]

The visions for a new Britain that emerged between 1940 and the
end of the war were not only a response to the current hostilities and
social conditions, but were also an attempt to put right the broken
promises of the First World War. Yet the importance of the memory
of the First World War does not surface in postwar Blitz memoirs, or
only tangentially in reference to the failures of the 1930s. Because the
civilian experiences of the Second World War, particularly in the
Blitz, were so central to the memory of the war and demands for
reconstruction, after the end of the war, the memory of the losses of
the First World War were subsumed into those of the Second.

Churchill as a War Leader

Similarly, the dissatisfaction with Conservative leadership in general,
as well as with the Prime Minister of 1940–45, rarely surfaces in
postwar memoirs. Contemporary diary entries give evidence of a

much more complex attitude to wartime leadership than postwar memoirs suggest. For example, popular dissatisfaction with Conservative leadership centered in the early war years on the figure of Neville Chamberlain. The perceived foreign policy failure of Chamberlain at Munich in 1938 added to existing dissatisfaction with interwar economic policy. Many London writers in 1940–41 were frank in their disapproval of Chamberlain, though not many were as frank as the nineteen-year-old civil servant who wrote about Chamberlain's resignation from office on October 3, 1940. 'And another grand Hooray! Goodbye Neville! Glad to see you go! There's only one bad thing about his resignation – it's forty years too late. Earl Neville of Chamberpoto? Or Earl Chamberlain of Munich? Which?'[17] Even as his death of cancer was announced on November 10, 1940, few reserved their judgment. G. W. King wrote that day: 'Mr Neville Chamberlain died to-day, aged 72. If only he had commenced to wage this war as strenuously as he fought for peace in 1938 there might have been a different tale to tell.'[18] Few were forgiving of Chamberlain's failed attempt to evade war, though sympathy for his early death was sometimes forthcoming, as Dr S. P. W. Chave wrote on November 10, 1940: 'The death of Neville Chamberlain was announced today. Poor old Neville. He had been very maligned since the Munich agreement, but he did hate war and he never lived to see victory.'[19]

Contemporary attitudes to Winston Churchill, Prime Minister from 1940 to 1945, were more complex. Churchill's general popularity as a wartime leader both during and after the war is undisputed. Of the 34 separate wartime polls conducted by the British Institute of Public Opinion, only once did his popularity fall below 80 per cent.[20] His powerful rhetoric in speeches and wartime broadcasts appealed to an ideal of the 'common people'. Even though Churchill drew his images of the common people from mythology and historical fantasy, rather than a shared social past, his invocations of Britain's lonely fight against tyranny and injustice gave the language of British politics a new resonance and inspired many Britons to fight on.

But Churchill's popularity as a war leader did not necessarily equate with popularity as a politician. Many politicians of his own party considered him highly gifted, but an ungentlemanly and untrustworthy man. His defection from the Conservatives in 1904 in defense of free trade, his return in 1924, his political excesses and lapses in judgment, and his raffish friends all contributed to his unsavory reputation. As David Cannadine notes: 'Before 1940, it was not easy for him to be taken seriously as the man of destiny he believed himself to be, when so many people in the know regarded him as little better than an ungentlemanly, almost déclassé, adventurer.'[21] While in Cannadine's example 'those in the know' were the Conservative party, their opinions extended to those outside of politics who nevertheless remembered his checkered military and political history.

Churchill's speeches were and are justly famous. To a wartime audience his speeches were often profoundly inspiring. After listening to Churchill speak, Vere Hodgson was full of praise:

> Mr Churchill's speech at the Pilgrim's Dinner stunning as usual. Wonderful to have a man of action who can put our emotions and longings into such deeply moving phrases. He is in the heat of the conflict, and yet he can speak as if he were a hundred years in the future, appraising our conduct. I like the way he faces the worst. I hope we deserve him. I think we do.[22]

Yet he brooked no criticism of his person or his government. Cecil Harnsworth King, director of the *Daily Mirror* and the *Sunday Pictorial*, described in his diary how his paper tried to find a compromise between supporting the government in the war effort, and not condoning the inefficiencies that were losing the war. He then recounted the series of scathing letters and interviews in which Churchill made it clear to King that 'in his view criticism *à la* Daily Mirror is treason'.[23] Many Londoners also felt that Churchill's rhetoric sometimes fell short of imparting actual information. A twenty-seven-year-old widow wrote at the very beginning of the Blitz on August 21, 1940: 'Churchill seems to have done his stuff excellently again last night. His speech was as usual splendid and most heartening, though to my mind it was slightly flawed by the glossing over of the Somaliland debate and the accustomed refusal to be drawn into any definite declaration of war aims.'[24] At the outbreak of the Blitz, which Churchill seemed to welcome, his defiant oratory often struck a callous note for those who were suffering through the raids.[25] A London architect expressed her disapproval of Churchill's rhetoric on September 12, 1940:

> To hear the BBC you would almost think that people in London like being bombed. I can't share the Prime Minister's confidence in our ability to withstand invasion. London's air-defences seem almost useless at night in spite of all his boasting of the RAF. Then there was his boasting at the time of the Norwegian invasion – I can't understand people's great confidence in him.[26]

A twenty-five-year-old postal sorter was even more scathing in a Christmas morning 1940 diary entry, as he woke in a Tube station:

> Woke up in the tube and stared at iron bolts whitewashed. Felt very exhilarated at this – I don't think. Thought a nasty lot of thoughts about Mr Churchill, imagining him with his fat ciger [sic] and possibly a few whiskey glasses – all in the tube station – I don't think. But of course there is more in it than that – and anyway I am a pacifist and shouldn't entertain such wicked thoughts as that.[27]

As the postal worker noted, there was 'more in it than that', but the gap between the level of physical and material sacrifice asked by Churchill and the comparative luxury he himself enjoyed was a sore point, especially when such exhortations were delivered in the midst of deadly air raids.

Some East End Jews, more aware of what German victory would

mean, recognized Churchill as their savior. This created a conflict
between those who admired his tenacity (which inspired Britain to
fight on and thus protect Jews from the fate of their European
families) and left-wing Jews who remembered Churchill's reactionary
domestic policies. Bernard Kops, a Jew from the East End, recalled
in his memoir Churchill's resolution to fight even after Dunkirk, and
the gratitude of Jews worldwide – except Kops's left-wing uncles:

> These English people ... were showing the other side of their
> coin and I was so grateful that I had been born in England,
> and Churchill's name was probably being blessed in every
> synagogue in the world. And in every Jewish home and in
> every Jewish heart, except, of course, those who couldn't
> forget the class war. 'But he's a bloody Conservative', one of
> my uncles said. Here we were locked in the middle of a life and
> death struggle and planes darting closer every day to London,
> and my uncle was still talking about the traitor Ramsay
> MacDonald and the stinking Conservative party.[28]

After the war, the symbolic importance of Churchill's words and
personality, in some ways augmented after his electoral defeat,
concealed these and other contemporary critiques of Churchill's
policies and politics. In postwar memoirs, the mythic view of
Churchill's leadership became well-established. Writers glossed over
their wartime doubts and anger in the warm glow of the Churchillian
symbol.[29] In their memoirs, few people recalled being anything but
supportive of Churchill during the war. Irene Brown recalled how
Churchill's 'we will never surrender' speech gave her and her family
new courage in the face of personal and financial loss during the
Blitz:

> Churchill was to speak that evening. We felt he could only tell
> us, 'Sorry folks we must surrender'. ... But OH NO – how
> wrong can you get? He said – *we will fight in the streets – on the
> beaches, etc.* All was transformed. Strangely, everyone felt

happier. Of course – that is what we must do. I love the man.
He gave us courage in our darkest hour.[30]

As this excerpt reveals, Churchill's heroic language and rhetoric
set the tone for popular memories and historical investigations of his
leadership and the war. Profiting from more free time after 1945,
Churchill set to work on writing the first history of the war.
Beginning in 1948, Churchill published a three-volume history of the
Second World War that drew on his voluminous correspondence.[31]
Placing himself at the centre of the action, Churchill constructed a
narrative of his principled statesmanship and the historical
inevitability both of his role as the savior of a war he had tried to
prevent in the 1930s, and of British victory. Subsequent historical
assessment and autobiographical treatments tend to reinforce this
view.[32] War victory privileged the positive aspects of his war leadership and policies. Churchill had won the war, so he could not be
criticized for his leadership, added to which his electoral defeat in
1945 made postwar criticism seem unfair. Yet Churchill's leadership
and policy decisions in the first ten months of his leadership in
1940–41 reflected the uncertainties, vacillations and differences of
his colleagues, far more than appear in his own later account.[33] In
both Churchill's history of the war and Londoners' postwar memoirs
of the Blitz, the fears and uncertainties of the war are glossed over in
a narrative of inevitable victory.

The rise in status of Churchill as a national icon continues. In
2002, he won a nation-wide BBC poll that voted him the Greatest
Briton, and in 2005, the £13.5 million Churchill Museum opened as
part of the Cabinet War Rooms. Here visitors can see Churchill and
his wife's private wartime apartments, including formal dining room,
as well as a museum dedicated to Churchill's life. That £11.5 million
of this project was raised from private donations reveals Churchill's
immense and growing popularity as a historical figure and as a tourist
attraction. The new museum reflects and will add to his increasingly
central position in the national history of the war. The popular
historical re-enactments of the civilian experiences of the Blitz

created in the 1980s in London museums, such as the Blitz Experience in the Imperial War Museum and the dingy and slightly surreal Blitz exhibit in the privately run Winston Churchill's London at War museum on Tooley Street, are poor by comparison.[34]

Reconstructing Memories

Even before the end of hostilities, participants recognized the political importance of the memory of the war, and the centrality of their experiences of the war to postwar national identity. Stephen Spender wrote in 1945:

> What we do with our memories is a psychological problem, which after the First World War we attempted to solve by burying them under war memorials. ... They mock us with not having built the world for which men gave their lives; and they demonstrate that the life we are living in peace lacks the virtues of their war. Unless we can incorporate the best of our war memories into the future, the peace will be an era of cynicism, with an undercurrent of regret tugging us towards another war.[35]

While Britain commemorated the First World War with monuments made ironic by the Second, the memories of the Second would serve as its memorial. Spender's assertion that it is the memories themselves that are important, not future actions based on those memories, demonstrate their symbolic importance, as well as the political role of the participants to whom they belong.[36] Incorporating memories into the future was not only important for individual psychological health. Memories of the Second World War in general, and the Blitz in particular, seemed also to offer a corrective to the inward-looking domestic British identity of the interwar years, and the failures of policy with which it was associated.

The way in which participants called upon their memories of the Blitz in the stories of their lives demonstrates more than their private experiences of the war. Their memories as participants and the national significance they ascribed to the war also offer a window into changing popular conceptions of the history and significance of the war in the times in which the participants wrote. The re-interpretations of the events of the Blitz in memoirs owe as much if not more to the political context of the time of their rewriting, as they do to the experiences themselves.

The first wave of memoirs were published in the immediate post-war years by senior civil servants and politicians. Of these, Churchill is the first and best example, but their ranks also include Robert Boothby, Parliamentary Secretary to the Ministry of Food, in 1947, and Communist Party MP William Gallacher, Communist Party member Phil Piratin and BBC Radio Times editor Maurice Gorham in 1948. Early memoirs tend to follow in Churchill's narrative style of epic struggle, though they did not always identify the same heroes and villains. A lull followed in publications until the 1960s, when private individuals began to publish records of their experiences. These new narratives, inspired by the popularity of social history and social history community groups, began to provide a public record of individual voices of the Blitz. Unpublished memoirs began to be deposited into archives at the Imperial War Museum, London borough Local Archives and the Working Class Autobiography project at Brunel University.[37]

Some memoirs of participants reveal the legacy of the sacrifices demanded during the war on their lives. Loss, grief and privation continued to affect survivors after the war. Painful memories, as well as destroyed neighborhoods, led many to move from their London neighborhoods after the war ended. Frances Faviell wrote in her 1959 memoir that she and her husband had moved away from Chelsea because all their former neighbors had died or left because of the devastation: 'It was too painful to return to that immediate neighbourhood even had we been able to find a house there.'[38] The disproportionate burden borne by those with limited means and in areas of heavy bombing like the East End made remembering the war painful. Dorothy Squires worked part time in an electrical factory in Enfield, and had two daughters in their teens during the war. She had few pleasant memories: 'What terrible times they were. ... There are so many unpleasant things happened during those war years that it would take years of writing to relate.'[39] May Rainer, who spent the years 1940–41 collecting insurance door-to-door, also remembered the war as a painful period: 'As far as the War was concerned we had to endure it but no one looks back on it with pleasure.'[40]

Even those who had initially felt themselves to have had a positive experience of the war could find they were later excluded from a shared popular memory. Alec Waugh had left London mid-way though the Blitz, and he returned to find himself no longer a Londoner:

> Yes I had a lucky war, but six years is a long time ... I never got back into my marriage, and I never quite became a part again of London life. I lacked the bond of shared experience. ... During the early bombings, when I had to spend a night out of London, I felt resentful at missing any part of London's Calvary. That bond became much stronger during the long, slow-passing years. I was surprised and touched when I went back to the Savile, to find how much the members liked each other. During those dreary slow-passing years the club had become their home, their bastion. They had come here night after night out of the bombing, out of the blackout. They had drawn sustenance from one another. There had grown a kin-ship between them.[41]

These memoirs present a postwar sadness and sense of diminution that is often glossed over in popular representations of the war.

Although war diarists kept diaries at least partly for themselves, the memoirists of the Blitz who began to publish during the 1960s and 70s had to present the importance of their narrative to the public in a postwar world. The postwar published accounts of journalists and public figures assumed a wider interest, and hinged on the elaboration of the author's experience as a 'true story', evident in the titles of works such as Ronald Gould's *Chalk up the Memory* (1976) and Nicolas Bentley's *A Version of the Truth* (1960).[42] Yet non-professional private writers, like many who appear here, often emphasized that the pressure to publish had come from outside, from friends and family or those in an official capacity, in order to establish their authorial authority. Ernestine Cotton dedicated her autobiography to her granddaughter, hoping it would encourage her interest in history.[43] Frances Partridge described the encouragement to publish on two sides: 'Why publish them? The suggestion that I should do so has come from two directions – firstly from those who want to be reminded of it, even down to the details of our adjustment to the daily grind, secondly from others who want to know ... what living through those years was like.'[44] Like Spender, Partridge presents her memories as valuable in and of themselves, both to remind others who shared them, and to teach those who did not.

While memoirs written by those in public roles, such as civil servants and professional authors, were published by the large national presses, those by civilians of no public rank, including most of the women's memoirs, were published by small presses, many formed from community activist or collective self-education groups.[45] A People's History group that not only helped with the writing but also often published individual or group memoirs encouraged Dolly Davey, among others.[46] In the 1980s, at a time when both Thatcherite policies and the Docklands development seemed to threaten London working-class culture, a Federation of Worker Writers and Community Publishers emerged in Britain, along with many autonomous social history projects.[47] In Hackney, the People's Autobiography Group, created in 1972, produced pamphlets on the neighborhood, and attempted to stimulate local research.[48] While these projects enjoyed a modicum of success, they could not reach the publishing figures of large publishing houses. The difference in publishing forums reflects both the marketability of the memoir and the differences in how national memory of the Blitz has been created in artistic subcultures, like the memoirs of Quentin Crisp and Theodora Fitzgibbon, or as part of military or political institutions.

Just as the members of the Savile Club drew on their common experiences after the war, so have participants called on their individual experiences as the basis of their authority to interpret the war's legacy. E. P. Thompson used his war experience as a member of the military to counter the public images of the war prevalent in the 1980s:

> One is not permitted to speak of one's wartime reminiscences today, nor is one under any impulse to do so. ... It is so, in part, because Chapman Pincher and his [like] have made an uncontested takeover of all the moral assets of that period; have coined the war into Hollywood Blockbusters and spooky paperbacks and television tedia; have attributed all the values of that moment to the mythic virtues of an authoritarian Right which is now, supposedly, the proper inheritor and guardian of the present nation's interests. My memories of that war are very different. I recall a resolute and ingenious civilian army, increasingly hostile to the conventional military virtues, which became – far more than my younger friends will begin to credit – an anti-fascist and anti-imperialist army. Its members voted Labour in 1945, knowing why, as did the civilian workers at home. ... Our expectations may have been shallow, but this was because we were overly utopian, ill-prepared for the betrayals at our backs.[49]

E. P. Thompson's sense of betrayal was in part a reaction to the 1980s attempts to publicly present the Second World War as a victory for British imperial might and self-sufficiency, with comparisons drawn from the 1982 Falklands War. Margaret Thatcher's Churchillian rhetoric in speeches during the war, and the nationalist fervor with which the London dailies welcomed it, invoked a memory of the Second World War as a nationalist military triumph. This memory of the war was tied to debates over the fate of the policies that had been born out of it. In Thatcher's autobiography, *The Downing Street Years* (1993), she wrote that the lessons of national and individual self-sufficiency that Britain had learned during the struggles of the war had been misinterpreted by the continuance of collectivist social policy:

> Some nostalgia for the austerity period apparently lingers. That is, I believe, an exercise in vicarious sacrifice, always more palatable than the real thing. Seen from afar, or from above, whether by a socialist gentleman in Whitehall or by a High Tory, socialism has a certain nobility: equal sacrifice, fair shares, everyone pulling together. Seen from below, however, it looked very different. Fair shares always somehow turn out to be small shares.[50]

The erosion of the institutions of the welfare state after 1979 and the end of the postwar consensual agreement between political parties to protect it seemed to those on the left, such as E. P. Thompson, to betray what they felt to be the lesson learned during the war. This made their wartime memories unbearably poignant. Naomi Mitchison, in the 1984 foreword to her published diary, wrote sadly of its optimism:

> Was I as I appear in the diary? I rather hope not as I don't like myself much, but with any luck the book will be read less for the diarist than for what we at the time thought was happening and how we acted. It reads sadly, as least I think so, because it is full of hope for a new kind of world, for something differ- ent, happier, more honest, for a new relationship between people who had been cut off from each other by money, power, and class structure. ... But the bright vision fades, always, always. Of course there have been changes for the common good. ... But realities have not kept up with expec- tations and personal relations are not changed that much. The welfare state is being eroded under our eyes.[51]

In the 1980s, both those on the Left and those on the Right felt betrayed by the nation's failure to remember the lessons of the war years.

The most recent publications of participant narratives are from the last generation to remember the Blitz: children. While some children who grew up in the war years remember them as times of excitement and unparalleled freedom, recent memoirs have painted a bleaker picture of wartime and postwar deprivation: a London physically reduced to rubble in parts, absent parents, lack of food and years of scarcity after the end of hostilities. Donald Wheal, author of *World's End: A Memoir of a Blitz Childhood* (2005), recalled in a Toronto *Globe and Mail* article that his strongest memory of the end of the war was the smell of charred buildings and the dust of broken bricks and fallen walls.[52] In some ways, publicly-invoked individual memories of the London Blitz have come full circle, as the last living survivors of the Blitz write of the legacy of grief, loss and austerity in their own lives, and bring to a close the final chapter of participants' remembrances of the war.

European Memories of World War Two

British victory encouraged a positive national public memory of the war, which emphasized a triumphal victory over the odds. The postwar nostalgia for a perceived time of unity in Britain's 'Finest Hour' has created a national memory of the war which glosses over doubts, fears and unrewarded hardships. Most participant narratives are easily absorbed into a positive national war memory, and the stories and persons of surviving civilians and veterans are celebrated.

The British process of memorialization of the war contrasts sharply with other European nations. Britain was not the sole European victor in 1945, but it was the only nation which had stood alone against the German threat in 1940, whose air defenses had prevented land invasion, and who had emerged from the war relatively unscathed. European nations such as France, Germany and Russia, whose war histories were marked by gradations of guilt,

collaboration, deprivation and trauma, have found it much more
difficult to create cohesive national histories of the war which reflect
or incorporate the memories of individual civilians. As Tony Judt
argues, European nations from 1945 to 1989 were concerned
primarily with forgetting the war, with the aim in both eastern and
western Europe to rebuild the economy and social cohesion.[53] Not
until the 1980s did European historians begin in earnest to debate
the legacy of the war for their national histories, and the place of
individual memories within that history.

In Germany, historiographical assessment of the war and its place
in German history must struggle with whether the aggressive
militarism and anti-Semitic horrors of the Third Reich were an
aberration in German history, and what role the Second World War
should play in German history of the present.[54] The Historians'
Debate of the 1980s over the centrality of the Holocaust in German
History, the furor over Daniel Goldhagen's assertion in *Hitler's
Willing Executioners* (1996) that German society was uniquely and
violently anti-Semitic, and the years of debates surrounding the
design of the Monument to the Murdered Jews of Europe in central
Berlin which finally opened in 2005, all question who has the
authority to interpret Germany's memory of war, and to what extent
must Germany's present be haunted by its war past. The role the
German citizen played in the Third Reich and in the implementation
of the Final Solution remains controversial, and published memories
of the war years in Germany have not come from self-confessed
perpetrators or colluders with the Nazis. Published memoirs and
diaries have come primarily from outside observers, such as Marie
Missie Vassiltchikov and Christabel Bielenberg, and thus avoid the
question of moral responsibility for Hitler's regime.[55] The writers are
also women, relegated to the domestic sphere under the Third Reich
and thus free of the taint of Nazi militarism. Even memoir titles
emphasize the author's resistance, as in *I Lived under Hitler: An
Englishwoman's Story of her life in Wartime Germany* (1957) and *Inside the
Gestapo: A Jewish Woman's Secret War* (1987).[56] The assertion of
resistance is central to published German war memoirs, as Ilse-

Margaret Vogel made clear in the introduction to *Bad Times, Good Friends: A Memoir – Berlin 1945* (2001):

> Some people may wonder why I never fled Germany entirely. The answer too is simple. My friends and I always believed the war would be over quickly, and Hitler would be defeated; there was no reason for us to flee our country. ... We also realized that, in our own way, we were helping to resist the Nazis. ... We all hated Hitler, his ideology, his lies, his crimes, a regime without freedom, without humanism, and so blatantly without justice. We cannot boast great deeds. We did not assassinate or physically harm any Nazis, but we did frequently risk our lives resisting them by helping people who, for racial or political reasons, were being pursued and persecuted.[57]

The exceptions to this insistence on resistance are memoirs written by those who were children during the Third Reich. Children, indoctrinated by Hitler Youth, taught to obey adult authority, and without an adult moral sense, can be forgiven by a public readership for their role in Nazi Germany, and offer an inner glimpse of that world.[58]

French historiography of the war years is also divided by questions of guilt, resistance and complicity. Henri Rousso, in *The Vichy Syndrome* (1991), was the first French historian to analyze the phases of public silence about France's wartime collaboration with Nazis and complicity in the Final Solution.[59] Not until 1995, in the 'Vel D'Hiv' speech of 16 July, did President Chirac acknowledge French responsibility for crimes committed by the Vichy state. While French films such as Marçel Ophul's *The Sorrow and the Pity* (1969) and Claude Lanzmann's *Shoah* (1985) dealt with collaboration within the countries under Nazi rule, questions of Nazi collaboration have not emerged in first-person memoirs. As in Germany, French war memoirs emphasize the author's resistance to German rule. Lucie Aubrac's memoir, *Outwitting the Gestapo* (1993), described her work in the French resistance between May 1943 and February 1944 and her role, while pregnant, in a plot to save her comrades and her husband imprisoned by Klaus Barbie in Lyon.[60] Such memoirs, with their dramatic stories of danger, betrayal and rescue, offer compelling reading as well as a positive example of the courage of French citizenry during the war.

What of other diaries and memoirs, which could defy or subvert these conventions?[61] It is likely that fewer war diaries were kept in mainland Europe, where the struggle for survival and need for conformity made such records dangerous. The destructiveness of the European war to both lives and property suggests that many diaries, had they been kept, would have been lost. And perhaps a record of guilt, complicity, and defeat cannot be written within the confines of a memoir, but must appear in depositions or testimonies, or remain buried. We are left with a partial record of civilian experiences of the war, and must learn to interpret the nuances of silence as we do words.

Russia and Eastern Europe's war history is defined by such silences. While these nations have an abundance of painful national memories in addition to those from the Second World War – such as Stalin's purges of the 1930s, and memories of Soviet occupation – until the 1980s and *glasnost* public rhetoric either denied or glossed over them. In private, people may have scorned the official memory of the past, but they only had their own individual and family recollections with which to counter it. This public history of denial created a culture of mistrust and cynicism, and a set of competing counter-histories 'of a mutually antagonistic and divisive nature', which undermine social and national unity.[62] As Catherine Merridale discovered in a series of 150 oral interviews between 1997 and 1998, Russians do not know how to talk about their war experiences, and their stories of pain, loss and shame remain deeply private. According to her findings, the predominant psychological and historiographical concept of war memory as 'trauma' does not hold true for individual Russians or the Russian example in general.[63]

The concept of traumatic memory pervades much historical writing about individual and group memories of World War Two, and is central to the historiography of the Holocaust. Trauma is a Freudian concept that describes an individual's inability to integrate traumatic memories into their conscious mind, the repression of the memory and the eventual process of 'working-through' that allows for a conscious integration of the event. Historians have applied the process to the communal history of the Holocaust, marked by forgetting or repression in the early postwar years, and the difficulty of integrating both the individual memories of survivors into their postwar lives, and the events of the Holocaust into wider narratives of history.[64]

The silences of the 1950s and 1960s have given way to a plethora of representations of the Holocaust in popular culture, most notably in widely popular films such as *Schindler's List* (1993), *Life is Beautiful* (1997) and *The Pianist* (2002), all honored in America by the Academy Awards. America also provides both presses and a popular market for the diaries and memoirs of European Jews who were victims of or survived the Holocaust. Such diaries exist in more numbers than other European memoirs, because of the importance Jews placed on keeping a record for posterity of their gradual loss of freedom, property and lives, and their determination to bear witness to the unimaginable things that were happening to them. The most famous diary was written by young Anne Frank in an Amsterdam attic, but many other ghetto diaries have survived and been published.[65] The desire to preserve individual memories, to not forget the atrocities of the Holocaust, has also led in recent years to the publication of many memoirs written by Holocaust survivors.[66] Yet as Michael Bernard-Donals argues, diaries which detail traumatic historical events, such as the liquidation of European Jewish ghettoes in 1942, do not necessarily give access to historical events themselves. Abraham Lewin, whose diary he analyzes, could not himself make sense of what he saw, and thus his words cannot transmit to the reader a sense of Warsaw in 1942 or 1943, or reveal a life of someone who died at the hands of the Nazis.[67] As Dominick La Capra argues, the relationship between history and memory after Auschwitz is 'exceptionally vexed'; memory can only give partial access to history.[68] Experiences and memories are constrained by language, and the writing of war memoirs and diaries are further constrained by opportunity, safety and audience. European debates on the place of individual memories in national traditions, and in the history of the Holocaust, point to the dangers of attempts to rigidly control the public memory of war. During the Second World War millions died without a record of their experiences, leaving behind the silences of lives cut short. Who can justly claim the authority to speak on their behalf?

London and the British Memory of the Second World War

During the Blitz, public and private narratives presented the Londoner as a new kind of national citizen. Fortitude during the raids made courage and valor seem uniquely and characteristically British. An Australian nurse who was trapped under the rubble of a bombed building for eighteen hours and who died as she was being unearthed was celebrated for her bravery by the rescue squad with a funeral wreath which said: 'Australian: A True Briton'.[69] The wartime fortitude of London was central to this vision of Britain, as Churchill's speech to the Ministry of Health on May 9, 1945 emphasized:

> London like a great rhinoceros, a great hippopotamus, saying: 'Let them do their worst. London can take it. London could take anything. My heart goes out to the Cockneys. Any visitors we have here today ... they echo what I say when I say: Good Old London!' In every capital of the victorious world there is rejoicing tonight, but in none is there any lack of respect for the part which London has played. I return my hearty thanks to you for never having failed in the long, monotonous days and the long nights black as hell. God bless you all. May you long remain as citizens of a great and splendid city. May you long remain as the heart of the British Empire.[70]

Just as Churchill situates London as the heart of the Empire, the London Blitz is central to memories of the Second World War in Britain. The London Blitz is what Pierre Nora calls a *lieux de mémoire*, a place of primary importance in the memory of the war, and a space in which participants, historians, and the creators and inheritors of national memory continue to thrash out new meanings and new applications for the memory of the war.

The sixtieth anniversary of VE and VJ days in 2005 underlined the complex historical legacy of remembering the war. A British past that seemed uncomplicatedly a source of British national pride was celebrated in the context of a present in which Britain was no longer a great power. Perhaps the reason why the war is so frequently remembered and the rights to its memory so hotly contested is that in hindsight it can be seen as a last moment of possibility, when the difficulties and defeats contained within victory were hidden in the future. Individual and public memories of the Blitz form part of a phenomenal national investment in the symbols of the war, which provide national symbols of heroism and national pride (as well as appeal to tourists).

The public memories of the Second World War in European nations are constrained by a postwar history which emphasized silence, and in a political and economic atmosphere that has seen increasing postwar *rapprochement* between European nations in the European Economic Community, now the European Union. The historiographical silences of France, Germany and Soviet Russia have begun to be explored, with all the controversy, tension and illumination to which such explorations will inevitably lead. Britain is at an advantage in that it has enjoyed sixty years of war remembrance and historical re-interpretation. But the danger remains that in a public culture with so much emphasis on representations of the war, the canonic images of Britain 'standing alone' will eclipse the complexities of the war experiences of British civilians. Such a loss would dishonor the contribution that so many writers, as in this study of Londoners writing during or about their lives during the Blitz, sought to give.

CONCLUSION

The 1940–41 bombing raids on London were a symbolic and social test of Britain's unity. In the interwar years Britain had faced the challenges of regionalized economic depression and unemployment, labor unrest, the independence of the white Dominions, modernist culture and a low birth rate, all of which worried those concerned with the fate of the nation. After the Fall of France in June 1940, British fortunes seemed at their lowest ebb, as they faced their German enemies alone. While the British Expeditionary Forces had proved themselves at Dunkirk, and the Royal Air Force in the Battle of Britain, the Blitz was the first test of civilian morale.

Witnesses in London during the Blitz thus had a strong sense of their own historical importance. They felt it was imperative that they record the details of their personal lives and their perceptions of the national crisis in Britain. They drew on older conceptions of British identity as stubborn, matter-of-fact and doggedly determined, and on the modern images of urban media. Their accounts of both positive and negative experiences combined the cultural and social authority of the individual urban spectator central to Modernism, Surrealism, and journalism with the metaphors of modern mass culture that many critics feared. Civilians remapped wartime London, transforming it from a city split between the consumer delights of the West End and the poverty and degradation of the East End into an imagined urban community unified by the democratic power of witnessing.

But the evidence in this same group of first-person sources reveals that underneath the democratic ideals, the social conditions of London during the Blitz continued to be markedly different for those with means to escape at least some of the privations of war and those without such means. The Blitz increased the material struggles among and between social classes, ethnicities, genders and the geographical boroughs of London, as each had access to varying levels of bureaucracy and social provisions. Public and official exhortations to maintain good morale and exemplary British fortitude hid the grass-roots struggles in London over entitlement to food, shelter and safety.

The institutions of the workplace, family and marriage came under increased public scrutiny and social pressures during the Blitz. They were also the focus of postwar plans for reconstruction. The social shift to a bureaucratized and naturalized domesticity enshrined in the 1942 Beveridge Report's plans for social insurance occurred during the war, not after the 1945 election. Like much of the public observation and commentary during the war, many of the social welfare provisions that emerged during the Blitz and formalized in the Report were prescriptive, and not a reward for popular wartime sacrifices. The year 1942 was the beginning of the social and political reinterpretation of the events of the Blitz as part of the search for an imagined social transformation to mirror the perceived changes in national political consciousness. Diaries and memoirs of the Blitz show the continuity of pre-war attitudes and allegiance and few conscious political shifts. The roots of the politicization of the Blitz lie in the political reinterpretation of the memories of Londoners, not in the experiences themselves.

Memory is crucial to national politics and identity. The memories of the First World War and the interwar years interpreted in the light of the political crises of 1939 and 1940 were crucial to contemporary perceptions of the Blitz. Similarly, postwar historical events and the political shifts of the postwar decades are vital to how the events of the Blitz have been interpreted by participants and by historians.

British national identity is based not only on a shared past or a collection of shared pasts, but also on the meaning and memories ascribed to past events. For instance, in contrast to the political and social importance of the Blitz, the German V-1 and V-2 raids on Britain in 1944–45 do not dominate in the national memory of the war and are not recalled as unifying national moments. The V-1s, pilotless aircraft launched from German bases in Northern France between June 13 and September 1944, killed 5000 people and injured 15,000 others. Just as the Allies overran the bombing bases in France, the V-2s, 45 foot rockets launched from mobile bases in Holland, began their attacks. Between September 1944 and the end of March, 518 V-2s had hit London and killed 2,724 people. The V-1 and V-2 attacks were distinct from the bombing raids of 1940–41 in a number of ways. There was only a twelve-second gap between a V-1's engine cutting out and it crashing to the ground. V-2s traveled the distance from Holland in four minutes, making any kind of warning impossible. Both types of bombs could come at any time of day or night, so that people existed in continual nervous tension, or continuously stayed in Tube shelters or the eight newly built deep shelters in London. The political climate had also changed. After six years of war and continued privations, Londoners were tired. Victory in Europe was in sight, and civilian resilience under the bombing could not be conceived as having a military or political purpose. All of these factors affect the relative silence around V-1 and V-2 attacks. The fact that these aerial attacks on civilian Londoners do not form part of a wider national myth also calls into question the link between morale and the British national character – that Londoners could react no other way than with fortitude. The fragility of morale in this later period of the war, when military success was assured, also provides another challenge to historical and historiographical beliefs in the inevitability of British victory.

When considering the effects of memory on the creation of national identities, what is left out is as important as what is put in. The Blitz is remembered so often because it was the first successful test of civilian morale, and because Winston Churchill and the Royal Family proved their popularity as leaders in times of national crisis.

Even in civilian memoirs, the memories of those in higher social positions are more likely to be published and to be passed on. National memory is also weighted towards the first to publish their accounts – one reason why Winston Churchill made sure to publish his memoirs first.

Though narrowly focused on eight months in one city, this book is a popular history of the Second World War. The diaries and memoirs of Londoners written during the Blitz reveal how civilians thought about the war and their own importance to it, how wartime hardships and difficulties affected their daily lives and how their war experiences and dreams for the future created a new vision of London and of postwar Britain. By recording and preserving the details of their daily lives, Londoners wrote and continue to write themselves into the history of 'The People's War' as well as the modern history of Britain.

NOTES

Introduction

1. Joan Bright Astley, *The Inner Circle: A View of War From the Top* (Boston: Little, Brown and Co., 1960), p. 63. Astley was responsible for a Special Information Centre in the War Cabinet Offices in London. The war won her professional acclaim and personal freedom: 'I was at a party when a lady bore down on me smiling sweetly: "You've had such a marvelous war," she said.' Astley, p. 13.

2. For more on sites of memory and modernity see Pierre Nora, *Realms of Memory* (New York: Columbia University Press, 1997) and Jay Winter, *Sites of Memory, Sites of Mourning* (Cambridge: Cambridge University Press, 1997).

3. Jonathan Rose, *The Intellectual Life of the British Working Classes* (New Haven: Yale University Press, 2001). The book is based on a reading of most of the two thousand nineteenth- and twentieth-century documents listed in Vincent, Burnett and Mayall's *The Autobiography of the Working Class* 3 Vols. (New York: New York University Press, 1984–9).

4. Sonya Rose, *Which People's War?* (Oxford: Oxford University Press, 2003), p. 26.

5. See Donald Thomas, *An Underworld at War* (London: John Murray, 2003) and Stuart Hylton, *Their Darkest Hour* (London: Sutton, 2001).

6. Henri Rousso, *The Haunting Past* (Philadelphia: University of Pennsylvania Press, 2002), p. 3.

7. As in Maurice Hawlbachs's conception that the collective memory of a culture has a social utility rooted in its moment of recall. Maurice Halbwach's, *On Collective Memory* ed. and trans. Lewis A. Coser (Chicago: University of Chicago Press, 1992).

8. Susan Sontag, *Regarding the Pain of Others* (London: Hamish Hamilton, 2003), p. 76.

9. Jan-Werner Muller, *Memory and Power in Post-war Europe* (Cambridge: Cambridge University Press, 2002), p. 3.

10. Geoff Eley, "Finding the People's War: Film, British Collective Memory, and World War II" *American Historical Review* 106.3 (2001): pp. 818–38. See also Judith Petersen, "How British Television Inserted the Holocaust into Britain's War Memory in 1995" *Historical Journal of Film, Radio and Television* 21.3 (2001): pp. 255–72.

11. I. H. Granger, *Imperial War Museum* [IWM] 94/45/2.

12. Alec Waugh, *Best Wine Last* (London: W. H. Allen, 1978), p. 169.

13. Constantine Fitzgibbon, *The Blitz* (London: Macdonald, 1970), Leonard Mosley, *Backs to the Wall* (London: Weidenfeld and Nicolson, 1971), and Norman Longmate, *How We Lived Then* (London: Hutchinson, 1971).

14. Richard Titmuss, *Problems of Social Policy: History of the Second World War, United Kingdom Civil Services* (London: HMSO and Longmans, 1950). Titmuss's positivism is reinforced in Arthur Marwick's "People's War and Top People's Peace? British Society and the Second World War" in *Crisis and Controversy* eds. Alan Sked and Chris Cook (London: Macmillan, 1976).

15. Angus Calder, *The People's War* (London: Jonathan Cape, 1969), p. 21.

16. Tom Harrisson, *Living through the Blitz* (London: Collins, 1976), p. 13.

17. Clive Ponting, *1940: Myth and Reality* (London: Hamish Hamilton, 1990), Angus Calder, *The Myth of the Blitz* (London: Jonathan Cape, 1991).

18. The same cannot be said for an authoritarian single-party state like the former Soviet Union. See Catherine Merridale, "War, Death and Remembrance in Soviet Russia" in *War and Remembrance in the Twentieth Century* eds. J. Winter and E. Sivan (Cambridge: Cambridge University Press, 1999), and *Night of Stone: Death and Memory in Twentieth-Century Russia* (London: Penguin, 2002).

19. James Olney, *Metaphors of the Self* (Princeton: Princeton University Press, 1972).

Chapter 1: Looking At London

1. Rose Macaulay, *Letters to a Sister* (London: Collins, 1964), p. 108.

2. As early as 1908, H. G. Wells had prophesized the blanket danger posed by the aerial bomber in *The War in the Air*. 'No place is safe, no place is at peace. ... The war comes through the air, bombs drop in the

night. Quiet people go out in the morning and see air-fleets passing overhead – dripping death – dripping death.' See also J. B. S. Haldane, *ARP* (London: Victor Gollancz, 1938), J. Thorburn Muirhead, *Air Attack on Cities: The Broader Aspects of the Problem* (London: George Allen & Unwin Ltd, 1938), Anthony Aldgate, *British Newsreels and the Second World War* (London: Scolar, 1979) and Elizabeth Kier, *Imagining War* (Princeton: Princeton University Press, 1997).

3. Vera Brittain, *England's Hour* (Toronto: Macmillan, 1941), p. ix.

4. Much of this debate originated in the postwar popularity of the war poets Wilfred Owen and Siegfried Sassoon, as well as the war memoirs of Robert Graves and the translated version of Erich Maria Remarque's *All Quiet on the Western Front* (1928). Vera Brittain's war memoir, *Testament of Youth* (1933), proved to be more popular than any of her many novels and continues to be reprinted.

5. This version is from Sir Harold Scott's *Your Obedient Servant* (London: Andre Deustch, 1959), p. 128.

6. L/Bdr Mark Bogush to wife Lily, Hackney Archives, M4586-4591.

7. *Churchill Speaks* ed. Robert Rhodes James (London: Chelsea House, 1980), p. 728.

8. Churchill saw not only London as the heart of the Empire, but himself as well. John Colville, his Assistant Private Secretary, recorded in his diary on January 24, 1941, that one workman had been overheard saying to another as Winston passed: '"There goes the bloody British Empire." Winston's face wreathed itself in smiles and, turning to me, he lisped, "*Very* nice." I don't think anything has given him such pleasure for a long time.' Colville, *The Fringes of Power* (London: Hodder and Stoughton, 1988), p. 341.

9. See for example Edward Murrow, *This is London* ed. Elmer Davis (New York: Simon and Shuster, 1941). For excerpts of other American journalism written between 1938 and 1946 see *Reporting World War Two: Parts One and Two* eds. Samuel Hynes, Anne Mathews, Nancy Caldwell Dorel and Roger J. Spillar (New York: New York Library of America, 1995).

10. Negley Farson, *Bomber's Moon* (New York: Harcourt and Brace, 1941), p. 15.

11. Diarist [D] 5349, Mass Observation Archive [MOA].

12. D 5427, MOA.

13. Stephen Spender, *World Within World* (New York; Modern Library, 2001), p. 299.

14. Robert Graves, *Goodbye to All That* (London: Cassell, 1966), p. 188.

15. Miss N. Bosanquet, IWM 81/33/1.

16. For more on prisoner-of-war diaries, see Laurie McNeill, "'Somewhere along the line I lost myself': Recreating Self in the War Diaries of Natalie Crouter and Elizabeth Vaughan" *Legacy* 19.1 (2002): pp. 98–105.

17. Harold Nicolson, *Diaries*, (London: Collins, 1967), p. 147.

18. Vere Hodgson, *Few Eggs and No Oranges* (London: Dennis Dobson, 1976), p. 13.

19. August 25, 1940: 'I am burying another tin box, containing my diaries for the first year of the war; Mortimer the gardener is again my accomplice.' *Chips: The Diaries of Sir Henry Channon* (London: Weidenfeld and Nicolson, 1967), p. 264.

20. For example, his analysis of British class politics in *The Road to Wigan Pier* (1933) combined his observations of the impoverished industrial communities of Northern England with autobiographical narrative.

21. See Peter Guerney, "Intersex and Dirty Girls: Mass-Observation and Working Class Sexuality in England in the 1930s" *Journal of the History of Sexuality* 8.3 (1997): pp. 256–90.

22. For more on the specific methodological issues of using MO material see Dorothy Sheridan, David Bloome and Brian Street, *Reading Mass-Observation Writing* (MOA Occasional Paper No. 1, University of Sussex Library, 1993). In "Writing to the Archive: Mass-Observation as Autobiography" in *Sociology* 27.1 (1993): pp. 27–40, Dorothy Sheridan, the archivist of the MO Archive, suggests that Mass Observation sources be read as part of a set of wider social and cultural practices. For my purposes, however, I will read them as autobiographical and historical commentary, as I see the 'continual slippage between what might be defined as "pure" subjective writing on the one hand and social reportage on the other' as a characteristic of most diaries written during the Blitz.

23. D 5244, MOA.

24. In the spring of 1940, the fall of Norway cut off the principal supply of the paper industry's wood pulp imports. The government set paper allocation for publishing companies at 60 per cent of their consumption during the 12 months before August 1939. This was an advantage for Penguin Books, who were publishing in paperback, and Macmillan, who had released the best-selling 1000-page novel *Gone With the Wind* in 1938. Despite restrictions on paper usage, demand for published books increased during the war, primarily because of the long evenings spent at home and in shelters. The publishing houses of Heinemann, Penguin and Macmillan all profited during the war, though the Stationer's Company Hall was demolished and the raids on the City on the night of December 29, 1940 destroyed 20 million books.

25. Peter Quennell, *The Wanton Chase* (London: Collins, 1980), p. 14.

26. See Neil Stammers, *Civil Liberties in Britain during the Second World War* (London, Croom Helm, 1982), and Paul O'Higgins, *Censorship In Britain* (London: Nelson, 1972). John Colville, Assistant Private Secretary to the Prime Minister, recorded his reactions to some of these reports in his diary, *The Fringes of Power* (1988).

27. Diana Cooper, *Trumpets from the Steep* (London: Soho Square, 1960), p. 70.

28. Naomi Mitchison, *Among You Taking Notes* (Oxford: Oxford University Press, 1986), p. 122.

29. Basil Woon, *Hell Came to London* (London: Peter Davies, 1941), p. viii.

30. Woon, p. 25.

31. James Olney, *Metaphors of Self: the Meaning of Autobiography* (Princeton: Princeton University Press, 1972). His later work adds a consideration of memory to his theories of autobiography, concluding that the autobiographical self cannot recall a past self, since both memory and narrative depend on time and change. See James Olney, *Memory and Narrative: The Weave of Life-Writing* (Chicago: University of Chicago Press, 1998). For more on the relational self and autobiography, see Paul John Eakin, *Touching the World: Reference in Autobiography* (Princeton: Princeton University Press, 1992) and his *Making Selves: How Our Lives Become Stories* (Ithaca: Cornell University Press, 1999).

32. Regina Kunzel, "Pulp Fiction and Problems Girls: Reading and Rewriting Single Pregnancy in the Postwar United States" *American Historical Review* 100.5 (1995): pp. 1465–87.

33. Michel de Certeau, *Practices of Everyday Life* trans. Steven Rendall (Berkeley: University of California Press, 1984).

34. David Gilbert, "'London in all its Glory – or How to Enjoy London': Guidebook Representations of Imperial London" *Journal of Historical Geography* 25.3 (1999): pp. 279–97.

35. See Peter Bailey, *Popular Culture and Performance in the Victorian City* (Cambridge: Cambridge University Press, 1999), and Erika Rappaport, *Shopping for Pleasure* (Princeton: Princeton University Press, 2000).

36. Susan Buck-Morss, "Dream World of Mass Culture: Walter Benjamin's Theory of Modernity and the Dialectics of Seeing" in *Modernity and the Hegemony of Vision* (Berkeley: University of California Press, 1993), p. 310. See also Walter Benjamin, "Paris, Capital of the Nineteenth Century" in *Reflections: Essays, Aphorisms and Autobiographical Writings* trans. E. Jephcott (New York: Schocken, 1978).

37. Norman Longmate, *How We Lived Then* (London: Hutchinson, 1971), p. 127.

38. Similarly, after the terrorist bombing attacks on New York City in September 2001, politicians and advertisers put out a more strident call for consumer consumption in the name of patriotism.

39. D 5401, MOA.

40. Joyce Weiner, IWM 77/176/1.

41. Naomi Royde- Smith, *Outside Information* (London: Macmillan, 1941), p. 119.

42. D 5039.9, MOA.

43. Nicolson, p. 109.

44. See Marshall Berman, *All That is Solid Melts into Air: The Experience of Modernity* (New York: Penguin Books, 1982).

45. Raymond Williams, "The Metropolis and the Emergence of Modernism" in Peter Brooker, ed. *Modernism/Postmodernism* (New York: Longman, 1992).

46. See David Morgan and Mary Evans, "The Spirit of the Times" in *The Battle for Britain* (London: Routledge, 1993), Angus Calder, "Deep England" in *The Myth of the Blitz* (London: Jonathan Cape, 1991) and Peter Miles and Malcolm Smith, *Cinema, Literature and Society: Elite and Mass Culture in Interwar Britain* (London: Croom Helm, 1987).

47. Nicolson, p. 145.

48. Charles Baudelaire, "The Painter of Modern Life" (1863) in *Baudelaire: Selected Writings on Art and Literature* trans. P. E. Charvet (New York: Viking, 1972), pp. 395–422.

49. See Mica Nava and Alan O'Shea, eds. *Modern Times* (London: Routledge, 1996) and Susan Buck-Morss, "The Flâneur, the Sandwichman and the Whore: the Politics of Loitering" *New German Critique* 39 (1986): pp. 99–140.

50. See Patricia J. Anderson, "A Revolution in Popular Art: Pictorial Magazines and the Making of a Mass Culture in England, 1832–1860" *Journal of Newspaper and Periodical History* 6.1 (1990): pp. 16–27, Patricia L. Garside, "Representing the Metropolis: The Changing Relationship between London and the Press, 1870–1939" *London Journal* 16.2 (1991): pp. 156–73, Jane Garrity, "Selling Culture to the 'Civilized': Bloomsbury, British *Vogue*, and the Marketing of National Identity" *Modernism/Modernity* 6.2 (1990): pp. 29–58.

51. Mrs M. Morris, IWM 80/38/1.

52. Hodgson, p. 95.

53. Similarly, Ritchie Calder wrote that the fires were so bright that at three in the morning: 'It is possible to see to type in a light as bright as an angry sunrise.' *Carry on London* (London: English Universities Press, 1941), p. 17.

54. Although visual forms of popular culture were embraced as new artistic media by such avant-garde modernist artists as Man Ray and Luis Buñuel.

55. See Alan O'Shea, "English Subjects of Modernity" in *Modern Times* (1996) and J. P. Mayer, *British Film Cinemas and Their Audiences* (London: Dennis Dobson, 1948).

56. Nicholas Pronay and Jeremy Croft, "British film censorship and propaganda policy during the Second World War" in James Curran and Vincent Porter, eds. *British Cinema History* (London: Weidenfeld and Nicolson, 1983), p. 149.

57. Mollie Panter-Downes, *London War Notes* (New York: Farrar and Giroux), pp. 100–1.

58. The Second World War was also one of the most popular subjects for film in the immediate postwar period. See John Ramsden, "Refocusing 'The People's War': British War Film of the 1950s" *Journal of Contemporary History* 33.1 (1998): pp. 35–64.

59. Jim Wolveridge, *Ain't it Grand, (Or This Was Stepney)* (London: Journeyman Press, 1981), p. 71.

60. Another raid spectator in Coventry also compared it to the film "The Last Days of Pompeii" in Norman Longmate's *Air Raid* (London: Hutchinson, 1976), p. 127.

61. Alan J. Bewell, "Portraits at Greyfriars: Photography, History and Memory in Walter Benjamin" in *Clio* 12.1(1982): pp. 17–29.

62. See Jane Fish, "It looked more natural: Miss Rosie Newman's Colour Film of the Second World War" *Imperial War Museum Review* 11 (1997): pp. 27–34.

63. Cecil Beaton, *The Years Between: Diaries 1939–1944* (London: Weidenfeld and Nicolson, 1965), p. 40. For his wartime photographs see *History Under Fire: 52 Photographs of Air Raid Damage to London Buildings 1940–1941* with a commentary by James Pope-Hennessy (London: Batsford, 1941) and *Time Exposure*, with a commentary by Peter Quennell (London: Batsford, 1941).

64. Beaton, *The Years Between*, p. 52.

65. For a more thorough discussion of visuality and modernism see Hal Foster, ed. *Vision and Visuality* (Seattle: Bay Press, 1988), Norman Bryson, *Vision and Painting* (New Haven: Yale University Press, 1983), Martin Jay, *Downcast Eyes* (Berkeley: University of California Press, 1993) and the discussion of the war photography of Lee Miller and the writing of H. D. in Jean Gallagher, "The World Wars and the Female Gaze" Ph.D. dissertation, City University of New York, 1994, UMI 9417462.

66. Victor Li, "Policing the City: Modernism, Autonomy and Authority" *Criticism* 34 (1992): pp. 261–79.

67. Lynda Nead, *Victorian Babylon: People, Streets and Images in Nineteenth-Century London* (New Haven: Yale University Press, 2000).

68. Edmund Burke, *A Philosophical Enquiry into the Origins of Our Ideas of the Sublime and Beautiful* (1757), ed. James T. Boulton (London: Routledge 1958; rev. ed., Oxford: Basil Blackwell, 1987).

69. Steven Cresap, "Sublime Politics: On the Uses of an Aesthetic of Terror" *Clio* 19.2 (1990): pp. 111–25.

70. Michael Mawson, ed., *Eyewitness in the Crimea: The Crimean War Letters (1854–1856) of Lt. Col. George Frederick Dallas* (London: Greenhill, 2001), p. 36.

71. Stephen Inwood, *A History of London* (London: Macmillan, 1998), pp. 701–2.

72. Michael MacDonagh, *In London During the Great War* (London: Eyre and Spottiswoode, 1935), p. 169.

73. Colville, p. 247, Nicolas Bentley, *A Version of the Truth* (London: Andre Deutsch, 1960) p. 102, Nicolson, p. 109.

74. Vivienne Hall, IWM DS/MISC/88 and Con Shelf.

75. Florence Speed, IWM 86/45/1.

76. Bruce Lockhart, *Comes the Reckoning* (London: Putnam, 1947), p. 102.

77. Edith Grimshaw, London Borough of Newham Library.

78. Hilde Marchant, *Daily Express* May 12, 1941, p. 1.

79. Michael Riffaterre, *Text Production* trans. Terese Lyons (New York: Columbia University Press, 1983).

80. Breton provided a more radical intellectual and literary exploration of the unconscious, while Dali's works exemplified the aesthetic or visual representation of it.

81. Mary Ann Caws, *The Art of Interference: Stressed Readings in Verbal and Visual Texts* (Princeton, N.J.: Princeton University Press, 1989), p. 90.

82. The exhibition was organized by Roland Penrose and David Gascoyne, and Paul Eluard and Andre Breton chose the work from abroad. It was also performative, as Salvador Dali, dressed in a diver's suit, lectured on his work and his love for his wife Gala, while holding two Irish wolfhounds on leads, and a young woman wandered the exhibition with her face covered by a mask of roses, with a model of a leg filled with roses in one hand, and a raw pork chop in another.

83. See James Buzard, "Mass-Observation, Modernism, and Auto-ethnography" *Modernism/Modernity* 4.3 (1997): pp. 93–122 and Antony Penrose, *The Lives of Lee Miller* (London: Thames and Hudson, 1988).

84. In 1947 two members of the English Surrealist group wrote a "Declaration of the Surrealist Group in England," which read in part, 'As soon as the war began, the English surrealist group underwent some more or less sly desertions, and in the succeeding months it showed itself rather vulnerable to the attacks of an occasional conformism. The most surprising case remains that of the sculptor Henry Moore, who went without warning from surrealism to the fabrication of sacerdotal ornaments, and sank afterwards to the monotonous production, in series, of sketches of air-raid shelters, a despicable popularization of his prewar "reclining figures". It is only fair to add that Moore's case does not palliate Herbert Read's eclecticism, which now reaches bewildering proportions, that David Gascoyne's hoaxes leave him prostrate and foaming at the mouth, and that Humphrey Jennings is decorated with the Order of the British Empire.' In *The Autobiography of Surrealism* ed. Marcel Jean (New York: Viking, 1980), p. 428.

85. I am indebted to Harold Mah for this comparison.

86. John Lehmann, *I am my Brother* (London: Longmans, 1960), p. 23.

87. Lehmann, p. 24.

88. S. G. Champion, IWM 77/178/1.

89. Max Cohen, *What Nobody told the Foreman.* (London: Butler and Tanner, 1953), p. 128.

90. Sir Hamilton Kerr, in "Pages from a Wartime Diary" *The National and English Review* 151 (1958): pp. 105–8, compared the 'odious dreams' of nighttime raids to the fact that the milk was on time in the morning.

91. Alan Goodlet, diary, Ealing Local History Library, September 8, 1940, and Cohen, p. 128.

92. Nicolson, p. 163.

93. Mrs Robert Henrey, *The Siege of London* (London: Dent, 1946), p. 41.

94. Freud coined the term uncanny, or *unheimlich*, to signify something both familiar yet strange. See Hal Foster, *Convulsive Beauty* (Cambridge, Mass.: MIT Press, 1997).

95. Mrs M. Morris, IWM 80/38/1.

96. Giles Tremlett, "Anarchists and the fine art of torture" *The Guardian* Monday, January 27, 2003.

97. Virginia Woolf, *The Diary of Virginia Woolf* (London: Harvester, 1984), pp. 316–17.

98. The nymph was the work of early Pre-Raphaelite sculptor Alexander Munro.

99. Quennell, p. 31.

Chapter 2: Raids and Rationing

1. Grace Foakes, *Life with Reuben* (London: Sheppeard & Walwyn, 1975), p. 66.
2. Margaret Kennedy, *Where Stands a Winged Sentry* (New Haven: Yale University Press, 1941), p. 140.
3. Henry Felix Srebnik, *London Jews and British Communism 1935–1945* (London: Valentine Mitchell, 1995), p. 64.
4. *The Jewish Chronicle* May 16, 1940.
5. For instance, on August 23, 1940, *The Jewish Chronicle* reported that Abraham Linskie of Salford was refused entry into the Home Guard, while his brother was accepted in Gorton. For a history of the *Chronicle* see David Ceasarini, *The Jewish Chronicle and Anglo-Jewry 1841–1991* (Cambridge: Cambridge University Press, 1994).
6. Angus Calder, *The People's War* (London: Granada, 1971), pp. 130–3. There were, however, many protests about Mosley and his wife's private apartment in Holloway prison and the servants they employed from the prison population. Their release in 1943, on grounds of ill-health, caused public and official protests. Willie Gallacher, the only communist Member of Parliament during the war, demanded in Parliament on November 23, 1943 why the same criteria for release did not apply to the imprisoned Mahatma Gandhi.
7. Frances Faviell, *A Chelsea Concerto* (London: Cassell, 1959), p. 32.
8. Faviell, p. 112.
9. Ritchie Calder, *The Lesson of London* (London: Secker and Warburg, 1941), p. 74. The *Jewish Chronicle* also reported on August 23, 1940 that many places of work, such as Hendon Hospital, had overt employment bans on Jews.
10. D 5098, MOA.
11. George Orwell, *The Complete Works Volume Twelve: A Patriot after All 1940–1941* ed. Peter Davison, (London: Secker and Warburg, 1998), p. 278.
12. *The Catholic Herald* October 25, 1940, p. 8.
13. D 5388, MOA.
14. *Jewish Chronicle* September 13, 1940, September 20, 1940, January 10, 1941.
15. Frank R. Lewey, *Cockney Campaign* (London: Stanley Paul, 1948), p. 76.
16. Diana Cooper, *Trumpets from the Steep* (London: Soho Square, 1960), p. 65.

17. Colville, p. 257.

18. Titmuss, p. 20.

19. Paul Addison, *The Road to 1945* (London: Jonathan Cape, 1975), p. 121.

20. David Thoms, "The Blitz, Civilian Morale and Regionalism 1940–1942" in *War Culture* eds. Kirkham and Thoms (London: Lawrence and Wishart, 1995), p. 4.

21. Ian McLaine, *Ministry of Morale*, (Boston: Allen and Unwin, 1979), p. 9.

22. McLaine, p. 119.

23. Churchill himself said in early 1940: 'In time of war, the machinery of government is so strong it can afford largely to ignore popular feeling.' In Clive Ponting, *1940: Myth and Reality* (London: Hamish Hamilton, 1990), p. 171.

24. S. Mogridge, IWM 85/19/1.

25. An inverse ratio presented in a Gallup poll published in May 1, 1941, as quoted in Allan Nevins, *This is England Today* (New York: Scribner & Sons, 1941), p. 43.

26. Weymouth, p. 188.

27. Ian Buruma, *The Wages of Guilt* (London: Jonathan Cape, 1999), p. 299.

28. For analyses of the difficulties European countries have in dealing with their public memories of the war see Tony Judt "The Past is Another Country: Myth and Memory in Postwar Europe" in *Daedalus* 121.4 (1992): pp. 93–118 and Kim Munholland, "Remembering Vichy France" *French Historical Studies* 18.3 (1994): pp. 801–20.

29. See Raphael Samuel, *Patriotism Volume 1: History and Politics* (London: Routledge, 1989), p. xxv.

30. Hodson, *Through the Dark Night*, p. 347.

31. Stephen Spender, *Civilians at War* (London, Harrap, 1945), p. 38.

32. 'Peter Conway,' pseudonym of George Alexis Milkomanovich Milkomane, *Living Tapestry* (London: Staples, 1946), p. 209.

33. Titmuss, p. 257.

34. Len Deighton, in *Blood, Tears and Folly* (London: Pimlico, 1995), estimated that the more fortunate districts of central London, Westminster, the City and Southwark, received 20–30 bombs per hundred square acres in the first two months of bombing, while the least fortunate areas, Surrey, the Docks, Shoreditch, Holborn and Chelsea, received 21–52 bombs per hundred square acres. Deighton, p. 392.

35. Constantine Fitzgibbon, *The Blitz* (London: Macdonald, 1970).

36. B. Beaven and D. Thoms, "The Blitz and Civilian Morale in Three Northern Cities 1940–1942" *Northern History* 32 (1996): pp. 195–203.

37. Yet the raid had a relatively low casualty rate, with 163 killed, twelve of whom were firemen, and 509 injured.

38. David Johnson, *The City Ablaze* (London: William Kimber, 1980), p. 209.

39. Fitzgibbon estimated that during the April 16 raid 685 planes dropped 890 tons of high explosives and 4,200 canisters of incendiaries, while in the April 19 raid 712 planes dropped 1,026 tons of high explosives and 4,252 incendiaries, and on May 10, 507 planes dropped 711 tons of high explosives and 2,393 incendiaries.

40. Johnson, pp. 208–10.

41. Lewey, p. 41.

42. Longmate, p. 121.

43. Titmuss, p. 342. This fear is evident in much governmental policy towards shelters, especially the closing in late March of 'Tunnel Town,' a large underground shelter housing 2000 people, large enough to run its own theatre and library. See the article in the *Daily Express* March 28, 1940.

44. *Daily Express* September 20, 1940.

45. *Daily Mirror* October 11, 1940.

46. "London to Dig more Tubes as Raid Shelters," *Daily Mirror* November 4, 1940.

47. See the memoir of William Gallacher, the lone Communist MP during the war: *The Last Memoirs of William Gallacher* (London: Lawrence and Wishart, 1966), and that of Phil Piratin, a Communist Party organizer and MP for Mile End/Stepney 1945–1950: *Our Flag Stays Red* (London: Thames Publications, 1948).

48. Based on a census report of 1940, cited in Fitzgibbon, p. 143, and Longmate, p. 128. These figures would have fluctuated over the course of the winter, with the highest concentration in the early fall and late spring, the periods of heaviest bombing.

49. London Transport estimates, in the *Daily Express* January 24, 1941.

50. Marie Lawrence, Richmond Local Studies Archive.

51. Longmate, p. 123.

52. I. H. Granger, IWM 94/45/2.

53. Macaulay, p. 112.

54. Nicolson, p. 117.

55. Lewey, p. 68.

56. Harrisson, p. 333.

57. *Daily Express*, September 9, 1940.

58. *Daily Express*, September 9, 1940.

59. Social geography, the analysis of social divisions and communities in space and place, has been the focus of much recent work on the history

of London. See Erika Rappaport, "'The Halls of Temptation': Gender: Politics and the Construction of the Department Store in Late Victorian London" *The Journal of British Studies* 35.1 (1996): pp. 58–83, Jon Lawrence, "Class and Gender in the Making of Urban Toryism, 1880–1914" *The English Historical Review* 108.428 (1993): pp. 628–52, Jon May, "Globalization and the Politics of Place: Place and Identity in an Inner London Neighborhood" *Transactions of the Institute of British Geographers* 21.1 (1996): pp. 194–215.

60. Ross McKibbin, *Classes and Cultures* (Oxford: Oxford University Press, 1998), 179.

61. Ritchie Calder, *The Lesson of London*, p. 39.

62. Ritchie Calder, *The Lesson of London*, p. 37.

63. Charles Graves, *Off the Record* (London: Hutchinson, 1941), p. v.

64. Cooper, p. 66.

65. Alexander Cadogan, *The Diaries of Sir Alexander Cadogan* (New York: Putnams, 1972), p. 332.

66. Beaton, *The Years Between*, pp. 52–3.

67. Stanley Jackson, *The Savoy* (London: Frederick Muller, 1964), pp. 179–80.

68. Fitzgibbon, p. 109.

69. Compton Mackenzie, *The Savoy of London* (London: Harrap, 1953), pp. 199–200.

70. Piratin, pp. 73–4.

71. Jackson, pp. 186–7.

72. Phyllis Warner, IWM 95/14/1.

73. Lehmann, p. 87.

74. Waugh, p. 171.

75. Lehmann, p. 82.

76. Winston Churchill, *Memoirs of the Second World War* (Cambridge: Riverside, 1959), p. 371.

77. Channon, p. 270.

78. Gordon, p. 141.

79. Reynolds, pp. 10–11.

80. See Ina Zweiniger-Bargielowska, *Austerity in Britain* (Oxford: Oxford University Press, 2000), Oxford University Institute of Statistics, *Studies in War Economics* (Oxford: Basil Blackwell, 1947) and Alan Booth, "Economists and Points Rationing in the Second World War" *Journal of European Economic History* 14.2 (1985): pp. 299–317.

81. Robert Boothby, *I Fight To Live* (London: Victor Gollancz, 1947), p. 221. The Milk-In-Schools portion of the program did survive for fifty years, to be discontinued by Margaret Thatcher.

82. Ellen Leopold, "London County Council Restaurants and the Decline of Municipal Enterprise" in Andrew Saint, ed. *Politics and the People of London: The London County Council 1889–1965* (London: Hambledon, 1989), pp. 202–3.

83. W. K. Hancock and M. W. Gowing, *British War Economy* (London: HMSO, 1949), p. 76.

84. The National Food Survey Committee, *The Urban Working-Class Household Diet 1940–1949* (London: His Majesty's Stationary Office, 1951), p. 10.

85. Zweiniger-Bargielowska, p. 152.

86. *Urban Working Class Diet*, p. 15.

87. Yet the needs of the worker were not always taken seriously, as in American writer Allan Nevins' statement: 'People are no worse for eating less red meat and sugar; and if a workman lacks a sufficient quantity of good hearty food it is usually because he is spending too much on beer, tobaccos and movies.' Nevins, p. 44.

88. Mrs M. Morris, IWM 80/38/1.

89. G. W. King, IWM 85/49/1.

90. D 5277, MOA.

91. Florence Speed, IWM 86/45/1.

92. Orwell, *A Patriot after All*, p. 453.

93. Hodgson, p. 119.

94. Mitchison, p. 120.

95. D 5427, MOA.

96. D 5427, MOA.

97. Priestley, p. 19.

98. See Ina Zweiniger-Bargielowska, "Rationing, Austerity and the Conservative Party Recovery after 1945" *The Historical Journal* 37.1 (1994): pp. 173–97.

99. I. H. Granger, IWM 94/45/2.

100. *Daily Express*, September 27, 1940, p. 1.

101. D 5103, MOA.

102. D 5103, MOA.

103. D 5427, MOA.

104. May Rainer, Brunel University Library.

105. D 5132, MOA.

106. James Lansdale Hodson, *Through the Dark Night* (London: Victor Gollancz, 1941), p. 340.

107. B. Garman, IWM 92/27/1.

108. W. Regan and Mrs Cox both record being looted. Norman Longmate cites an auxiliary fireman saying: 'Everybody loots ... the

ARP, Wardens, Demolition Men … the Police.' *How We Lived Then*, p. 134.

109. *The Sunday Express* December 8, 1940, p. 7. They stole a mink coat and a skunk cape.
110. Miss V. Bawtree, IWM 91/5/1.
111. D 5427, MOA.

Chapter 3: Workers and Civil Defence

1. Ben Robertson, *I Saw England* (New York: Knopf, 1941), p. 127.
2. D 5427, MOA.
3. Sonya Rose, "Resuscitating Class" *Social Science History* 22.1 (1998): pp. 19–27.
4. Arthur Marwick, "People's War and Top People's Peace? British Society and the Second World War" in *Crisis and Controversy* eds. Alan Sked and Chris Cook (London: Macmillan, 1976) and A. J. P. Taylor *English History 1914–1945* (Oxford: Oxford University Press, 1965).
5. See Jose Harris, "Did British workers want the welfare state? G. D. H. Cole's Survey of 1942" in *The Working Class in Modern British History* (Cambridge: Cambridge University Press, 1983), David Goldthorpe et al. *The Affluent Worker: Political Attitudes and Behaviour* (Cambridge: Cambridge University Press, 1968), David Cannadine, *The Rise and Fall of Class in Britain* (New York: Columbia University Press, 1999) and Penny Summerfield, "The Leveling of Class" in *War and Social Change* ed. Harold Smith (Manchester: Manchester University Press, 1986).
6. Stephen Inwood, *A History of London* (London: Macmillan, 1998), p. 724.
7. See Miriam Glucksmann, *Women Assemble* (London: Routledge, 1990).
8. Inwood, p. 727.
9. Angus Calder, *The People's War*, p. 73.
10. See Jim Tomlinson, *Employment Policy: The Crucial Years 1939–1955* (Oxford: Clarendon, 1987), and Richard Toye, "Keynes, the Labour Movement and how to pay for the war" *Twentieth Century British History* 10.3 (1999): pp. 255–81.
11. MO Diarist 5039.3 recorded seeing 'Go To It' knit into the design of a woman's sweater on September 4, 1940.
12. Angus Calder, *People's War*, p. 117.
13. Angus Calder, *People's War*, p. 234.
14. G. C. Peden, *British Economic and Social Policy: Lloyd George to Thatcher* (London: Philip Allan, 1991) p. 120.

15. Angus Calder, *The People's War*, p. 228.
16. Harold Perkin, *The Rise of Professional Society* (London: Routledge, 1989), pp. 407–8.
17. *Britain Looks Ahead: British Official Statements Volume III* (New York: British Information Services, 1943), p. 25.
18. *Britain Looks Ahead*, p. 25.
19. In the papers of Mrs Florence Elkus, IWM Con Shelf.
20. Vera Douie, *Daughters of Britain* (Oxford: Vincent-Baxter Press, 1949), p. 158.
21. Harold Smith, "The effect of the war on the status of women" in *War and Social Change* (Manchester: Manchester University Press, 1986), pp. 211–12.
22. See Christine Gledhill and Gillian Swanson, eds., *Nationalising Femininity* (Manchester: Manchester University Press, 1996), Julia Swindells, "Coming Home to Heaven: Manpower and Myth in 1944 Britain" *Women's History Review* 4.2 (1995): pp. 223–34, Antonia Lant, *Blackout* (Princeton: Princeton University Press, 1991) and Denise Riley, "Some Peculiarities of Social Policy Concerning Women" in *Behind the Lines* eds. P. and M. Higonnet (New Haven: Yale University Press, 1987).
23. *The Sunday Express* September 15, 1940, p. 6.
24. Robertson, pp. 137–8.
25. Ritchie Calder, *Carry On London*, pp. 159–60.
26. Spender, p. 14.
27. Spender, p. 34.
28. W. Eric Jackson, *Achievement: A Short History of the London County Council* (London: Longmans, 1965), p. 33.
29. Sir Harold Scott, p. 108.
30. Many of these pinned maps can be seen in London's local borough archives.
31. Key's achievement was recognized by the government in his appointment as a Regional Commissioner in 1941. A. D. Harvey, "Local Authorities and the Blitz" *Contemporary Review* (1990): pp. 197–201.
32. Stepney's ARP Controller had to be replaced by the Ministry of Home Security on October 4, 1940 and then again ten weeks later. Harvey, p. 198.
33. S. M. S. Woodcock, IWM 87/36/1.
34. Gladys Langford, Islington Local Council Central Reference Library Y X079 LAN. See for instance, Patricia Knowlden's *The Long Alert 1937–1945* (Orpington: A. G. Bishops and Sons, 1988).
35. B. Garman, IWM 92/27/1.

36. William Regan, IWM 88/10/1 and Con. Shelf.

37. Cyril Demarne, *The London Blitz: A Fireman's Tale* (London: Newham Parent's Centre Publications, 1980), p. 146.

38. Demarne, p. 15.

39. F. W. Hurd, IWM 80/30/1.

40. Bentley, p. 188.

41. Yvonne Green, IWM 99/9/1. A plaque commemorating her sacrifice was erected in the Chelsea Old Church in June 2007.

42. *Front Line: The Story of Civil Defence 1940–1941* (London: Ministry of Information for Ministry of Home Security, 1942), p. 145.

43. *Front Line*, p. 152.

44. Douie, p. 158.

45. Elizabeth Watson, *Don't Wait for It* (IWM: Department of Printed Books, 1941; reprinted 1994).

46. Letter from Mary Glasgow, 8 Justice Walk, Chelsea. In the papers of Miss J. Oakman, IWM 91/20/1.

47. A. S. G. Butler, *Recording Ruin* (London: Constable, 1942), p. 9.

48. S. G. Champion, IWM 77/178/1.

49. Lehmann, pp. 128–9.

50. Graves, p. 16.

51. Florence Speed, IWM 86/45/1.

52. Nellie Carver, IWM 90/16/1.

53. Canon J. H. Rumens, IWM 87/8/1.

54. D 5244, MOA.

55. Willmott, pp. 44–5.

56. G. W. King, IWM 85/49/1.

57. George Beardsmore, *Civilians at War* (London: John Murray, 1985), p. 96.

58. Cooper, p. 285.

59. Quennell, p. 13.

60. Anthony Weymouth, *Plague Year* (London: Harrap, 1942), p. 185.

61. Phyllis Warner, IWM 95/14/1.

62. Marie Lawrence, Richmond Local Studies Archive.

63. Nellie Carver, IWM 90/16/1.

64. I. H. Granger, IWM 94/45/2.

65. Gladys Langford, Islington Central Reference Library YX079 LAN.

66. D 5129, MOA.

67. Max Cohen, *What Nobody Told the Foreman* (London: Spalding and Levy, 1953), p. 121.

68. Cohen, pp. 130–1.

69. Phyllis Damonte, IWM 95/32/1.

70. See Eugenio F. Biagini, ed. *Citizenship and Community* (Cambridge: Cambridge University Press, 1996), and Julia Parker, *Citizenship, Work and Welfare* (London: Macmillan, 1998).

71. Similarly the Labour government under Tony Blair emphasized the status of work as the basis of citizenship. For more on contemporary citizenship and work debates see John Edwards and Jean-Paul Revauger, eds. *Employment and Citizenship in Britain and France* (Aldershot: Ashgate, 2000).

72. Marx wrote that labor was a commodity that had both a use-value linked to production, and an exchange-value linked to the market. The heading's inversion of Marx's theory emphasizes the government's fear of wartime Marxist radicalization of workers. This anxiety led to a ban on the export of nine left-wing newspapers in 1940, and the suppression of the Marxist newspaper the *Daily Worker* in January 1941.

73. Reginald Bell, *The Bull's Eye* (London: Cassell, 1943), p. 93.

Chapter 4: Children and the Family

1. Derek Lambert, *The Sheltered Days* (London: Andre Deutsch, 1965), p. 57.

2. Susan Pedersen, *Family, Dependence, and the Origins of the Welfare State* (Cambridge: Cambridge University Press, 1993), p. 5.

3. Pat Starkey, *Families and Social Workers: The Work of Family Service Units 1940–1985* (Liverpool: Liverpool University Press, 2000), Jane Lewis, *The Voluntary Sector, The State and Social Work in Britain* (Aldershot: Edward Elgar, 1995), and Carol Dyhouse, *Feminism and the Family in England 1880–1939* (London: Basil Blackwell, 1989).

4. Carolyn Steedman, *Landscape for a Good Woman* (London: Virago, 1986), p. 65.

5. Leonore Davidoff, Megan Doolittle, Janet Fink, and Katherine Holden, *The Family Story: Blood: Contract and Intimacy 1830–1960* (London: Longman, 1996), p. 200.

6. P. J. Atkins, "The Spatial Configuration of Class Solidarity in London's West End 1792–1939" *Urban History Yearbook* 17 (1990): pp. 36–65, and Eliot Slater and Moya Woodside, *Patterns of Marriage* (London: Cassell, 1951), p. 31.

7. Sheila B. Kammerman and Alfred J. Kahn, *Family Change and Family Policies in Great Britain, Canada, New Zealand and the United States* (Oxford: Clarendon Press, 1997), p. 34.

8. Richard Titmuss gives the statistics of the first scheme of national evacuation in 1939 as: 1,500,000 mothers and children evacuated from urban areas, 2,000,000 people who left of their own accord, 140,000 sick discharged from hospitals and most evacuated.

9. Addison, *The Road to 1945*, p. 130.

10. Jeffrey Weeks, *Sex, Politics and Society: the Regulation of Sexuality since 1800* (London: Longman, 1990), p. 232.

11. Herbert Morrison in Swindon, December 20, 1942, in *Britain Looks Ahead* (New York: British Information Services), p. 40.

12. Geoffrey Field, "The Working Class Family in Wartime Britain" *International Labour and Working Class History* 38 (1990): pp. 3–28.

13. William Regan, IWM 88/10/1.

14. Miss G. T. Thomas, IWM 90/30/1.

15. Quentin Reynolds, *A London Diary* (New York: Faber and Faber, 1941).

16. The fragments and an explanatory note are archived in the IWM DS/MISC/88.

17. Jerry White, *The Worst Street in North London* (London: Routledge, 1986), Nancy Tomes, "A Torrent of Abuse: Crimes of Violence Between Working Class Men and Women in London 1840–1875" *Journal of Social History* 11.3(1978): pp. 328–45.

18. Stephen Mack and Joanna Humphries, in *The Making of Modern London: 1939–1945 London at War* (London: Sidgwick and Jackson, 1986) described rich youths who went 'slumming' in the tube shelters, as well as the reactions of the shelterers who felt they were being 'looked down upon'. Jim Wolveridge also described this in his memoir *Ain't it Grand (or This was Stepney)*.

19. Bentley, pp. 193–4.

20. Watson, pp. 14–15.

21. Conway, p. 25.

22. D 5401, MOA.

23. Lehmann, p. 131.

24. Sefton Delmer, *Black Boomerang* (New York: Viking, 1962), p. 22.

25. Orwell, September 21, 1940, *A Patriot After All*, p. 267.

26. Orwell, October 25, 1940, *A Patriot After All*, p. 278.

27. Field, p. 4.

28. D 5245, MOA.

29. D 5039, MOA.

30. Cooper, pp. 64–5.

31. Doris Pierce, *Memories of the Civilians' War 1939–1945* (London: Temple, 1996), p. 29.

32. D 5244, MOA.

33. Florence Speed, IWM 86/45/1.

34. Florence Speed, IWM 86/45/1.

35. Steedman, p. 6.

36. Lambert, p. 64.

37. Mrs H. Faber, IWM 96/26/1.

38. Roy Ridgway, IWM 67/347/1.

39. Titmuss, p. 410.

40. Jeffrey Weeks, *Sex, Politics and Society* (London: Longman, 1990), p. 210.

41. Upper and upper-middle class children were more often evacuated overseas, in the care of governmental organizations such as the Children's Overseas Reception Board, or evacuated privately within Britain. For histories of evacuation see Carlton Jackson, *Who will take our Children?* (London: Methuen, 1985) and Travis Crosby, *The Impact of Civilian Evacuation in the Second World War* (London: Croom Helm, 1986).

42. Titmuss, p. 516. See also John Welshman, "Evacuation and Social Policy During the Second World War: Myth and Reality" *Twentieth Century British History* 9.1 (1998): pp. 28–53.

43. See Richard Padley and Margaret Cole, *Evacuation Survey* (London: Routledge, 1940) and Mrs Strachey, *Borrowed Children: A Popular Account of Some Evacuation Problems and Their Remedies* (New York: The Commonwealth Fund, 1940).

44. National Federation of Women's Institutes, *Town Children through Country Eyes* (1940), pp. 3–4.

45. *Town Children*, p. 5. James Hinton has argued that an analysis of the leaders and actions of the Women's Voluntary Service reveal how the war reinforced the continuities of class. James Hinton, *Women, Social Leadership, and the Second World War: Continuities of Class* (Oxford: Oxford University Press, 2002).

46. Ritchie Calder, *Carry On London*, p. 128.

47. Titmuss, p. 423.

48. I have not found a diary or memoir of a mother evacuated with her children, though several were written by teachers.

49. Edward Dorking, IWM 97/28/1. Memoirs of children who had been evacuated from London during the war include J. R. Sweetland, IWM 97/21/1, Edward Dorking, IWM 97/28/1, M. J. Reynolds, IWM 96/18/1, May Hobbs, *Born to Struggle* (London: Quartet, 1973), May Baker, IWM 96/26/1, R. W. Hill, IWM 97/24/1, Richard Pooley, *The Evacuee* (Hull: Anglo American Publicity Services, 1972). May Hobbs and Richard Pooley both spoke of the unkindness and suspicion with which evacuees were greeted, Pooley eventually being forced to steal food to supplement his meager meals. May Baker recalled kindness, as

did the brother of John Major, Terry Major-Ball in *Major Major* (London: Duckworth, 1994).

50. Penny Elaine Starns and Martin L. Parsons, "Against Their Will: The Use and Abuse of British Children during the Second World War" in *Children and War: An Anthology* (New York: New York University Press, 2003), pp. 266–78.

51. M. J. Reynolds, IWM 96/18/1.

52. Titmuss, p. 349.

53. Titmuss, p. 249.

54. D 5037, MOA.

55. *Daily Mirror* November 7, 1940, p. 3.

56. J. B. S. Haldane, *ARP* (London: Victor Gollancz, 1938), p. 11.

57. Mrs C. Eustace, IWM 83/27/1.

58. D 5388, MOA.

59. Marie Paneth, *Branch Street* (London: George Allen & Unwin, 1943), p. 86.

60. Paneth, p. 120.

61. Harry Walters, *The Street* (London: Centreprise, 1975), p. 11.

62. Hodson, p. 317.

63. Florence Speed, IWM 86/45/1.

64. S. M. S. Woodcock, IWM 87/36/1.

65. Kammerman and Khan, p. 72.

66. John Bowlby, *Forty-Four Juvenile Thieves: Their Character and Home Life* (London, 1946), pp. 49–54. His ideas were elaborated in a report on mental health to the World Health Organization, and in the popular Penguin version of his *Child Care and the Growth of Love* published in 1953.

67. The sinking of the ship *The City of Benares*, on September 17, 1940, killing 73 children and their 6 guardians, and the shipping stringency put an end to overseas evacuation.

68. Vera Brittain, *Wartime Chronicle*, p. 50.

69. Channon, p. 260.

70. D 5277, MOA.

71. Anthony Weymouth, *A Psychologist's Wartime Diary* (London: Harrap, 1940), p. 177.

72. *Daily Mirror*, September 9, 1940.

73. May Hobbs, *Born to Struggle* (London: Quartet, 1973).

74. Ferguson and Fitzgerald, *Studies in the Social Services* (1954) in Wendy Webster, *Imagining Home: Gender, 'Race' and National Identity, 1945–64* (London: UCL Press, 1998), p. 12.

75. Foakes, p. 80.

76. Titmuss, p. 410.
77. Lewey, pp. 51–8. *Front Line* (London: HMSO, 1942).
78. Titmuss, p. 412.
79. *The Jewish Chronicle* "Little Rebels in the Home" March 21, 1940, p. 24.
80. Peter Loewenberg, "The Psychohistorical Origins of the Nazi Youth Cohort" *The American Historical Review* 76.5 (1971): pp. 1457–502.
81. Lyndsey Stonebridge, "Anxiety at a Time of Crisis" *History Workshop Journal* 45 (1998): pp. 171–82.
82. Janis, p. 95.
83. Gordon, p. 152.
84. Recent publications aim to rectify this silence. In the context of the Second World War, Anthony Tuttle analyzes the psychological effect of the war on American children in *Daddy's Gone to War* (Oxford: Oxford University Press, 1993). Editors Glen Elder Jr., John Modell and Ross Parke, in *Children in Time and Place* (Cambridge: Cambridge University Press, 1993), gather articles which combine psychology, sociology and history, and Anthony Fletcher and Stephen Hussey, in *Childhood in Question* (Manchester: Manchester University Press, 1999), explore children's subjectivities through legal and welfare records between 1650 and 1960.
85. Partridge, p. 92.
86. Joyce Smith, IWM 96/19/1.
87. Geoffrey Dellar, IWM P321.
88. C. Brownbill, IWM 88/49/1.
89. Colin Perry, *Boy in the Blitz* (London: Leo Cooper, 1972), p. 108.
90. Mary Comyns, Enfield Local History Library.
91. R. A. Weir, IWM 88/49/1.
92. Miss P. M. Donald, IWM 96/19/1.
93. Perry, p. 87.
94. Mary Comyns, Enfield Local History Library.
95. David C. Rubin, ed. *Remembering Our Past: Studies in Autobiographical Memory* (Cambridge: Cambridge University Press, 1996). Psychologists at first posited a theory to explain why adolescent memories were clearer and given more importance by the subject by suggesting the possibility of differential encoding of memories at that age. This theory has been recently modified to include the possibility of non-cognitive factors, such as identity formation.
96. Kops, p. 68.
97. Forbes, p. 53.
98. After having been told by their teacher of their friend's death, they began to fight in the schoolyard at recess. The teacher stopped the

fight, accusing them of having no respect for death and saying 'If Mervyn is killed we'll all know how to behave, won't we?' and he was sent off to be caned. Mervyn Haisman and L. E. Snellgrove, *Dear Merv, Dear Bill* (Llandysul, Wales: Gomer, 1992), p. 124.

99. *Dear Merv, Dear Bill*, p. 163.

Chapter 5: Love in the Blitz

1. Quentin Crisp, *The Naked Civil Servant* (London: Jonathan Cape, 1968), p. 154.

2. For the First World War, see Angela Woollacott, "'Khaki Fever' and its Control: Gender, Class, Age and Sexual Morality on the British Homefront in the First World War" *The Journal of Contemporary History* 29.2 (1994): pp. 325–47 and Philippa Levine, "Battle Colors: Race, Sex and Colonial Soldiery in World War One" *Journal of Women's History* 9.4 (1998): pp. 104–30. For the Second World War, see Sonya Rose, "Girls and G.I.s: Race, Sex, and Diplomacy in Second World War Britain" *The International History Review* 19.1 (1997): pp. 146–60, and Phil Goodman, "Patriotic Femininity" Women's Morals and Men's Morale during the Second World War" *Gender and History* 10.2 (1998): pp. 278–93.

3. George Ryley Scott, *Sex Problems and Dangers in Wartime* (London: T. Werner Laurie, 1940), p. 41. Scott was also the author of histories of cockfighting, torture, prostitution and corporal punishment.

4. The memoir Scott quoted was Helen Zenna Smith's *Not So Quiet on the Western Front: The Stepdaughters of War* (1930). Other First World War memoirs also described the new attitudes to the body that women's experiences at the front and mixing with and caring for soldiers gave them. Vera Brittain, in *Testament of Youth* (1935) wrote that instead of being embarrassed, contact with soldiers' bodies made her think of her fiancé, and thus filled her with compassion. See also Enid Bagnold, *A Diary Without Dates* (1935) and Mary Borden, *The Forbidden Zone* (1930). Men at the front also wrote about a new awareness of their bodies, whether it was their pathetic vulnerability, in Wilfred Owen's poetry, or their robust corporeality, in Isaac Rosenburg's poetry.

5. See Sonya Rose, "Sex, Citizenship, and the Nation in World War II Britain" *American Historical Review* 103.4 (1998): pp. 1147–76 and Uta G. Poiger, "Rock 'n' Roll, Female Sexuality and the Cold War Battle over German Identities" *The Journal of Modern History* 68.3 (1996): pp. 577–616.

6. Lawrence Knopp, "Sexuality and Urban Space: A Framework for Analysis" in *Mapping Desire: Geographies of Sexuality* eds. D. Bell and G. Valentine (London: Routledge, 1995), p. 149.

7. See Matt Houlbrook, *Queer London: Perils and Pleasures in the Sexual Metropolis, 1918–1957* (Chicago: University of Chicago Press, 2005), Marc Stein, *City of Sisterly and Brotherly Loves: Lesbian and Gay Philadelphia 1945–1972* (Chicago: University of Chicago Press, 2000), Nan Almilla Boyd, *Wide Open Town: A History of Queer San Francisco* (Berkeley: University of California Press, 2003), George Chauncey, *Gay New York: Gender, Urban Culture and the Making of the Gay Male World, 1890–1940* (New York: Basic Books, 1994) and Dorothy Rowe, *Representing Berlin: Sexuality and the City in Imperial and Weimar Germany* (Aldershot: Ashgate, 2003).

8. See Alan Berube, *Coming Out Under Fire: The History of Gay Men and Women in World War Two* (New York: The Free Press, 1990) and John Costello, *Love, Sex and War* (London: Pan, 1985), which deals with the United States and Britain.

9. J. Robert Lilly, *La Face Cacheé des GIs: Les Viols Commis* (Paris: Payot, 2003); Maria Höhn, *GIs and Frauleins: The German- American Encounter in 1950s West Germany* (Chapel Hill: The University of North Carolina Press, 2002).

10. Matt Houlbrook, "Towards a Historical Geography of Sexuality" *Journal of Urban History* 27.4 (2001): pp. 497–504.

11. David T. Evans, *Sexual Citizenship* (London: Routledge, 1993), p. 12. See Michel Foucault, *History of Sexuality: An Introduction, Vol. 1* (1976), *The Use of Pleasure: The History of Sexuality, Vol. 2* (1984), *The Care of the Self: History of Sexuality: Vol. 3* (1984).

12. Peter Guerney, "Intersex and Dirty Girls: Mass-Observation and Working Class Sexuality in England in the 1930s" *Journal of the History of Sexuality* 8.2 (1997): pp. 256–90.

13. D 5244, MOA.

14. Mass-Observation, *War Begins at Home* ed. Charles Madge and Tom Harrisson (London: Chatto and Windus, 1940), p. 229.

15. John R. Gillis, *For Better or For Worse: British Marriages 1600 to the Present* (Oxford: Oxford University Press, 1985), p. 261.

16. S. Mogridge, IWM 85/19/1, p. 38.

17. D 5285, MOA.

18. Reynolds, p. 90.

19. D 5728, MOA. While all diarists who wrote for Mass Observation were and are guaranteed anonymity, Olivia Cockett's family has agreed for her diary to be published and her identity to become known. See Olivia

Cockett, *Love and War in London: A Woman's Diary 1939–1942* ed. Robert W. Malcolmson. (Waterloo: University of Waterloo Press, 2005).

20. D 5728, MOA.
21. Mrs M. L. C. Griffiths, IWM 86/5/1.
22. Joan Johnstone, papers, Waltham Forest Archive, 10062.
23. Judith Walkowitz, *Prostitution and Victorian Society* (Cambridge: Cambridge University Press, 1980).
24. See Mark W. Turner, *In a Queer Place*, Chedgzoy, Francis and Pratt, eds. (Aldershot: Ashgate, 2002), pp. 89–109, Frank Mort, "Cityscapes: Consumption, Masculinities and the Mapping of London since 1950" *Urban Studies* 35.5-6 (1998): pp. 889–907, and Gordon Westwood, pseud. of M. G. Schofield, *A Minority: A Report on the Life of the Male Homosexual in Great Britain* (London: Longmans, 1960).
25. Ryley Scott, p. 39.
26. Andrew Sinclair, *War Like A Wasp* (London: Hamish Hamilton, 1989), p. 9. See also Robert Hewison, *Under Siege: Literary Life in London 1939–1945* (London: Weidenfeld and Nicolson, 1977).
27. Joan Wyndham, *Love Lessons* (London: Heinemann, 1985). See also her *Love is Blue* (1986).
28. He was also the husband of the novelist Vita Sackville-West.
29. Lehmann, p. 136.
30. His memoirs described random beatings, harassment by the police, and the disqualification from the army on the grounds of homosexuality: 'Even while I was merely having my eyes tested, I was told, "you've dyed your hair. This is a sign of sexual perversion. Do you know what those words mean?" I replied I did and that I was homosexual. ... Within a minute the entire governing body had gone into a spasm of consternation behind a hessian screen leaving the would-be members of the forces to shiver in their nakedness and to urinate into an assortment of bottles.' Crisp, p. 115.
31. Knopp, p. 151.
32. Carole Vance and the contributors to *Pleasure and Danger* (Boston: Routledge and Kegan, 1984) explored the ways in which pleasure and danger capture women's experience of sexuality. In the case of the Blitz, the physical danger represented by bombs extended to everyone, therefore including men in this sexual dialectic.
33. Quennell, p. 20.
34. Crisp, pp. 155–6.
35. Fitzgibbon, p. 63.
36. Charles Graves, *Off the Record* (London: Hutchinson, 1941), p. 56.

37. Possibly the most popular, and hardest-working, woman in Britain was Miss Olive Kent, the one-legged jitterbugging champion of Swansea, who, after being featured in the *Daily Mirror* in March 1940, had three hundred suitors from the Armed Forces write to her. She kept up correspondence with all of them, using all her free time, and a complex indexing system. *Daily Mirror* October 9, 1940.

38. Lehmann, p. 136.

39. Faviell, p. 27.

40. The Vicar of Preston also showed a more permissive attitude towards soldiers. As a memorial to their RAF officer son who was killed in action, J. E. W. Wallis and his wife opened the vicarage to officers and their wives and sweethearts, where they could recapture the atmosphere of home and enjoy privacy. The *Daily Mirror* article lingered over the details of 'cozy nooks' and shaded lights, and highlighted the vicar's offer to lend his private suite where 'no others will be admitted. Those who ask first will have the study to themselves.' *Daily Mirror* November 27, 1940.

41. Peter Gay, *Schnitzler's Century: The Making of Middle-Class Culture, 1815–1914* (New York: W. W. Norton, 2002).

42. Christopher Breward, *The Hidden Consumer: Masculinities, Fashion and City Life, 1860–1914* (Manchester: Manchester University Press, 1999), Alan Kidd and David Nicholls, eds. *Culture, Gender and Identity: The British Middle Class, 1795–1939* (Manchester: Manchester University Press, 1999) and Frank Mort, *Cultures of Consumption: Masculinities and Social Space in Late Twentieth-Century Britain* (London: Routledge, 1996).

43. Waugh, p. 167.

44. Waugh, pp. 171–3.

45. Waugh, pp. 174–5.

46. In a self-referential tangent, Waugh even contrasted the story of his love affair with Diana to a previously told love story in a previous autobiography.

47. Quennell, p. 36.

48. Quennell, p. 38.

49. Quennell wrote that the mistake was made because Z. was wearing Quennell's dressing gown when he opened the door, though how the curate knew the gown to be Quennell's is a matter of conjecture. Quennell, pp. 38–9.

50. Quennell, p. 36.

51. *Daily Mirror* November 11, 1940.

52. Quennell, pp. 39–40.

53. Nicolson, p. 112.

54. Conway, p. 81.

55. He wrote: 'As I dropped off to sleep through sheer fatigue I wondered how I should show that pound note in the personal accounts I have kept ever since I was a boy at school.' Conway, p. 83.

56. Opportunities to measure marital behavior opened up with the publication in 1830 of the first of the Registrar General's *Annual Reports ... of Births, Deaths, Marriages in England*. For more on declining fertility see Richard Soloway, "The perfect Contraceptive: Eugenics and Birth Control Research in Britain and America in the Interwar Years" *Journal of Contemporary History* 30.4 (1995): pp. 637–64, Wally Seacombe, "Starting to Stop: Working Class Fertility Decline in Britain" *Past and Present* 126 (1990): pp. 151–88.

57. See Leonore Davidoff, Megan Doolittle, Janet Fink and Katherine Holden, *The Family Story* (London: Longman, 1996) Janet Finch and Penny Summerfield, "Social Reconstruction and the Emergence of the Companionate Marriage, 1945–1959" in *Marriage, Domestic Life and Social Change* (London: Routledge, 1991) and Frank Mort, *Dangerous Sexualities: Medico-Moral Politics in England since 1830* (London: Routledge, 1987).

58. Weeks, p. 201.

59. Jane Lewis, "Public Institution and Private Relationship: Marriage and Marriage Guidance, 1920–1968" *Twentieth Century British History* 1990 2: pp. 233–63.

60. Weeks, p. 200.

61. Woodside and Slater, pp. 166–7.

62. See Liz Stanley, "Mass-Observation's 'Little Kinsey' and the British Sex Survey Tradition" in *Sexual Cultures* eds. Jeffrey Weeks and Janet Holland (London: Macmillan, 1996).

63. Angela Woollacott, "'Khaki Fever' and its Control". See also Judy Giles, "'Playing Hard to Get': Working-Class Women, Sexuality and Respectability in Britain 1918–1940" *Women's History Review* 1.2 (1992): pp. 239–55 and Ellen M. Holtzman, "The Pursuit of Married Love: Women's Attitudes towards Sexuality and Marriage in Great Britain 1918–1939" *Journal of Social History* 16.2 (1982): pp. 39–52.

64. Weeks, p. 212.

65. Mary Comyns, diary. Enfield Local History Library. Author's emphasis.

66. George Ryley Scott, *Sex Problems and Dangers in Wartime* (London: T. Werner Laurie, 1940).

67. Hansard, *Parliamentary Debates* Volume 398, 16 March, 1944, p. 418. The question concerned Regulation 33b, the mandatory treatment of VD in the Armed Forces.

68. Paul Jackson, *One of the Boys: Homosexuality in the Military during World War II*, (Kingston, Ont.; Montreal, Que.: McGill-Queen's University Press, 2004).

69. Felicity Ashbee, IWM 97/34/1.

70. For an American perspective on the link between a burgeoning sexuality and national security, see Geoffrey Smith, "Interrogating Security: A Personal Memoir of the Cold War" in *Whose National Security?* (Toronto: Between the Lines, 2000).

71. Woodside and Slater, Chapter VIII.

72. Mrs M. Morris, IWM 80/38/1.

73. Faviell, p. 136.

74. D 5245, MOA.

75. R. B. Outhwaite, *Marriage and Society* (New York: St. Martin's Press, 1982).

76. *Daily Express* November 2, 1940.

77. Gillis, p. 288.

78. Susan Kingsley Kent, in *Making Peace*, (Princeton: Princeton University Press, 1993), identified an interwar ideal of marriage as the means by which to reconcile the sexual antagonism of the First World War though harmonious marital sexuality. The conception of sexuality as a way to reduce antagonism and yet increase the legitimate birthrate was an underpinning of the new interwar marriage therapists and the ideal of 'companionate marriage.'

79. Damonte, p. 3.

80. Damonte, p. 5.

81. Verily Anderson, *Spam Tomorrow* (Bath: Chivers Large Print, 1996), p. 96.

82. Woodside and Slater.

83. Hugh Dalton, *The Second World War Diary of Hugh Dalton* (London: Jonathan Cape, 1986), p. 94.

84. Gordon, pp. 135–6.

85. D 5037, MOA.

86. Nicolson, p. 157–8.

87. D 5342, MOA.

88. Her husband's ill-temper was not all due to the tensions of war, as the following passage reveals: April 24, 1941. 'Offered two bull's eyes to W. H. furious, hates the smell of peppermint or sound of people crunching sweets.'

89. Partridge, p. 9.

90. Nigel Nicolson, one of the sons of the couple, broke the silence in 1973 by publishing a memoir of their relationship entitled *Portrait of a*

Marriage based on their letters and an unpublished autobiography of Sackville-West's. It was received with much hostile criticism, and seen by many critics as tainting the literary and public reputation of both.

91. Vivienne Hall, IWM DSMISC/88 and Con Shelf.
92. D 5278 MOA.
93. D 5342, MOA.
94. D 5342, MOA.
95. D 5342, MOA.
96. Edith Evans, *Rough Diamonds* (Bognor Regis: New Horizons, 1982), pp. 405–8.
97. Weeks, p. 232.
98. From the 1955 Royal Commission on Marriage and Divorce. Quoted in Janet Finch and Penny Summerfield, "Social Reconstruction and Companionate Marriage" in *Marriage, Domestic Life and Social Change* ed. David Clark (London: Routledge, 1991).
99. Laurence Stone, *Road to Divorce* (Oxford: Oxford University Press, 1990), p. 401.
100. Weeks, p. 213. The 1937 Law was also framed as an attempt to end the charades of collusion which meant that well-off couples could hire a woman to be seen in a hotel bed with the husband, thus providing 'proof' of marital infidelity and securing a divorce.
101. See Laurie McNeill, "'Somewhere Along the Line I Lost Myself': Recreating Self in the War Diaries of Natalie Crouter and Elizabeth Vaughn" *Legacy* 19.1 (2001): pp. 98–105, Herman Kruk, *Last Days of the Jerusalem of Lithuania: Chronicles from the Vilna Ghetto and the Camps 1939–1944* (New Haven: Yale University Press, 2002).
102. For more on decoding historical silences see Diana Gittins, "Silences: The Case of a Psychiatric Hospital" in *Narrative and Genre* eds. M. Chamberlain and P. Thompson (London: Routledge, 1998).

Chapter 6: Remembering the Blitz

1. Henry Longhurst, *My Life and Soft Times* (London: Cassell, 1971), p. 141.
2. The others were in 1906 and 1997. Yet in Britain as a whole the voting pattern in 1945 had only shifted 12 per cent, though in London and the Home Counties, North-West Kent and the West Midlands the swing was closer to 20 per cent.
3. R. B. MacCallum, *The British General Election of 1945* (Oxford: Oxford University Press, 1947), p. 270.

4. Hamilton Fyfe, *Britain's Wartime Revolution* (London: Victor Gollancz, 1944), p. 8.

5. See Paul Addison, *The Road to 1945* (London: Jonathan Cape, 1975), Arthur Marwick, "People's War and Top People's Peace? British Society and the Second World War" in *Crisis and Controversy* eds. A. Sked and C. Cook, (London: Macmillan, 1976), Stephen Brooke, *Labour's War* (Oxford: Clarendon, 1992), Corelli Barnett, *The Audit of War* (London: Macmillan, 1986), Henry Pelling, *Britain and the Second World War* (Glasgow: Collins, 1970) and Stephen Fielding, Peter Thompson and Nick Tiratsoo *England Arise! The Labour Party and Popular Politics in 1940s Britain* (Manchester: Manchester University Press, 1995).

6. Geoff Eley, "Finding the People's War: Film, British Collective Memory, and World War Two" *American Historical Review* 106.3 (2001): pp. 818–38.

7. H. Hopkins, *The New Look* (London: Secker and Warburg, 1963), p. 31.

8. Written by Peter Howard of the *Daily Express*, and Michael Foot and Frank Owen of the *Evening Standard* under the pseudonym 'Cato', *Guilty Men* was written during the evacuation from Dunkirk and accused the leaders of Britain between 1931 and 1940 of failing to protect the population by rearming.

9. Adrian Gregory, *The Silence of Memory: Armistice Day 1919–1946* (Oxford: Berg, 1994), p. 163.

10. Gregory, p. 169.

11. Dr S. P. W. Chave, IWM 79/27/1.

12. Sydney Walton, *Letters from the White Cottage* (London: Epworth Press, 1942), pp. 82–3.

13. D 5089, MOA.

14. Gladys Langford diary, Islington Council Central Reference Library Y X079 LAN.

15. Storm Jameson, *Journey from the North* (London: Collins and Harvill Press, 1970), p. 71.

16. S. Mogridge, IWM 85/19/1.

17. D 5039.9, MOA.

18. G. W. King, diary, IWM 85/49/1.

19. Dr S. P. W. Chave, IWM 79/27/1.

20. Fielding, Thompson and Tiratsoo, p. 59.

21. David Cannadine, *Aspects of Aristocracy* (New Haven: Yale University Press, 1994), p. 147.

22. Hodgson, p. 131.

23. Harnsworth King, p. 98.

24. D 5438, MOA.

25. See for example an anecdote told by an East Londoner in the 1972 documentary *The World At War*, in which he recalls seeing an East End woman castigating Churchill, 'We're the ones taking it, not you.'

26. D 5402, MOA.

27. D 5089, MOA.

28. Kops, p. 62.

29. See John Ramsden, "How Winston Churchill became 'The Greatest Living Englishman'" *Contemporary British History* 12.3 (1998): pp. 1–40.

30. Irene Brown, *One Woman's War* (London: Excalibur, 1991), p. 81.

31. Winston Churchill, *Volume 1: The Gathering Storm* (1948), *Volume 2: Their Finest Hour* (1949) and *Volume 3: The Grand Alliance* (1950).

32. This is the view not only of Churchill's official biographer, Martin Gilbert, but also of such recent works as John Lukacs, *Five Days in London: May 1940* (New Haven: Yale University Press, 1999).

33. See Sheila Lawlor, *Churchill and the Politics of War 1940–1941* (Cambridge: Cambridge University Press, 1994) and Paul Addison, *Churchill on the Home Front 1900–1955* (London: Jonathan Cape, 1992).

34. See Lucy Noakes, *War and the British: Gender and National Identity 1939–91* (London: I.B.Tauris, 1998) and Kirkham and Thoms for discussions of these specific sites, and Raphael Samuel *Theatres of Memory: Volumes I and II* (1994 and 1998) and the three volumes of *Patriotisms* (1989) he edited on the commodification of historical sites and the commercialization of history in general.

35. Spender, Civilians in War and After, p. 103.

36. Spender's interpretation of war memorials as a way for individuals and society to forget, rather than to remember are also interesting in the context of the historiography of the memory of the First World War. See Paul Fussell, *The Great War and Modern Memory* (Oxford: Oxford University Press, 1975), Samuel Hynes, *A War Imagined* (New York: Atheneum, 1991), and Jay Winter, *Sites of Memory, Sites of Mourning* (Cambridge: Cambridge University Press, 1995).

37. The Working Class Autobiographies Collection held at Brunel University was compiled by John Burnett, David Vincent and David Mayall in the making of their bibliography.

38. Faviell, p. 252.

39. Dorothy Squires, Brunel University Library, p. 63.

40. May Rainer, Brunel University Library.

41. Waugh, p. 211.

42. See Leigh Gilmore, *Autobiographics: a Feminist Theory of Women's Self-Representation* (Ithaca: Cornell University Press, 1994), who explores 'the

ways in which self-representation is constitutively shaped though proximity to those discourses' definition of authority,' p. 13.

43. Ernestine Cotton, IWM 93/3/1.

44. Partridge, p. 9.

45. Gerry Gregory, "Community Publishing as Self-Education" in *Writing in the Community* ed. David Barton and Roz Ivanic (London: Sage, 1991).

46. Dolly Davey, *A Sense of Adventure* (London: SE1 People's History Project, 1981).

47. See Mary Jo Maynes, "Autobiography and Class Formation in Nineteenth-Century Europe: Methodological Considerations" *Social Science History* 16.3 (1992): pp. 517–37 and Marianne Debouzy, "In Search of Working Class Memory: Some Questions and a Tentative Assessment" *History and Anthropology* 2 (1986): pp. 261–85.

48. The influence of this project continues today. My visit to the Rose Lipman Library in Hackney in 2000 revealed a small reading room crowded with people researching their family histories.

49. E. P. Thompson, "A State of Blackmail" in *Writing by Candlelight* (London: Merlin, 1980), pp. 130–1.

50. Margaret Thatcher, *The Downing Street Years* (London: Harper Collins, 1993), pp. 11–12.

51. Mitchison, pp. 12–13.

52. *Globe and Mail*, Saturday, April 30, 2005, "Europe lay in ruins, with more struggles to come" by Doug Saunders, F1, F8.

53. Tony Judt, "The Past is Another Country: Myth and Memory in Postwar Europe" *Daedalus* 121.4 (1992): pp. 83–118.

54. See C. S. Maier, *The Unmasterable Past: History, Holocaust, and German National Identity* (Cambridge Mass: Harvard University Press, 1998), Jeffrey Herf, *Divided Past: The Nazi Past in the Two Germanys* (Cambridge Mass.: Harvard University Press, 1997), Nancy Wood, *Vectors of Memory: Legacies of Trauma in Postwar Europe* (Oxford: Berg, 1999), Omer Bartov, *Mirrors of Destruction: War, Genocide and National Identity* (Oxford: Oxford University Press, 2000) and Daniel Goldhagen, *Hitler's Willing Executioners: Ordinary Germans and the Holocaust* (New York: Knopf, 1996).

55. Marie Missie Vassiltchikov, *Berlin Diaries, 1940–1945* (New York: Vintage, 1988) and Christabel Bielenberg, *The Past is Myself* (London: Chatto and Windus, 1968). See also Ruth Andreas-Friedrich, *Berlin Underground, 1938–1945* trans. Barrows Mussey (New York: Paragon House, 1995), Ursula von Kardorff, *Diary of a Nightmare: Berlin 1942–1945* trans. Ewan Butler (New York: John Day, 1965).

56. Sybil Bannister, *I Lived under Hitler: An Englishwoman's Story of her life in Wartime Germany* (London: Rockliff, 1957), and Helene Moskiewicz, *Inside the Gestapo: A Jewish Woman's Secret War* (New York: Dell, 1987).

57. Ilse-Margaret Vogel, *Bad Times, Good Friends: A Memoir – Berlin 1945* (Riverdale-on-Hudson, New York: The Sheep Meadow Press, 2001), pp. x–xi.

58. Marianne MacKinnon, *The Naked Years: Growing up in Nazi Germany* (London: Trafalgar Square, 1992) and Henry Metelman, *Hitler Youth: Growing Up in Germany in the 1930s* (New York: Spellmount, 2004).

59. See Henri Rousso, *The Vichy Syndrome* trans. Arthur Goldhammer (Cambridge Mass.: Harvard University Press, 1991) and Kim Munholland, "Wartime France: Remembering Vichy" *French Historical Studies* 18.3 (1994) pp. 801–20.

60. Lucie Aubrac, *Outwitting the Gestapo* trans. Konrad Bieber (Lincoln: University of Nebraska Press, 1993). See also Elisabeth Sevier, *Resistance Fighter: A Teenage Girl in World War Two France* (New York: Sunflower University Press, 1998).

61. I have only read European memoirs that have been translated into English, but have failed to find scholarly references to un-translated European war diaries memoirs. This would suggest that Britain and America are the primary market for such memoirs, a market which would strictly define the limits of the genre.

62. Judt, p. 101.

63. Catherine Merridale, *Nights of Stone*.

64. See Saul Friedlander, *Probing the Limits of Representation: Nazism and the "Final Solution"* (Cambridge, Mass.: Harvard University Press, 1992), Saul Friedlander, "Trauma, Transference and 'Working Through' in Writing the History of the Shoah" *History and Memory* 7.1 (1992): pp. 34–59, Cathy Caruth, *Unclaimed Experience: Trauma, Narrative and History* (Baltimore: The John Hopkins University Press, 1996), and James E. Young, "Between History and Memory: the Uncanny Voices of Historian and Survivor" *History and Memory* 9.1-2 (1997): pp. 47–58.

65. See Anne Frank, *The Diary of a Young Girl* (New York: Anchor, 1995), Alan Adelson, ed. *The Diary of David Sierakowiak: Five Notebooks from the Lodz Ghetto* (New York: Oxford University Press, 1996), Raul Hilberg, ed. *The Warsaw Diary of Adam Czerniakow* (New York: Stein and Day, 1982), Chaim Aron Kaplan, *Scroll of Agony: The Warsaw Diary of Chaim Kaplan* ed. Israel Gutman trans. Abraham I. Katsh (Bloomington: Indiana University Press, 1999) and the postwar memoirs of David Kahane, *Lvov Ghetto Diary* (Amherst: University of Massachusetts Press, 1990) and Janina Bauman, *Winter in the Morning:*

A Young Girl's Life in the Warsaw Ghetto and Beyond (London: Little, Brown, 1997).

66. See for example Hedi Fried, *The Road to Auschwitz: Fragments of a Life* ed. Michael Meyer, (University of Nebraska Press, 1996).

67. Michael Bernard-Donals, "History and Disaster: Witness, Trauma and the Problem of Writing the Holocaust. *Clio* 30.2 (2001): pp. 143–68. For recent scholarly analyses of Anne Frank and her diary in the context of debates about trauma see Victoria Stewart, "Anne Frank and the Uncanny" *Paragraph* 24.1 (2001): pp. 99–113 and Marouf Hasian Jr., "Anne Frank, Bergen-Belsen and the Polysemic Nature of Holocaust Memories" *Rhetoric and Public Affairs* 4.3 (2001): pp. 349–74.

68. Dominick LaCapra, *History and Memory after Auschwitz* (Ithaca: Cornell University Press, 1998).

69. Ritchie Calder, *Carry On London*, p. 113.

70. *Churchill Speaks* ed. Robert Rhode James (London: Chelsea House, 1980), pp. 863–4.

BIBLIOGRAPHY

Primary Sources

Newspapers

Daily Express
Daily Mirror
The Illustrated London News
The Jewish Chronicle
The London Times
The People
The Sunday Express
The Globe and Mail (Canada)

Pamphlets, Plans and Articles

Abercrombie, Patrick. *Greater London Plan 1944*. London: His Majesty's Stationary Office, 1945.

A People at War. New York: British Information Services, 1943.

Britain and The Common Pool. New York: British Information Services, 1944.

Britain Looks Ahead: British Official Statements Vol. III. New York: British Information Services, 1943.

Britain Plans: British Official Statements 1941–1942. New York: British Information Services, 1942.

Douie, Vera. *Daughters of Britain*. Oxford: Vincent-Baxter Press, 1949.

Fire over London 1940–1941. London: Hutchinson, 1941, reprinted IWM Historical Pamphlet Series, no. 3.

Five Years of War. New York: British Information Services, 1944.

Front Line: The Story of Civil Defence 1940–1941. London: Ministry of Information for Ministry of Home Security, 1942.

Glover, C. W. *Civil Defence*. London: Chapman and Hall, 1938.

Glover, Edward. "Notes on the Psychological Effects of War Conditions on the Civilian Population." *International Journal of Psycho-Analysis* 22 (1941): pp. 132–46.

Goldsmith, Margaret. *Women at War*. London: Lindsey Drummond, 1943.

Haldane, J. B. S. *ARP*. London: Victor Gollancz, 1938.

Impresario, pseud. *The Market Square: The Story of the Ration Book 1940–1944*. 1944, reprinted IWM Historical Pamphlet Series, no. 6.

John Britain. New York: British Information Services, 1944.

Jones, Sydney R. *London Triumphant*. London: Studio Publications, 1942.

Korn, A. and F. Samuely. "A Master Plan for London." *Architectural Review* 91 (1942): pp. 143–50.

Montagu, Ivor. *The Traitor Class*. London: Lawrence and Wishart, 1940.

Muirhead, J. Thorburn. *Air Attack on Cities*. London: George Allen & Unwin, 1938.

National Federation of Women's Institutes. *Town Children through Country Eyes*. 1940.

The National Food Survey Committee. *The Urban Working-Class Household Diet 1940–1949*. London: His Majesty's Stationary Office, 1951.

Nicolson, Harold. *Why Britain is at War*. Middlesex: Penguin Special, 1939.

Oxford University Institute of Statistics. *Studies in War Economics*. Oxford: Basil Blackwell, 1947.

Padley, Richard and Margaret Cole. *Evacuation Survey*. London: Routledge, 1940.

Peace Aims: British Official Statements. New York: British Information Services, 1941.

Price, John. *British Trade Unions and the War.* London: Ministry of Information, 1945.

Rasmussen, Steen Eiler. *London: The Unique City.* 1937, reprinted Cambridge: MIT Press, 1967.

Scott, George Ryley. *Sex Problems and Dangers in Wartime.* London: T. Werner Laurie, 1940.

Strachey, Mrs. *Borrowed Children: A Popular Account of Some Evacuation Problems and Their Remedies.* New York: The Commonwealth Fund, 1940.

The Battle of Britain. London: His Majesty's Stationer's Office, 1941.

The First Four Years. New York: British Information Services, 1943.

The Improvements and Town Planning Committee of the Common Council of the City of London. *Reconstruction in the City of London.* London: Guildhall, 1944.

The War Seen From Britain 1939–1945. London: Ministry of Information, 1945.

Unwin, Stanley. *Publishing in Peace and War.* London: George Allen Unwin, 1944.

Wauters, Arthur. *Eve in Overalls.* London, 1944. Reprinted IWM Dept. of Printed Documents, 1994.

Journalism and Personal Narratives Published During the War

Timoleon, pseud. *King's Cross to Waverley.* London: William Hodge, 1944.

Beaton, Cecil. *History Under Fire: 52 Photographs of Air Raid Damage to London Buildings 1940–1941.* London: Batsford, 1941.

—— *Time Exposure.* London: Batsford, 1941.

Bell, Reginald. *The Bull's Eye.* London: Cassell, 1943.

Brittain, Vera. *England's Hour.* Toronto: Macmillan, 1941.

Butler, A. S. G. *Recording Ruin.* London: Constable, 1942.

Calder, Ritchie. *Carry On London.* London: English Universities Press, 1941.

—— *Lesson of London.* London: Secker and Warburg, 1941.

Carter, Ernestine, ed. *Grim Glory: Pictures of Britain Under Fire*. London: Scribners, 1941.

Charlton, L. E. O. *War Over England*. London: Longmans, 1936.

Farson, Negley. *Bomber's Moon*. New York: Harcourt & Brace, 1941.

Fyfe, Hamilton. *Britain's Wartime Revolution*. London: Victor Gollancz, 1944.

Graves, Charles. *Off the Record*. London: Hutchinson, 1941.

—— *Londoner's Life*. London: Hutchinson, 1942.

—— *Great Days*. London: Hutchinson, 1944.

Hodson, James Lansdale. *Through the Dark Night*. London: Victor Gollancz, 1941.

—— *Before Daybreak*. London: Victor Gollancz, 1941

—— *Towards the Morning*. London: Victor Gollancz, 1941.

Kennedy, Margaret. *Where Stands a Winged Sentry*. New Haven: Yale University Press, 1941.

Lewey, Frank. *Cockney Campaign*. London: Stanley Paul, 1948.

MacDonagh, Michael. *In London During the Great War*. London: Eyre and Spottiswoode, 1935.

Mass-Observation. *War Begins at Home*. ed. Charles Madge and Tom Harrisson, London: Chatto and Windus, 1940.

Marchant, Hilde. *Women and Children Last*. London: Victor Gollancz, 1941.

Morgan, Charles. *The House of Macmillan*. London: Macmillan, 1943.

Murrow, Edward. *This is London*. New York: Simon and Shuster, 1941.

Nevins, Allan. *This is England Today*. New York: Scribner and Sons, 1941.

Paneth, Marie. *Branch Street*. London: George Allen & Unwin, 1943.

Priestley, J. B. *Postscripts*. London: William Heinemann, 1940.

Rosman, Alice Grant. *Nine Lives: A Cat of London in Peace and in War*. New York: Putnam, 1941.

Reynolds, Quentin. *A London Diary*. New York: Faber and Faber, 1941.

Robbins, Gordon. *A Fleet Street Blitzkrieg Diary*. London: Ernest Benn, 1944.

Robertson, Ben. *I Saw England.* New York: Knopf, 1941.

Royde-Smith, Naomi. *Outside Information.* London: Macmillan, 1941.

Spender, Stephen. *Citizens in War and After.* London: Harrap, 1945.

Strange, William. *Into The Blitz.* Toronto: Macmillan, 1941.

Weymouth, Anthony. *Plague Year.* London: George G. Harrap, 1942.

────── *A Psychologist's War-time Diary.* London: Longmans, 1940.

Wilson, Rev. H. A. *Death Over Haggerston.* London: Mowbray, 1941.

Woon, Basil. *Hell Came to London.* London: Peter Davies, 1941.

Anonymous Diaries

"An Everyday War": An Anonymous Diary Of a Chelsea Resident Written During the War. Kensington Local Studies Library 940.548.EVE AR/RS.

War Diary of the English Electrical Company. London: LTA Robinson, 1945.

Correspondence

While London Burns: Letters Written to America: July 1940–June 1941. London: Constable, 1942.

Allan, Mea, letters to friend May. IWM 95/8/7.

Base, Edith. *Dearest Phylabe.* Niwot: University Press of Colorado, 1996.

Barnard, Mrs E. P., letter to Nellie. IWM 92/9/1.

Bogush, L/Bdr Mark and wife Lily, March, 1941. Hackney Archives M4586-4591.

Bosanquet, Miss Nancy, letters to parents. IWM 81/33/1.

Bowman, Mrs W. C. letters from England to her in U.S. IWM 85/45/1.

Brockway, Sylvia, ed. *Respectfully Yours, Annie.* New York, E. P. Dutton, 1942.

Day-Lewis, T., ed. *Last Letters Home.* London: Pan Books, 1995.

Eccles, Sybil and David. *By Safe Hands: Letters of Sybil and David Eccles: 1939–1942.* London: Bodley Head, 1983.

Elkus, Mrs Elizabeth, letters from parents, friends and relatives. IWM Con Shelf.

Fyfe, Miss G. S., letters to adopted son. IWM 86/64/3.

Granger, I. H., letters to Harrison Brown. IWM 94/45/2 and Con. Shelf.

Green, Mrs Yvonne, letters to mother. IWM 99/9/1.

Grenfell, Joyce. *Darling Ma: Letters to her Mother 1932–1944*. London: Coronet, 1988.

Griffiths, Mrs M. L. C., letters to daughter. IWM 86/5/1.

Grigg, Alice, condolence letter to Mrs Simmonds. Bexley Local History Library PE/MIS/21.

Haisman, Mervyn and L. E. Snellgrove. *Dear Merv, Dear Bill*. Wales: Gomer, 1992.

Hodgson, Vere, letters and diary. Kensington Local Studies Library, MS 22466-22472.

Jesse, F. Tennyson and H. M. Harwood, eds. *While London Burns*. London: Constable & Co. 1942.

Johnstone, Joan, papers. London Borough of Waltham Forest Archive, Deposit #10062

Loundes, Susan, ed. *Diary and Letters of Marie Belloc Loundes 1911–1947*. London: Chatto and Windus, 1971.

Macaulay, Rose. *Letters to a Sister*. London: Collins, 1964.

MacLean, Dr Charles Forbes, letters to daughter. IWM 94/42/1.

Graham, J. A. Maxtone. *Women of Britain: Letters from England*. New York: Harcourt, Brace & Co. 1941.

McMullan, Mrs Gertrude, correspondence with Miss H. Buckenham. Kensington Local Studies Library, MS 36148-36247.

Mawson, Michael ed. *Eyewitness in the Crimea: The Crimean War Letters (1854–1856) of Lt. Col. George Frederick Dallas*. London: Greenhill, 2001.

Miles, Alan, letters to parents from evacuated child. Lewisham Local History Library A 97/23.

Walton, Sydney. *From the White Cottage*. London: Epworth Press, 1942.

Weir, R. A., letter from a child in a shelter. IWM 88/49/1.

Wells, Maureen. *Entertaining Eric: Letters from Surrey 1941–1944*. London: Imperial War Museum, 1988.

Women's Diaries

Bawtree, Miss V., diary. IWM 91/5/1.

Bloom, Ursula. *War Isn't Wonderful.* London: Hutchinson, 1961.

Bloomfield, Mrs Mary, diary. IWM 77/177/1.

Bowen, Elizabeth. "London 1940." In *Collected Impressions.* London: Longmans, 1950.

Brittain, Vera. *Wartime Chronicle: Diary 1939–1945.* London: Victor Gollancz, 1989.

Carpenter, Mrs L. M., diary. IWM 92/49/1.

Carver, Miss Nellie Violet, diary. IWM 90/16/1.

Cox, Mrs Gladwys, diary. IWM 86/46/1

Crawley, Miss K. M., diaries and correspondence with parents. IWM 94/29/1 and Con Shelf.

Desch, Miss R. C., diary. IWM 89/19/1

Panter-Downes, Mollie. *London War Notes 1939–1945.* New York: Farrar, Straus and Giroux, 1971.

Downs, Mrs A., diary. Bexley Local History Library PE/Bre/1-5.

Eustace, Mrs C., diary with clippings IWM 83/27/1.

Ford, Erica Lesley, diaries Ealing Local History Library.

Grimshaw, Edith, diary. London Borough of Newham Archive, Jun 12/1940– Jan 2/41.

Hall, Miss Vivienne, diary. IWM DS/MISC/88 and Con Shelf.

Hodgson, Vere. *Few Eggs and No Oranges: How Unimportant People lived through the War Years 1940–1945.* London: Dennis Dobson, 1976.

Jameson, Storm. *The Diary of Mary Hervey Russell.* London: Macmillan, 1945.

Jellis, Irene, diary. Bexley Local History Library, c. 521687.

Johnson, Miss Daisy, diary. IWM 89/14/1.

Langford, Gladys, diaries. Islington Council Central Reference Library Y XO79 LAN.

Last, Nella. *Nella Last's War.* ed. Richard Broad and Suzie Fleming. Bristol: Falling Wall Press, 1981.

Lawrence, Marie, diary. London Borough of Richmond Local Studies Archive.

Millin, Sarah Gertrude. *Fire Out of Heaven*. London: Faber and Faber, 1947.

Mitchison, Naomi. *Among You Taking Notes*. ed. Dorothy Sheridan, Oxford: Oxford University Press, 1986.

Morris, Mrs M., diary. IWM 80/38/1.

Nixon, Barbara. *Raiders Overhead: The Record of a London Warden*. London: Lindsey Drummond, 1943.

Oakman, Josephine May, ARP logs and diary. IWM 91/20/1.

Partridge, Frances. *A Pacifist's War*. London: Hogarth Press, 1978.

Ryle, Peggy. *Missing in Action, May–September 1944*. London: WH Allen, 1979.

Shepperd, Mrs Anne (Queenie), diary. IWM 95/13/1.

Speed, Miss Florence M., diary. IWM 86/45/1.

Stevenson, Mrs M. E., diary and correspondence. IWM 86/56/1.

Thomas, Miss G. T., diary. IWM 90/30/1.

Thompson, Miss Joan, diary. IWM 90/16/1.

Tyler, Violet, diary. Lewisham Local Studies Library A 98/99.

Uttin, Rose Eleanor, diary. IWM 88/50/1.

Veazy, Mrs Joan, diary. IWM PP/MCR/199.

Warner, Phyllis, diary. IWM 95/14/1.

Weeks, Mrs S., account of first German air raid over London. IWM 88/49/1.

Weiner, Miss Joyce, diary. IWM 77/176/1.

Woolf, Virginia. *The Diary of Virginia Woolf Vol. 5: 1936–1941*. ed. Anne Olivier Bell. New York: Harvest, 1984.

Wyndham, Joan. *Love Lessons*. London: Heinemann, 1985.

—— *Love is Blue*. London: Heinemann, 1986.

Diarist [D] 5240, Mass Observation Archive [MOA].

D 5244, MOA.

D 5245, MOA.

D 5240, MOA.

D 5247, MOA.

D 5269, MOA.

D 5277, MOA.

D 5278, MOA.

D 5280, MOA.

D 5285, MOA.

D 5305, MOA.

D 5342, MOA.

D 5349, MOA.

D 5388, MOA.

D 5401, MOA.

D 5402, MOA.

D 5422, MOA.

D 5425, MOA.

D 5427, MOA.

D 5438, MOA.

D 5250, MOA.

Women's Autobiographies

Abel, Florence. "A Cockney Looks Back." Waltham Forest Archive, W. 60.01.

Anderson, Verily. *Spam Tomorrow*. Bath: Chivers Large Print, 1996.

Ashbee, Felicity, memoir. IWM 97/34/1.

Astley, Joan Bright. *The Inner Circle: A View of War from the Top*. Boston: Little, Brown & Co, 1960.

Bell, Mrs P., memoir. IWM 86/4/1

Blewitt, Mrs J. Cox, memoir. IWM PP/MCR/360.

Broadway, Mrs H., memoir. IWM 95/13/1.

Burkin, Henrietta, autobiography. Brunel University Library.

Byers, Mrs Irene, memoir. IWM 88/10/1.

Cooper, Diana. *Trumpets from the Steep*. London: Soho Square, 1960.

Churchill, Sarah. *A Thread in the Tapestry*. London: Andre Deustch, 1967.

Cotton, Mrs Ernestine Hunt, memoir, IWM 93/3/1.

Damonte, Mrs Phyllis M, memoir. IWM 95/32/1.

Davey, Dolly. *A Sense of Adventure*. London: SE1 People's History Project, 1981

Dugget, Irene F., memoir. Waltham Forest Archive 21627.

Edwards, Hazel. *War Among the Ruins*. Oxford: Phoenix Press, 1996.

Evans, Edith. *Rough Diamonds*. Bognor Regis: New Horizons, 1982.

Evans, Rosemary, memoir. Waltham Forest Archive, W. 60 EVA.

Faviell, Frances. *A Chelsea Concerto*. London: Cassell, 1959.

Fitzgibbon, Theodora. *With Love*, London: Century, 1982.

Foakes, Grace. *My Life with Reuben*. London: Shepeard and Walwyn, 1975.

Freedman, Mrs Rosa, memoir. IWM P360.

Garrett, Kay, autobiographical letter. Brunel University Library.

Gordon, Jane. *Married to Charles*. London: Heinemann, 1950.

Haldane, Charlotte. *Truth Will Out*. London: George Weidenfeld and Nicolson, 1949.

Henrey, Mrs Robert. *The Siege of London*. London: Dent, 1946.

—— *London*. London: Dent, 1948.

Hughes, Marian. *No Cake, No Jam*. Leicester: Ulverscraft, 1994.

Jameson, Storm. *Journey from the North*. London: Collins and Harvill Press, 1970.

Knowlden, Patricia. *The Long Alert 1937–1945*. Kent: A.J. Bishop, 1988.

Lowe, Rose. *Daddy Burtt's for Dinner: Growing up in Hoxton Between the Wars*. London: Centreprise Publishing Project, 1981.

Pierce, Doris V. *Memories of the Civilian's War 1939–1945*. London: Temple, 1996.

Rainer, May. "Emma's Daughter." unpublished memoir. Brunel University Library.

Roberts, Florrie. *The Ups and Downs of Florrie Roberts*. London: Peckham Publishing Project, 1980.

Rogers, Joan A. "Memories of Homerton Recalled." *Cockney Ancestor*. 62 (1994): pp. 50–2.

Roose, Miss B. L., "Got Any Gum Chum?" IWM 89/14/1

Squires, Dorothy, autobiography. Brunel University Library.

Steedman, Carolyn. *Landscape for a Good Woman*. London: Virago, 1986.

Storey, Joyce. *Joyce's War*. Oxford: Isis, 1990.

Stark, Freya. *Dust in the Lion's Paw*. London: John Murray, 1961.

Valery, Anne. *Talking about the War*. London: Michael Joseph, 1991.

Thatcher, Margaret. *The Downing Street Years*. London: HarperCollins, 1993.

Watson, Elizabeth. *Don't Wait for It: Impressions of War*, 1941. Reprinted IWM Dept. of Printed Documents, 1994.

Whiteing, Eileen. *Some Sunny Day*. London: Sutton Libraries, 1983.

Wild, Mrs S. P., memoir. IWM 92/22/1.

Willmott, Phyllis. *Coming of Age in Wartime*. London: Peter Owen, 1988.

Collections

Pullen, Doris, ed. *Wartime Memories*. Devon: Merlin Books, 1986.

Schimanski, Stefan and Henry Treece, eds. *Leaves in the Storm*. London: Lindsay Drummond, 1947.

Men's Diaries

Agate, James. *A Shorter Ego*. London: Harrap, 1946.

Artiss, P. H., diary. IWM PP/MCR/230.

Backhouse, F., diary. IWM 90/16/1.

Baker, Richard Brown. *The Year of the Buzz Bomb: A London Diary 1944*. New York: Exposition Press, 1952.

Beaton, Cecil. *The Years Between: Diaries 1939–1944*. London: Weidenfeld and Nicolson, 1965.

Brown, T. E., Hackney Archive, D/F/BRO/1-7/ARP.

Beardsmore, George. *Civilians at War: Journals, 1938–1946*. London: John Murray, 1984.

Blackerby, Robert J., City of Westminster Archives Centre # 1489.

Cadogan, Alexander. *The Diaries of Sir Alexander Cadogan, 1938–1945*. ed. David Dilks. New York: G.P. Putnam's Sons, 1972.

Champion, S. G., diary. IWM 77/178/1.

Channon, Henry. *Chips: The Diaries of Sir Henry Channon*. ed. Robert Rhode James. London: Weidenfeld and Nicolson, 1967.

Chave, Dr Sidney Percy William, diary. IWM 79/27/1.

Colville, John. *The Fringes of Power*. London: Hodder and Stoughton, 1988.

Coward, Noel. *The Noel Coward Diaries*. eds, G. Payne and S. Morley. London: Weidenfeld & Nicolson, 1982.

Dalton, Hugh. *The Second World War Diary of Hugh Dalton 1940–1945*. ed. Ben Pimlott. London: Jonathon Cape, 1986.

Hurd, F. W., diary. IWM 80/30/1.

Gander, L. Marsland, diary. IWM 78/62/1.

Garman, B., ARP logbook. IWM 92/2/1.

Goodlet, Alan, diaries. Ealing Local History Library.

Jarvis, Dr H. C. M., diary. IWM 89/16/2.

Kerr, Sir Hamilton. "Pages from a War-Time Diary." *The National and English Review*. 151 (1958): pp. 105–8.

King, G. W., diary. IWM 85/49/1.

King, Cecil Harnsworth. *With Malice Towards None: A War Diary*. ed. W. Armstrong. London: Sidgwick and Jackson, 1970.

Lees-Milne, James. *Ancestral Voices Prophesying Peace: Diaries 1942– 1945*. London: John Murray, 1995.

Mohan, Rev. and Mrs B. P., IWM 96/49/1.

Nicolson, Harold. *Diaries*. ed. Nigel Nicolson. London: Collins, 1967.

Orwell, George. *The Complete Works Volume Twelve: A Patriot after All 1940–1941*. ed. Peter Davison. London: Secker and Warburg, 1998.

Regan,W. B., diary and account of an air raid by his wife. IWM 88/10/1 and Con Shelf.

Ridgway, Roy, diary. IWM 67/347/1.

Rumens, Canon J. H., diary. IWM 87/8/1.

Waugh, Evelyn. *The Diaries of Evelyn Waugh*. ed. Michael Davies. London: Weidenfeld and Nicolson, 1976.

Williamson, A. F., diary. IWM 95/4/1.

Woodcock, S. M. S., diary. IWM 87/36/1.

Wrigley, W. R., diary. IWM 76/10/1.

Diarist [D] 5003 Mass Observation Archive [MOA].

D 5032, MOA.

D 5037, MOA.

D 5039.3, MOA.

D 5039.9, MOA.

D 5061.1, MOA.

D 5089, MOA.

D 5098, MOA.

D 5103, MOA.

D 5129, MOA.

D 5130, MOA.

D 5132, MOA.

D 5136, MOA.

D 5163, MOA.

D 5193.1, MOA.

Men's Autobiographies

Bentley, Nicolas. *A Version of the Truth*. London: Andre Deustch, 1960.

Blake, Lewis. *Bromley in the Front Line*. Published by author, 1980.

Boothby, Robert. *I Fight to Live*. London: Victor Gollancz, 1947.

Boorman, John. *Hope and Glory*. London: Faber and Faber, 1987.

Churchill, Winston. *Memoirs of the Second World War*, abridged edn. Cambridge: Riverside Press, 1959.

—— *Memoirs: Volume 1: The Gathering Storm*. Boston: Houghton Mifflin, 1948.

—— *Memoirs: Volume 2: Their Finest Hour*. Boston: Houghton Mifflin, 1949.

—— *Memoirs: Volume 3: The Grand Alliance*. Boston: Houghton Mifflin, 1950.

Compton, Denis. *Playing for England*. London: Sampson Low, Marston & Co., 1948.

Conway, Peter. *Living Tapestry*. London: Staples, 1946.

Coward, Noel. *The Autobiography of Noel Coward*. ed. S. Morley. London: Methuen, 1986.

Cohen, Max. *What Nobody told the Foreman*. London: Butler and Tanner, 1953.

Cooper, Alfred. *Old Men Forget*. New York: Carroll and Graf Publishers, 1988.

Crisp, Quentin. *The Naked Civil Servant*. London: Jonathan Cape, 1968.

Dean, Basil. *The Theatre at War.* London: Harrap, 1956.

Delmer, Sefton. *Black Boomerang.* New York: Viking Press, 1962.

Demarne, Cyril. *The London Blitz: A Fireman's Tale.* London: Newham Parents' Centre Publishing, 1980.

Dickinson, Patric. *The Good Minute.* London: Victor Gollancz, 1965.

Gallacher, William. *The Last Memoirs of William Gallacher.* London: Lawrence & Wishart, 1966.

—— *The Rolling of the Thunder.* London: Lawrence and Wishart, 1948.

Gorham, Maurice. *Sound and Fury.* London: Percival Marshall, 1948.

Gould, Sir Ronald. *Chalk up the Memory.* Birmingham: George Philip Alexander, 1976.

Haines, Geoffrey. "Notes and Recollections: Vol. 7: 1938–1943." Wandsworth Local History Library.

Hamburger, Michael. *Strings of Beginnings.* London: Skoob, 1973.

Heard, P. A. *An Octogenarian's Memoirs.* Devon: Arthur H. Stockwell, 1974.

Hill, Archie. *Cage of Shadows.* London: Hutchinson, 1977.

Hyde, Douglas. *I Believed.* London: The Reprint Society, 1952.

Lancaster, Osbert. *All Done from Memory.* Boston: Houghton Mifflin, 1953.

Lehmann, John. *I Am my Brother.* London: Longmans, 1960.

Levinson, Maurice. *The Trouble with Yesterday.* London: Peter Davies, 1946.

Lockart, R. H. Bruce. *Comes the Reckoning.* London: Putnam, 1947.

Longhurst, Henry. *My Life and Soft Times.* London: Cassell, 1971.

Macmillan, Harold. *The Blast of War.* London: Macmillan, 1967.

Maclaren-Ross, J. *Memoirs of the Forties.* London: Allan Ross, 1965.

Middlebrook, Wilfred. "Trumpet Voluntary," unpublished memoir, Brunel University Library.

Mogridge, S., memoir written in 1942. IWM 85/19/1.

Pickles, Wilfred. *Between You and Me.* London: Werner Laurie, 1949.

Piratin, Phil. *Our Flag Stays Red.* London: Thames Publications, London, 1948.

Quennell, Peter. *The Wanton Chase.* London: Collins, 1980.

Raymond, Ernest. *Please You Draw Near.* London: Cassell, 1969.

Scott, Sir Harold. *Your Obedient Servant.* London: Andre Deustch, 1959.

Shakespeare, Sir Geoffrey. *Let Candles Be Brought In.* London: Macdonald, 1949.

Spender, Stephen. *World Within World.* New York: Modern Library 1951, reprinted 2001.

Thomas, Cameron. "Remembering the London Blitz." *National Geographic* July 1991: pp. 60–77.

Thompson, E. P. *Writing by Candlelight.* London: Merlin, 1980.

Turner, E. W. "Some Memories of a Walthamstow Teenager". Waltham Forest Archive 10097.

Waugh, Alec. *Best Wine Last.* London: W.H. Allen, 1978.

Wolveridge, Jim. *Ain't it Grand (or this was Stepney).* London: Journeyman Press, 1981.

Wyatt, Woodrow. *Confessions of an Optimist.* London: Collins, 1985.

Children's Diaries

Brownbill, C., diary. IWM 88/49/1.

Comyns, Mary, diary. Enfield Local History Library.

Dellar, G., diary. IWM P321.

Donald, Miss P. M., diary. IWM 89/14/1.

Perry, Colin. *Boy in the Blitz.* London: Leo Cooper, 1972.

Smith, Miss Hilda Joyce, diary. IWM 96/19/1.

Children's Autobiographies

Avery Valerie. *London Morning.* London: William Kimber, London 1964.

Baker, Mrs May, memoir. IWM 96/26/1.

Breed, Bryan. *I Know a Rotten Place.* London: Arlington Books, 1975.

Brown, Irene. *One Woman's War.* London: Excalibur, 1991.

Dorking, Edward A., memoir. IWM 97/28/1.

Faber, Mrs H., memoir. IWM 96/26/1.

Forbes, Bryan. *Notes for a Life.* London: Collins, 1974.

Ford, Dennis, memoir. IWM 97/24/1.

Hill, R. W., memoir. IWM 97/24/1.

Hobbs, May. *Born to Struggle*. London, Quartet, 1973.

Johnson, B. S., ed. *The Evacuees*. London: Victor Gollancz, 1968.

Kops, Bernard. *The World is a Wedding*. London: McKibbon & Kee, 1963.

Lambert, Derek. *The Sheltered Days*. London: Andre Deutsch, 1965.

Major-Ball, Terry. *Major Major*. London: Duckworth, 1994.

Massey, Victoria. *One Child's War*. London: BBC, 1983.

Pluckwell, George. *Children of the War*. London: Regency Press, 1966.

Pooley, Richard. *The Evacuee*. Hull: Anglo American Publicity Services, 1972.

Reynolds, M. J., memoir. IWM 96/18/1.

Russell, Peter. *Butler Royal*. London: Hutchinson, 1982.

Siddal, Margaret. *Safe as Houses*. Devon: Devonshire House, 1995.

Sweetland, J. R., memoir. IWM 97/21/1.

Walters, Harry. *The Street*. London: Centreprise Publishing Project, 1975.

Westall, Robert, ed. *Children of the Blitz*. Harmondsworth: Viking, 1985.

Wheal, Donald. *World's End: A Memoir of a Blitz Childhood*. London: Century, 2005.

European Diaries and Memoirs

Andreas-Friedrich, Ruth. *Berlin Underground, 1938–1945*. trans. Barrows Mussey. New York: Paragon House, 1995.

Aubrac, Lucie. *Outwitting the Gestapo*. trans. Konrad Bieber. Lincoln: University of Nebraska Press,1993.

Bannister, Sybil. *I Lived under Hitler: An Englishwoman's Story of her Life in Wartime Germany*. London: Rockliff, 1957.

Bauman, Janina. *Winter in the Morning: A Young Girl's Life in the Warsaw Ghetto and Beyond*. London: Little Brown, 1997.

Bielenberg, Christabel. *The Past is Myself*. London: Chatto and Windus, 1968.

Czerniakow, Adam. *The Warsaw Diary of Adam Czerniakow*. ed. Raul Hilberg. New York: Stein and Day, 1982.

Frank, Anne. *The Diary of a Young Girl*. New York: Anchor, 1995.

Fried, Hedi. *The Road to Auschwitz: Fragments of a Life.* ed. Michael Meyer. Lincoln: University of Nebraska Press, 1996.

Kahane, David. *Lvov Ghetto Diary.* Amherst: University of Massachusetts Press, 1990.

Kaplan, Chaim Aron. *Scroll of Agony: The Warsaw Diary of Chaim Kaplan.* ed. Israel Gutman. trans. Abraham I. Katsh. Bloomington: Indiana University Press, 1999.

von Kardorff, Ursula. *Diary of a Nightmare: Berlin 1942–1945.* trans. Ewan Butler. New York: John Day, 1965.

MacKinnon, Marianne. *The Naked Years: Growing up in Nazi Germany.* London: Trafalgar Square, 1992.

Metelman, Henry. *Hitler Youth: Growing Up in Germany in the 1930s.* New York: Spellmount, 2004.

Moskiewicz, Helene. *Inside the Gestapo: A Jewish Woman's Secret War.* New York: Dell, 1987.

Sevier, Elisabeth. *Resistance Fighter: A Teenage Girl in World War Two France.* New York: Sunflower University Press, 1998

Sierakowiak, David. *The Diary of David Sierakowiak: Five Notebooks from the Lodz Ghetto.* ed. Alan Adelson. New York: Oxford University Press, 1996.

Vassiltchikov, Marie Missie. *Berlin Diaries: 1940–1945.* New York: Vintage, 1988.

Vogel, Ilse-Margaret. *Bad Times, Good Friends: A Memoir – Berlin 1945.* Riverdale-on-Hudson, New York: The Sheep Meadow Press, 2001.

Secondary Sources

Addison, Paul. *Churchill on the Home Front 1900–1955.* London: Jonathan Cape 1992.

—— *The Road to 1945.* London: Jonathan Cape, 1975.

Assmann, Jan. "Collective Memory and Cultural Identity." *New German Critique* 65 (1995): pp. 125–33.

Bailey, Peter. *Popular Culture and Performance in the Victorian City.* Cambridge: Cambridge University Press, 1999.

Barnett, Corelli. *The Audit of War.* London: Macmillan, 1986.

Barton, David and Roz Ivanic, eds. *Writing in the Community*. London: Sage, 1991.

Bartov, Omer. *Mirrors of Destruction: War, Genocide and National Identity*. Oxford: Oxford University Press, 2000.

Baudelaire, Charles. "The Painter of Modern Life," (1863) in *Baudelaire: Selected Writings on Art and Literature*. trans. P. E. Charvet. New York: Viking 1972.

Beaven, B. and D. Thoms. "The Blitz and Civilian Morale in Three Northern Cities 1940–1942." *Northern History* 32 (1996): pp. 195–203.

Beaven, Brad and John Griffiths. *Mass-Observation and Civilian Morale: Working-Class Communities During the Blitz 1940–1941*. MOA Occasional Paper No. 8, University of Sussex Library, 1998.

Bell, David and Gill Valentine. *Mapping Desires: Geographies of Sexualities*. London: Routledge, 1995.

Berman, Marshall, *All That is Solid Melts into Air: The Experience of Modernity*. New York: Penguin Books, 1982.

Bernard-Donals, Michael. "History and Disaster: Witness, Trauma and the Problem of Writing the Holocaust. *Clio* 30.2 (2001): pp. 143–68.

Berube, Alan. *Coming Out Under Fire: The History of Gay Men and Women in World War Two*. New York: The Free Press, 1990.

Bewell, Alan J. "Portraits at Greyfriars: Photography, History and Memory in Walter Benjamin." *Clio* 12.1 (1982): pp. 17–29.

Biagini, Eugenio F., ed. *Citizenship and Community*. Cambridge: Cambridge University Press, 1996.

Bloom, David, Dorothy Sheridan and Brian Street. *Reading Mass-Observation Writing: Theoretical and Methodological Issues in Researching the MOA*, MOA Occasional Paper No. 1. University of Sussex Library, 1993.

Booth, Alan. "Economists and Points Rationing in the Second World War," *Journal of European Economic History* 14.2 (1985): pp. 299–317.

Boyd, Nan Almilla. *Wide Open Town: A History of Queer San Francisco*. Berkeley: University of California Press, 2003.

Breward, Christopher. *The Hidden Consumer: Masculinities, Fashion and City Life, 1860–1914*. Manchester: Manchester University Press, 1999.

Brooke, Stephen. *Labour's War*. Oxford: Clarendon, 1992.

Brooker, Peter, ed. *Modernism/Postmodernism*. New York: Longman, 1992.

Buck-Morss, Susan. "Dream World of Mass Culture: Walter Benjamin's Theory of Modernity and the Dialectics of Seeing." in *Modernity and The Hegemony of Vision*. Berkeley: University of California Press, 1993.

—— "The Flâneur, the Sandwichman and the Whore: the Politics of Loitering." *New German Critique* 39 (1986): pp. 99–140.

Burke, Edmund. *A Philosophical Enquiry into the Origins of Our Ideas of the Sublime and Beautiful* (1757). ed, James T. Boulton. London: Routledge 1958; rev. ed., Oxford: Basil Blackwell, 1987.

Burnett, John, David Vincent and David Mayall, eds. *The Autobiography of the Working Class*. Brighton: Harvester Press, 1984–1989.

Buruma, Ian. *The Wages of Guilt: Memories of War in Germany and Japan*. London: Jonathan Cape, 1994.

Buzard, James. "Mass-Observation, Modernism, and Auto-ethnography." *Modernism/Modernity* 1997 4.3 (1997): pp. 93–122.

Calder, Angus. *The Myth of the Blitz*. London: Jonathan Cape, 1991.

—— *The People's War*. London: Granada, 1971.

Cannadine, David. *Aspects of Aristocracy*. New Haven: Yale University Press, 1994.

—— *The Rise and Fall of Class in Britain*. New York: Columbia University Press, 1999.

Carruth, Cathy. *Unclaimed Experience: Trauma, Narrative and History*. Baltimore: John Hopkins University Press, 1996.

Caws, Mary Ann. *The Art of Interference: Stressed Readings in Verbal and Visual Texts*. Princeton NJ: Princeton University Press, 1989.

Ceasarini, David. *The Jewish Chronicle and Anglo-Jewry 1841–1991*. Cambridge: Cambridge University Press, 1994.

de Certeau, Michel. *Practices of Everyday Life*. trans. Steven Rendall. Berkeley: University of California Press, 1984.

Chamberlain, Mary and Paul Thompson, eds. *Narrative and Genre*. London: Routledge, 1998.

Chauncey, George. *Gay New York: Gender, Urban Culture and the Making of the Gay Male World, 1890–1940*. New York: Basic Books, 1994.

Churchill Speaks. ed. Robert Rhode James. London: Chelsea House, 1980.

Clark, David, ed. *Marriage, Domestic Life and Social Change*. London: Routledge, 1991.

Costello, John. *Love, Sex and War*. London: Pan, 1985.

Cresap, Steven. "Sublime Politics: On the Uses of an Aesthetic of Terror," *Clio* 19.2 (1990): pp. 111–25.

Crosby, Travis. *The Impact of Civilian Evacuation in the Second World War*. London: Croom Helm, 1986.

Davidoff, Leonore, Megan Doolittle, Janet Fink, and Katherine Holden. *The Family Story: Blood: Contract and Intimacy 1830–1960*. London: Longman, 1996.

Debouzy, Marianne. "In Search of Working Class Memory: Some Questions and a Tentative Assessment." *History and Anthropology* 2 (1986): pp. 261–85.

Dyhouse, Carol. *Feminism and the Family in England 1880–1939*. London: Basil Blackwell, 1989.

Eakin, Paul John. *Touching the World: Reference in Autobiography*. Princeton: Princeton University Press, 1992.

—— *Making Selves*. Ithaca: Cornell, 1999.

Edwards, John and Jean-Paul Revauger, eds. *Employment and Citizenship in Britain and France*. Burlington USA: Ashgate, 2000.

Elder Jr., Glen, John Modell and Ross Parke, eds. *Children in Time and Place*. Cambridge University Press, 1993.

Eley, Geoff, "Finding the People's War: Film, British Collective Memory, and World War Two." *American Historical Review* 106.3 (2001): pp. 818–38.

Evans, David T. *Sexual Citizenship*. London: Routledge, 1993.

Field, Geoffrey. "Perspectives on the Working Class Family in Wartime Britain, 1939–1945." *International Labour and Working Class History* 38 (1990): pp. 3–28.

Fielding, Steven. "Don't Know and Don't Care: Popular Political Attitudes in Labour's Britain, 1945–51." in *The Attlee Years*, ed. Nick Tiratsoo. London: Pinter, 1991.

Fielding, Steven, Peter Thompson and Nick Tiratsoo. *England Arise! The Labour Party and Popular Politics in 1940s Britain*. Manchester: Manchester University Press, 1995.

Fish, Jane. "It looked more natural: Miss Rosie Newman's Colour Film of the Second World War." *Imperial War Museum Review* 11 (1997): pp. 27–34.

Fitzgibbon, Constantine. *The Blitz*. London: Macdonald, 1970.

Fletcher, Anthony and Stephen Hussey, eds. *Childhood in Question*. Manchester: Manchester University Press, 1999.

Foster, Hal. *Convulsive Beauty*. Cambridge, Mass.: MIT Press, 1997.

Friedlander, Saul, ed. *Probing the Limits of Representation*. Cambridge: Harvard University Press, 1992.

—— "Trauma, Transference and 'Working Through' in Writing the History of the *Shoah*." *History and Memory* 7.1 (1992): pp. 34–59.

Fussell, Paul. *The Great War and Modern Memory*. Oxford: Oxford University Press, 1975.

Gallagher, Jean. "The World Wars and the Female Gaze." Ph.D. dissertation, City University of New York, 1994, UMI 9417462.

Garrity, Jane. "Selling Culture to the 'Civilized': Bloomsbury, British Vogue, and the Marketing of National Identity." *Modernism/Modernity* 6.2 (1990): pp. 29–58.

Garside, Patricia L. "Representing the Metropolis: The Changing Relationship between London and the Press, 1870–1939." *London Journal* 16:2 (1991): pp. 156–73.

Gilbert, David. "London in all its Glory – or How to Enjoy London: Guidebook Representations of Imperial London." *Journal of Historical Geography* 25.3 (1999): pp. 279–97.

Giles, Judy. "'Playing Hard to get': Working-Class Women, Sexuality and Respectability in Britain 1918–1940." *Women's History Review* 1.2 (1992): pp. 239–55.

Gillis, John R. *For Better or For Worse: British Marriages 1600 to the Present*. Oxford, Oxford University Press, 1985.

Gilmore, Leigh. *Autobiographics: a Feminist Theory of Women's Self-Representation*. Ithaca: Cornell University Press, 1994.

Gledhill, Susan and Gillian Swanson, eds. *Nationalising Femininity*. Manchester: Manchester University Press, 1996.

Glucksmann, Miriam. *Women Assemble*. London: Routledge, 1990.

Goldhagen, David. *Hitler's Willing Executioners: Ordinary Germans and the Holocaust*. New York: Knopf, 1996.

Goldthorpe, David, et al. *The Affluent Worker: Political Attitudes and Behaviour*. Cambridge: Cambridge University Press, 1968.

Goldthorpe, John H. *Social Mobility and Class Structure in Modern Britain*. Oxford: Clarendon, 1980.

Goodman, Phil. "'Patriotic Femininity': Women's Morals and Men's Morale during the Second World War." *Gender and History* 10.2 (1998): pp. 278–93.

Gregory, Adrian. *The Silence of Memory: Armistice Day 1919–1946*. Oxford: Berg, 1994.

Gregory, Gerry. "Community Publishing as Self-Education." in *Writing in the Community*. eds. David Barton and Roz Ivanic. London: Sage, 1991.

Gurney, Peter. "'Intersex' and 'Dirty Girls': Mass-Observation and Working Class Sexuality in England in the 1930s" *Journal of the History of Sexuality* 8.3 (1997): pp. 256–90.

Halbwachs, Maurice. *On Collective Memory*, ed. and trans. Lewis A. Coser. Chicago: University of Chicago Press, 1992.

Harris, José. "Did British Workers Want the Welfare State? G. D. H. Cole's Survey of 1942." in *The Working Class in Modern British History*. ed. Jay Winter. Cambridge: Cambridge University Press, 1983.

Harrisson, Tom. *Living through the Blitz*. London: Collins, 1976.

Harvey, A. D. "Local Authorities and the Blitz." *Contemporary Review* (1990): pp. 197–201.

Hasian Jr., Marouf. "Anne Frank, Bergen-Belsen and the Polysemic Nature of Holocaust Memories." *Rhetoric and Public Affairs* 4.3 (2001): pp. 349–74.

Herf, Jeffrey. *Divided Past: The Nazi Past in the Two Germanys*. Cambridge, Mass.: Harvard University Press, 1997.

Hewison, Robert. *Under Siege: Literary Life in London 1939–1945*. London: Weidenfeld and Nicolson, 1977.

Higonnet, Margaret et al., eds. *Behind the Lines: Gender and the Two World Wars*. New Haven: Yale University Press, 1987.

Hodgson, John. *The Search for the Self: Childhood and Autobiography and Fiction since 1940*. Sheffield: Sheffield Academic Press, 1994.

Höhn, Maria. *GIs and Frauleins: The German-American Encounter in 1950s West Germany*. Chapel Hill: The University of North Carolina Press, 2002.

Holtzman, Ellen. "The Pursuit of Married Love: Women's Attitudes towards Sexuality and Marriage in Great Britain 1918–1939." *Journal of Social History* 16.2 (1982): pp. 39–52.

Hopkins, H. *The New Look*. London: Secker and Warburg, 1963.

Houlbrook, Matt. "Towards a Historical Geography of Sexuality." *Journal of Urban History* 27.4 (2001): pp. 497–504.

—— *Queer London: Perils and Pleasures in the Sexual Metropolis, 1918–1957*. Chicago: University of Chicago Press, 2005.

Hylton, Stuart. *Their Darkest Hour*. London: Sutton, 2001.

Hynes, Samuel, Anne Mathews, Nancy Caldwell Dorel and Roger J. Spillar. *Reporting World War Two: Parts One and Two*. New York: Library of America, 1995.

Inwood, Stephen. *A History of London*. London: Macmillan, 1998.

Jackson, Carlton. *Who will take our Children?* London: Methuen, 1985.

Jackson, Paul. *One of the Boys: Homosexuality in the Military during World War II*. Kingston, Ont.; Montreal, Que.: McGill-Queen's University Press, 2004.

Jackson, W. Eric. *Achievement: A Short History of the London County Council*. London: Longmans, 1965.

Janis, Irving L. *Air War and Emotional Stress*. Ann Arbour: University Microfilms, 1963.

Jay, Martin. *Downcast Eyes*. Berkeley: University of California Press, 1993.

Jean, Marcel, ed. *The Autobiography of Surrealism*. New York: Viking Press, 1980.

Jeffrey, Tom. *Mass-Observation: A Short History*. MOA Occasional Paper No. 10. University of Sussex Library, 1999.

Johnson, David. *The City Ablaze*. London: William Kimber, 1980.

Judt, Tony. "The Past is Another Country: Myth and Memory in Postwar Europe." *Daedalus* 121.4 (1992): pp. 93–118.

Kammerman, Sheila B. and Alfred J. Kahn. *Family Change and Family Policies in Great Britain, Canada, New Zealand and the United States.* Oxford: Clarendon Press, 1997.

Kent, Susan Kingsley. *Making Peace: The Reconstruction of Gender in Interwar Britain.* Princeton: Princeton University Press, 1993.

Kidd, Alan, and David Nicholls, eds. *Culture, Gender and Identity: The British Middle Class, 1795–1939.* Manchester: Manchester University Press, 1999.

Kier, Elizabeth. *Imagining War.* Princeton: Princeton University Press, 1997.

Kirkham, Pat and David Thoms, eds. *War Culture: Social Change and Changing Experience in World War Two Britain.* London: Lawrence and Wishart, 1995.

Kunzel, Regina. "Pulp Fiction and Problems Girls: Reading and Rewriting Single Pregnancy in the Postwar United States." *American Historical Review* 100.5 (1995): pp. 1465–87.

LaCapra, Dominick. *History and Memory after Auschwitz.* Ithaca: Cornell University Press, 1998.

Lant, Antonia. *Blackout.* Princeton: Princeton University Press, 1991.

Lawlor, Sheila. *Churchill and the Politics of War 1940–1941.* Cambridge: Cambridge University Press, 1994.

Lawrence, Jon. "Class and Gender in the Making of Urban Toryism, 1880–1914." *The English Historical Review* 108.428 (1993): pp. 628–52.

LeGoff, Jacques. *History and Memory.* New York: Columbia University Press, 1992.

Lewis, Jane. "Public Institution and Private Relationship: Marriage and Marriage Guidance 1920–1968." *Twentieth Century British History* 1.3 (1990): pp. 233–63.

—— *The Voluntary Sector, The State and Social Work in Britain.* Aldershot, Hants.: Edward Elgar, 1995.

Leys, Ruth. "Traumatic Cures: Shell Shock, Janet, and the Question of Memory." *Critical Inquiry* 20.4 (1994): pp. 623–62.

Li, Victor. "Policing the City: Modernism, Autonomy and Authority." *Criticism* 34 (1992): pp. 261–79.

Lilly, J. Robert. *La Face Cacheé des GIs: Les Viols Commis*. Paris: Payot, 2003.

Longmate, Norman. *How We Lived Then*. London: Hutchinson, 1971.

Loewenberg, Peter. "The Psychohistorical Origins of the Nazi Youth Cohort." *The American Historical Review* 76.5 (1971): pp. 1457–502.

Lukacs, John. *Five Days in London: May 1940*. New Haven: Yale University Press, 1999.

MacCallum, R. B. *The British General Election of 1945*. Oxford: Oxford University Press, 1947.

Mack, Joanna and Steve Humphries. *London at War*. London: Sidgwick and Jackson, 1985.

Maier, C. S. *The Unmasterable Past: History, Holocaust, and German National Identity*. Cambridge, Mass.: Harvard University Press, 1998.

Marwick, Arthur. "People's War and Top People's Peace? British Society and the Second World War." in *Crisis and Controversy*. eds. Alan Sked and Chris Cook. London: Macmillan, 1976.

—— *The Home Front*. London: Thames and Hudson, 1976.

May, Jon. "Globalization and the Politics of Place: Place and Identity in an Inner London Neighborhood." *Transactions of the Institute of British Geographers* 21.1 (1996): pp. 194–215.

Maynes, Mary J. "Autobiography and Class Formation in Nineteenth-Century Europe: Methodological Considerations." *Social Science History* 16.3 (1992): pp. 517–37.

McKibbin, Ross. *Classes and Cultures*. Oxford: Oxford University Press, 1998.

McLaine, Ian. *Ministry of Morale*. Boston: Allen & Unwin, 1979.

McNeill, Laurie. "'Somewhere along the line I lost myself': Recreating Self in the War Diaries of Natalie Crouter and Elizabeth Vaughan." *Legacy* 19.1 (2002): pp. 98–105.

Merridale, Catherine. "War, death and remembrance in Soviet Russia" in *War and Remembrance in the Twentieth Century*. eds. J. Winter and E. Sivan. Cambridge: Cambridge University Press, 1999.

—— *Night of Stone: Death and Memory in Twentieth-Century Russia*. London: Penguin, 2002.

Miles, Peter and Malcolm Smith. *Cinema, Literature and Society*. Beckenham: Croom Helm, 1988.

Morgan, David and Mary Evans. *The Battle for Britain: Citizenship and Ideology in the Second World War*. London: Routledge, 1993.

Mort, Frank. "Cityscapes: Consumption, Masculinities and the Mapping of London since 1950." *Urban Studies* 35.5-6 (1998): pp. 889–907.

―― *Dangerous Sexualities: Medico-Moral Politics in England since 1830*. London: Routledge, 1987.

―― *Cultures of Consumption: Masculinities and Social Space in Late Twentieth-Century Britain*. London: Routledge, 1996.

Mosley, Leonard. *Backs to the Wall*. London: Weidenfeld & Nicholson, 1971.

Muller, Jan-Werner. *Memory and Power in Post-war Europe*. Cambridge: Cambridge University Press, 2002.

Munholland, Kim. "Wartime France: Remembering Vichy." *French Historical Studies* 18.3 (1994): pp. 801–20.

Nava, Mica and Alan O'Shea, eds. *Modern Times*. London: Routledge, 1996.

Nead, Lynda. *Victorian Babylon: People, Streets and Images in Nineteenth-Century London*. New Haven: Yale University Press, 2000.

Nicolson, Nigel. *Portrait of a Marriage*. London: Weidenfeld and Nicolson, 1973.

Noakes, Lucy. *War and the British: Gender and National Identity 1939–91*. London: I.B.Tauris, 1998.

Nora, Pierre. *Realms of Memory*. English-language edn. ed. by Lawrence D. Kritzman, trans. by Arthur Goldhammer. New York: Columbia University Press, 1997.

O'Higgins, Paul. *Censorship in Britain*. London: Nelson, 1972.

Olney, James. *Memory and Narrative: The Weave of Life Writing*. Chicago: University of Chicago Press, 1998.

―― *Metaphors of Self: The Meaning of Autobiography*. Princeton: Princeton UP, 1972.

Outhwaite, R. B. *Marriage and Society*. New York: St. Martin's Press, 1982.

Parker, Julia. *Citizenship, Work and Welfare*. London: Macmillan, 1998,

Peden, G. C. *British Economic and Social Policy: Lloyd George to Thatcher*. London: Philip Allan, 1991.

Pedersen, Susan. *Family, Dependence and the Origins of the Welfare State*. Cambridge, Cambridge University Press, 1993.

Petersen, Judith. "How British Television Inserted the Holocaust into Britain's War Memory in 1995." *Historical Journal of Film, Radio and Television* 21.3 (2001): pp. 255–72.

Peistsch, H. et al., eds. *European Memories of the Second World War*. New York: Berghan Books, 1999.

Pelling, Henry. *Britain in the Second World War*. London: Collins, 1970.

Perkin, Harold. *The Rise of Professional Society*. London: Routledge, 1989.

Phillips, Adam."Bombs Away." *History Workshop Journal* 45 (1998): pp. 183–98.

Poiger, Uta. "Rock 'n' Roll, Female Sexuality and the Cold War Battle over German Identities." *The Journal of Modern History* 68.3 (1996): pp. 577–616.

Ponting, Clive. *1940: Myth and Reality*. London: Hamish Hamilton, 1990.

Pronay, Nicholas and Jeremy Croft. "British Film Censorship and Propaganda Policy during the Second World War." in James Curran and Vincent Porter, eds. *British Cinema History*. London: Weidenfeld and Nicolson, 1983.

Ramsden, John. "How Winston Churchill became 'The Greatest Living Englishman.'" *Contemporary British History* 12.3 (1998): pp. 1–40.

―― "Refocusing 'The People's War': British War Films of the 1950s." *Journal of Contemporary History* 33.1 (1998): pp. 35–64.

Rappaport, Erika. *Shopping for Pleasure*. Princeton: Princeton University Press, 2000.

―― "'The Halls of Temptation': Gender: Politics and the Construction of the Department Store in Late Victorian London." *The Journal of British Studies* 35.1 (1996): pp. 58–83.

Riffaterre, Michael. *Text Production.* trans. Terese Lyons. New York: Columbia University Press, 1983.

Riley, Denise. "Some Peculiarities of Social Policy Concerning Women in Wartime and Postwar Britain." in *Behind the Lines,* ed. Margaret and Patrice Higonnet. New Haven: Yale University Press, 1987.

Rose, Jonathan. *The Intellectual Life of the British Working Classes.* New Haven: Yale University Press, 2001.

Rose, Sonya. *Which People's War?* Oxford: Oxford University Press, 2003.

––––– "Sex, Citizenship and the Nation in World War Two Britain." *American Historical Review* 103.4 (1998): pp. 1147–76.

––––– "Girls and G.I.s: Race, Sex, and Diplomacy in Second World War Britain." *The International History Review* 19.1 (1997): pp. 146–60.

––––– "Resuscitating Class." *Social Science History* 22.1 (1998): pp. 19–27.

Rousso, Henri. *The Haunting Past.* trans. Ralph Schoolcraft, Philadelphia: University of Pennsylvania Press, 2002.

––––– *The Vichy Syndrome.* trans. Arthur Goldhammer. Cambridge, Mass.: Harvard University Press, 1991.

Rowe, Dorothy. *Representing Berlin: Sexuality and the City in Imperial and Weimar Germany.* Aldershot: Ashgate, 2003.

Rubin, David. C., ed. *Remembering Our Past: Studies in Autobiographical Memory.* Cambridge: Cambridge University Press, 1996.

Saint, Andrew, ed. *Politics and the People of London.* London: Hambledon, 1989.

Samuel, Raphael. *Patriotism: The Making and Unmaking of British National Identity: Vols 1 & 2.* London: Routledge, 1984, 1989.

Seacombe, Wally. "Starting to Stop: Working Class Fertility Decline in Britain." *Past and Present* 126 (1990): pp. 151–88.

Shapira, Anita. "The Holocaust: Private Memories, Public Memory." *Jewish Social Studies* 4.2 (1998): pp. 40–58.

Sheppard, Francis. *London: A History.* Oxford: Oxford University Press, 1998.

Sheridan, Dorothy. "Writing to the Archive: Mass-Observation as Autobiography." *Sociology* 27.1 (1993): pp. 27–40.

Sinclair, Andrew. *War Like A Wasp*. London: Hamish Hamilton, 1989.

Smith, Geoffrey. "Interrogating Security: A Personal Memoir of the Cold War." in *Whose National Security?* Toronto: Between the Lines, 2000.

Smith, Harold, ed. *War and Social Change*. Manchester: Manchester University Press, 1986.

Soloway, Richard. "The Perfect Contraceptive: Eugenics and Birth Control Research in Britain and America in the Interwar Years." *Journal of Contemporary History* 30.4 (1995): pp. 637–64.

Sontag, Susan. *Regarding the Pain of Others*. London: Hamish Hamilton, 2003.

Srebnik, Henry Felix. *London Jews and British Communism 1935–1945*. London: Valentine Mitchell, 1995.

Stammers, Neil. *Civil Liberties in Britain during the Second World War*. London: Croom Helm, 1982.

Stanley, Liz. "Mass-Observation's 'Little Kinsey' and the British Sex Survey Tradition." in *Sexual Cultures*. eds. Jeffrey Weeks and Janet Holland. London: Macmillan, 1996.

Starkey, Pat. *Families and Social Workers: The Work of Family Service Units 1940–1985*. Liverpool: Liverpool University Press, 2000.

Stein, Marc. *City of Sisterly and Brotherly Loves: Lesbian and Gay Philadelphia 1945–1972*. Chicago: University of Chicago Press, 2000.

Stewart, Victoria. "Anne Frank and the Uncanny." *Paragraph* 24.1 (2001): pp. 99–113.

Stone, Laurence. *Road to Divorce*. Oxford: Oxford University Press, 1990.

Stonebridge, Lyndsey. "Anxiety at a Time of Crisis." *History Workshop Journal* 45 (1998): 171–82.

Sutcliffe, Anthony, ed. *Metropolis 1890–1940*. London: Mansell, 1984.

Swindells, Julia. "Coming Home to Heaven: Manpower and Myth in 1944 Britain." *Women's History Review* 4.2 (1995): pp. 223–34.

Thomas, Donald. *An Underworld at War*. London: John Murray, 2003.

Thompson, Paul and Mary Chamberlain, eds. *Narrative and Genre*. London: Routledge, 1998.

Titmuss, Richard. *Problems of Social Policy: History of the Second World War, United Kingdom Civil Services*. London: HMSO and Longmans, 1950.

Tomes, Nancy. "A Torrent of Abuse: Crimes of Violence between Working Class Men and Women in London 1840–1875." *Journal of Social History* 11.3 (1978): pp. 328–45.

Tomlinson, Jim. *Employment Policy: The Crucial Years 1939–1955*. Oxford: Clarendon, 1987.

Toye, Richard. "Keynes, the Labor Movement and How to Pay for the War." *Twentieth-Century British History* 10.3 (1999): pp. 255–81.

Turner, Mark. *In a Queer Place*. Chedgzoy, Francis and Pratt, eds. Aldershot: Ashgate, 2002.

Tuttle, Anthony. *Daddy's Gone to War*. Oxford: Oxford University Press, 1993.

Tylee, Claire. *The Great War and Women's Consciousness*. Iowa: University of Iowa Press, 1990.

Vance, Carol, ed. *Pleasure and Danger*. Boston: Routledge and Kegan, 1984.

Walkowitz, Judith. *Prostitution and Victorian Society*. Cambridge: Cambridge University Press, 1980.

Webster, Wendy. *Imagining Home: Gender, 'Race' and National Identity, 1945–64*. London: UCL Press, 1998.

Weeks, Jeffrey. *Sex, Politics and Society: The Regulation of Sexuality since 1800*. London: Longman, 1990.

Welshman, John. "Evacuation and Social Policy During the Second World War: Myth and Reality." *Twentieth-Century British History* 9.1 (1998): pp. 28–53.

Westwood, Gordon, pseud. M. G. Schofield. *A Minority: A Report on the Life of the Male Homosexual in Great Britain*. London: Longmans, 1960.

White, Jerry. *The Worst Street in North London*. London: Routledge, 1986.

Williams, Raymond. "The Metropolis and the Emergence of Modernism." in Peter Brooker, ed. *Modernism/Postmodernism*. New York: Longman, 1992.

Winter, Jay. *Sites of Memory, Sites of Mourning*. Cambridge: Cambridge University Press, 1995.

Wood, Nancy. *Vectors of Memory: Legacies in Trauma in Postwar Europe*. Oxford: Berg, 1999.

Young, James E. "Between History and Memory." *History and Memory* 9.1-2 (1997): pp. 47–58.

Zeigler, Philip. *London at War*. New York: Knopf, 1995.

Zweiniger-Bargielowska, Ina. "Rationing, Austerity and the Conservative Party Recovery after 1945." *The Historical Journal* 37.1 (1994): pp. 173–97.

—— *Austerity in Britain*. Oxford: Oxford University Press, 2000.

INDEX